THIS IS A CARLTON BOOK

Text copyright © 2004, 2007 David Southwell
Design copyright © 2004, 2007 Carlton Publishing Group

This edition published in 2007 by Carlton Books Ltd
20 Mortimer Street
London
W1T 3JW

A CIP catalogue for this book is available from the British Library.

ISBN 978-1-84442-232-6

Project Editor: Gareth Jones, Lara Maiklem
Art Editor: Vicky Holmes, Anna Pow
Design: Adam Wright
Picture Research: Steve Behan
Production: Lisa Moore

Printed in Dubai

CONSPIRACY FILES

PARANOIA SECRECY INTRIGUE

David Southwell
& Sean Twist

CARLTON
BOOKS

CONTEN

TS

INTRODUCTION

Everything you have been taught to believe is wrong. History is a lie. There is a secret earth from which you have been prevented ever finding out about. Your life has been controlled from the moment of your birth by sinister, secret forces. You are not paranoid enough because yes, they really are out to get you. Everything is a conspiracy and you have been duped.

From the best-selling comics of Warren Ellis to Mel Gibson movies and thousands of late-night phone-ins, conspiracies are everywhere you look. Mulder and Scully even became global icons, thanks to their quest to discover the truth behind a huge range of conspiracies and expose them. Conspiracy theories have become an integral part of our culture and the age of global communication has seen them multiply and spread like never before. When John F Kennedy Jnr's plane hit the water in July 1999, it took a full 24 hours for the first murmurs of conspiracy to surface. And when the first jet collided on 9/11, conspiracy theories were in full circulation before the first tower fell. When the Stone Cutters in *The Simpsons sing*, "Who controls the British Crown? Who keeps the metric system down? We do! We do!" many laugh nervously, believing this parody to be closer to the truth than the TV news that is suppressed by the "real forces in control".

So why does this happen and why do we seem to need conspiracy theories? In part, it is a reaction to our times. We live in an age when most of us have no trust in the political, scientific, business and military establishment; when we are saturated with information that we are often at a loss to comprehend. The world is full of frightening, inexplicable events that we cannot understand or control. Conspiracies theories provide a narrative (it is no coincidence that another word for them is "plots") to explain what is going on. Knowing about a conspiracy helps us feel less powerless. Instead of being merely helpless, unknowing victims of some dark machination, we become insiders to the secret. It may also be that we need conspiracy theories. Societies have always found it necessary to devise scapegoats – to explain the evils of the world is the responsibility of the few. This possibility highlights one of the most dangerous aspects of conspiracy theories: some of them are little more than cleverly constructed propaganda designed to provide an excuse for distrusting those who are different to us. We should not forget that the Nazis were the acknowledged masters of the conspiracy theory. Their rise to power and subsequent persecution of Jews, socialists, gypsies and other groups was underpinned by a variety of carefully crafted *right* Bill Clinton apologized to survivors of a conspiracy to conduct medical tests on the inhabitants of Tuskegee.

conspiracy theories, which took in not only the German population but also their many other supporters across the globe.

Of course, another reason why conspiracy theories are everywhere is because they are so damn entertaining! Where else can you find stories with a cast containing extra-terrestrials, film stars, heads of state and age-old secret societies? They even have the added spice of possibly being true, as you can never prove a really big conspiracy is false. After all, if it is big enough and successful enough, all of the usual investigating authorities are bound to be part of it. However, it is important to remember that not all conspiracy theories are only believed by the paranoid fantasists who originally dreamt them up. A few years ago it was rumoured that there was a conspiracy to cover up the fact that since 1932, the US government had been conducting an experiment on more than 200 poor, unwitting, black men in Tuskegee, Alabama in order to study the effects of syphilis. It seemed wildly implausible that the respected Center for Disease Control would allow these people to die, and their wives and children to acquire the disease without telling them. Common sense suggested it was ridiculous to think that the authorities would plot to do something like this and then conspire to cover it up. Yet the sceptics were proved to be spectacularly wrong in doubting the conspiracy. The truth about the Tuskegee conspiracy was eventually exposed and President Clinton travelled to Tuskegee to apologize to the survivors of this shameful incident in American history.

Welcome to the worldview of conspiracy theorists — as Warren Ellis would call them — the mystery archaeologists of a world we are not meant to see; the people who peer into the dark corners of the planet and unearth the truth from centuries of accumulated lies and cover-ups. So, as you read this book and leave behind the safe, secure world of official versions and commonly accepted views, as you enter into the scary world of bizarre, mind-boggling and often implausible conspiracies, remember Tuskegee. Remember, you may not be paranoid enough. Remember, everything you know is wrong.

CELEBRITIES

KURT COBAIN

At 8:40am on April 8, 1994, an electrician who had come to fit security lighting to a luxury home in Seattle found the body of Kurt Cobain. A shotgun wound to the head had killed him. Beside his body was found a box of drug paraphernalia, including syringes and burnt spoons. A shotgun lay across his chest and it was claimed a "goodbye" note was found in the room. An open and shut case of suicide then? Only for the local police. Conspiriologists were hardly going to be satisfied with the cursory examination of Seattle's boys in blue and the media frenzy of reporting following Cobain's untimely end.

The 27-year-old lead singer and songwriter of Nirvana was not only an internationally acclaimed rock star, but an icon and inspiration to many members of Generation X. His fans viewed him as more than another star; to them he was a leader, a hero. His funeral brought Seattle to a state of gridlock and there were copycat suicides across the world. Cobain died at the peak of his power. His music had reached out and touched millions and incredible success had brought him the unwanted status of spokesman for a generation as well as the grunge rock movement.

Punk rock was an escape for Cobain; drugs were an escape for Cobain. At first it seemed entirely in keeping with his character that he might have sought death as the ultimate escape from the pain and depression that had dogged him throughout his young life. However, despite the common knowledge that Cobain was a troubled man, many have found it hard to believe that he took his own life and conspiracy theories concerning his demise have proliferated while his records continue to sell.

The common thread in the numerous allegations in circulation is that despite his troubled state of mind – exemplified by a close shave with death via a heroin overdose in a Rome hotel a month before – Cobain was actually starting to sort himself out and planning positive changes in his life. A messy divorce from his wife and fellow rock star Courtney Love and a high-profile custody battle for their daughter may have been on the cards, but Cobain was not one to wimp out. He had shown toughness before and was a man who had fought his way from a backwoods redneck town to global status. Many of those who have studied the case feel that sinister forces were working in Seattle to ensure an untimely end for Cobain. They have certainly come up with some unsettling questions surrounding his alleged suicide.

left Kurt Cobain – was his death suicide or murder?

above Courtney Love, Kurt's widow, hired a private detective to find her missing husband.

THE STRANGE PART

On Easter Sunday, April 3, 1994, Courtney Love called private detective Tom Grant, a California-based private detective. The previous day Cobain had climbed over the wall of Exodus Rehab Clinic and had flown back to Seattle. Despite the fact that her husband was meant to be suicidal, had almost died in an overdose less than a month before and was returning to a home containing a shotgun, Love decided not to go to Seattle to find him herself. Instead, she hired Grant and despatched him to track down Cobain with the rather flippant and enigmatic phrase, "Save the American icon, Tom." Grant searched for Cobain at the Seattle house on April 7, at 2:45am and 9:45pm, but did not find the body that was hidden in the greenhouse on top of the garage. It was eventually discovered the next day.

THE USUAL SUSPECTS

Someone Close to Kurt

Tom Grant, whom Love subsequently hired for seven months to investigate Cobain's death, is just one of many who believe that Cobain must have been murdered by someone close to him. Given that the murderer and other conspirators must have had his trust and good access to him, many theorists believe the finger points to a family member, close friend or employee.

Record Industry Executives

It is widely rumoured that Cobain was more concerned about leaving the music industry than leaving the world of the living. A dead rock icon is worth a lot more in terms of back catalogue sales than a live one who is no longer interested in a music career. Record industry executives are well-known for possessing a moral sense that makes alley cats look like upstanding members of the community and with millions of dollars at stake, murder might have been seen as preferable to Cobain's retirement.

THE UNUSUAL SUSPECTS

Kurt Cobain

It would not be a rock 'n' roll conspiracy theory if there were not some conspiriologists who believe that Cobain is still alive. The inconsistencies surrounding his apparent death can be fully explained by his faking it to escape from his wife, by the pressures of being a celebrity and by the drugs scene.

Military Industrial Complex

Cobain's role as spokesman for a generation that was apathetic about political concerns could have made him a danger to the Military Industrial Complex (MIC) if he had decided to galvanize the disaffected young of the globe by taking an anti-war stance over the developing conflict in Yugoslavia. To ensure healthy weapon sales and lack of public interest, a pre-emptive strike may have been called for.

MOST CONVINCING EVIDENCE

There is a whole raft of hard crime scene evidence that raises questions over the idea that Cobain killed himself. One of his credit cards was missing and someone had attempted to use it after the time the autopsy says he was shot and before the body was discovered. There were no fingerprints on this shotgun or shells, which suggests the weapon had been wiped, and his body was found to contain an incapacitating level of heroin that should have prevented him from being able to fire the gun. The "suicide" note was actually a note explaining why he was quitting the record industry and many handwriting experts believe that someone other than Cobain had added the last four lines relating to his wife and daughter.

MOST MYSTERIOUS FACT

It has been reported that a "Dream Machine" – a trance-inducing contraption made from a light bulb, record player and cardboard cylinder with slits in it – was found in the greenhouse with Cobain. Brion Gysin, a friend and collaborator with author William S Burroughs – one of Cobain's acknowledged heroes – first created the Dream Machine. A group calling themselves "Friends Understanding Kurt" have pointed out that there have been previous recorded incidents where the use of a Dream Machine has been associated with suicides.

SCEPTICALLY SPEAKING

A deeply troubled man with an enormous drug habit and an interest in firearms – that makes it just so hard to understand why anyone thinks Cobain may have taken his own life, doesn't it? Given that he was once photographed with a gun in his mouth, Cobain actually pulling the trigger one day isn't exactly the most surprising ending to his story. It might be a puzzle for some to figure out why people buy Britney Spears' records, but even with the odd circumstances surrounding Cobain's end there is little mystery about why the sharp money is on suicide in this case.

THE ASSASSINATION OF JFK

November 22, 1963, is a day not easily forgotten. Even now, countless millions of people can recall what they were doing on the day President John F Kennedy was shot.

It was a bright, clear and almost summer-like day in Dallas. The sky above the Texas School Book Depository was free from clouds. There could be no better day for a parade to welcome the President and yet, within seconds, several bullets had struck the presidential limousine at Dealey Plaza, and history was changed forever.

Despite the suppression of vast amounts of evidence and the best attempts of the Warren Commission, in the aftermath of the assassination, to promote the idea that JFK was killed by Lee Harvey Oswald acting alone, 73 per cent of Americans believe that their President was the victim of a conspiracy.

It's a view that is backed up by the report of the Select Committee on Assassinations of the House of Representatives, which stated: "The Committee believes, on the basis of the evidence available to it, that President John F Kennedy was assassinated as the result of a conspiracy."

A close look at the assassination of JFK produces convincing evidence that Oswald was not acting alone and that a cover-up at the highest levels is still in operation. It becomes more a question of who was behind the conspiracy than whether it was a conspiracy at all.

THE STRANGE PART

Despite the official government opinion that the President was killed by a single shot, there were seven wounds found on JFK and on Governor Connally, one of the other passengers in the car. The angles and trajectories of the wounds make a single gunman fairly unfeasible. Lee Harvey Oswald, who was arrested for the murder, was himself assassinated before he could be brought to trial.

THE USUAL SUSPECTS

The CIA

Kennedy was about to disband the CIA due to its corruption, its inability to oust Castro from Cuba, and its general hostility to him since the Bay of Pigs debacle. It is alleged that, in self-defence, the CIA plotted with the Mafia and FBI to kill Kennedy and frame a former double-agent, Oswald, as the killer.

Cuban Communists/KGB

Fidel Castro and his KGB allies were still smarting from

above President Kennedy on that fateful day in Dallas – just moments before his death.

Kennedy's victory in the Cuban Missile Crisis. As revenge they plotted his murder. Their involvement in his death was discovered by the CIA and FBI who had to cover it up to prevent a public outrage that could have led to a World War III.

Mafia

JFK and his Attorney-General brother, Robert Kennedy, were close to winning their crusade against organized crime. Attempts to blackmail Kennedy over his adultery had failed, so the Mafia decided to have him rubbed out. It is known that Oswald had connections to Mafia members; just why did small-time Dallas mobster Jack Ruby so conveniently shoot Oswald?

Military Industrial Complex

Kennedy had plans to pull out of Vietnam. This obviously angered the Military Industrial Complex, which thrives on war. Were connections in the shadowy worlds of the Secret Service and Mafia used to conduct a coup and place Vice President Johnson in the White House? Interestingly, just four days after JFK's assassination, Johnson sent more troops to Vietnam, completely ignoring JFK's recommendations.

Also suspected: the Masons; MJ-12 (Majestic 12, the top-secret defence committee overseeing America's negotiations with the aliens that do all those abductions); Richard Nixon; and the American oil barons.

THE UNUSUAL SUSPECTS

The Canadian Liberal Party

Over recent years, evidence has emerged linking prominent Mafia captain Lucian Rivard to both Jack Ruby and the Liberal Party of Canada. Rivard is also linked to Oswald's recorded time in Montreal. When the Mafia man was jailed in 1964 to await extradition to the US, officers of the Canadian Justice Department, and members of the ruling Liberal Party, offered bribes to the American lawyers to try and secure his release. Despite the lack of motive, this has been enough for some people to suggest that the true answer to the conspiracy to assassinate JFK will be found in Canada.

Jackie Kennedy

The wildest and most discredited conspiracy theory surrounding the assassination is that Jackie Kennedy, sickened by her husband's continuous adultery, arranged for the Mafia to wipe him out and spare her the public humiliation of a divorce.

MOST CONVINCING EVIDENCE

One thing that swings it in the favour of the conspiracy theories is the impossibility of the "single bullet theory" accepted by the Warren Commission. It claimed that the one shot Oswald took from a sixth-floor window entered Kennedy's back, yet rose and flew out of his neck, altering its trajectory to cause the seven wounds found in Kennedy and Governor Connally, in the seat ahead of the President's.

MOST MYSTERIOUS FACT

President Kennedy's brain went missing under mysterious circumstances a number of years ago. This is highly suspicious and also very convenient, as modern scientific tests cannot now be carried out to establish the trajectory of the fatal bullets. The tests would have answered once and for all the question of whether there was a second (or even a third) gunman.

SCEPTICALLY SPEAKING

The legendary grassy knoll from where the second gunman was supposed to have shot Kennedy would have been so busy that surely someone would have spotted the thirty or so gunmen that would have to have been there to account for all the proposed conspiracy theories.

BRUCE LEE

Sometimes death does not end the web of intrigue that has grown up around a celebrity during his life. In fact, sometimes death is only the start of greater and stranger speculations.

In late July, 1973, when they laid to rest the body of Bruce Lee, dressed in the Chinese costume he wore in the movie *Enter The Dragon*, in Seattle's Lakeview Cemetery, they did not succeed in burying the mystery surrounding his death.

A much-loved but controversial figure who made many enemies, Lee was 32 and at the height of his career when he suddenly died after falling into a coma. The subsequent coroner's report was inconclusive and the numerous medical experts who looked at the case could only agree on one thing – that death had been brought about by a swelling of his brain.

On the fateful day of his death, Lee met film producer Raymond Chow at his home in the early afternoon and spent a couple of hours working with him on the film *The Game Of Death*. The pair then went over to the home of Taiwanese actress Betty Tingpei, who was starring in the movie. Chow left for a meeting and Lee complained of having a headache. Tingpei gave him an Equagesic tablet – a form of powerful aspirin – and he took a nap. Chow rang Tingpei to invite her and Lee out for dinner, but the actress could not wake the sleeping star. By the time Lee arrived at the Queen Elizabeth hospital he was dead.

Dr Lycette of the hospital felt that the death was a result of Lee being hypersensitive to compounds in the Equagesic tablet, but other medical authorities disagreed and rumours of a conspiracy began to spread throughout Hong Kong and the rest of the martial arts world.

THE STRANGE PART

Months before he was officially declared dead, rumours had been circulating around Hong Kong that Lee had died. These grew so strong that journalists on one of Hong Kong's largest newspapers wouldn't believe he was alive until they had spoken personally to Lee and subjected him to some rigorous questioning. This does tend to suggest that his eventual death may not have been as unexpected as the official version of events suggests.

THE USUAL SUSPECTS

The Triads

In the Seventies Chinese criminal organizations, such as the Triads, often demanded protection money from Hong Kong-based movie stars. Lee was known to have stood up to their demands and may have been poisoned as a result of this

brave move – he was so adored by the Hong Kong public that he had to be disposed of in a subtle way.

Secret Martial Art Masters

A popular and plausible conjecture is that Lee was killed on the instructions of a cabal of secret martial art masters who were angered that he had taught too many of their secrets to foreigners. It is true that Lee had already had many problems with the traditional Chinese martial arts establishment. Given the nature of the dim mak known to these masters, this theory is not easily dismissed. (Dim mak is a death touch that can be administered by glancing contact and is impossible for an autopsy to detect.) Also suspected: a secret group of Hong Kong movie producers; a cabal of Hollywood Masons; Chinese Communists; defeated opponents; and the British Intelligence Service.

THE UNUSUAL SUSPECTS

Ancient Chinese Demons

It is rumoured that Lee felt his family was suffering from an ancient curse that ensured that the first-born son of any generation would be haunted by demons. The tradition of this curse in his family was so strong that when Bruce was born he was originally given a girl's name to confuse the demonic powers. More than one conspiracy theorist feels that this theory has been strengthened by the strange case of the death of Brandon Lee, Bruce's son, who died after a mysterious handgun accident during the filming of movie blockbuster *The Crow*.

Bruce Lee

An even wilder conspiracy theory proposes that Lee is still alive and that he staged his supposed death in an attempt to escape from either the pressures of fame or the evil intent of various Triad gangs. Those that believe this hypothesis also think that Lee may return at some unspecified point in the future. He certainly is not spotted as much as Elvis.

MOST CONVINCING EVIDENCE

One thing that persuades many that there is a conspiracy behind Bruce Lee's death is the confusion over the medical evidence surrounding his demise. The coroner's report proved inconclusive and the medical authorities put forward no less than five different theories to explain what caused the swelling of the brain that led to his untimely death.

MOST MYSTERIOUS FACT

When interviewed, Lee frequently reflected on the possibility of an early death and at times almost appeared to welcome the prospect. His wife Linda is quoted as saying that Bruce had no wish to live to old age as he found the prospect of losing his physical abilities too horrifying to contemplate. Death as an escape from failing strength and fading prowess as a master of martial art combat may not have been the only reason Lee contemplated dying young. It is known that he took the idea of the first-born of his family being cursed by demons seriously enough to try and protect his son Brandon by employing traditional magic.

SCEPTICALLY SPEAKING

Much of the speculation of the circumstances surrounding the conspiracy can be explained by the fact that when Raymond Chow announced Lee's death on television he omitted the fact that he had not died at home but in the apartment of Betty Tingpei. The attempt to cover up this possibly embarrassing detail may have led many people to become convinced that there was a lot more going on behind the scenes, especially when there was an unsolved medical puzzle over the exact cause of the fatal swelling of the brain.

below Thirty years after his death, Bruce Lee remains martial arts' legend.

inset Lee's son Brandon died in mysterious circumstances during the shooting of the movie *The Crow*.

THE SHOOTING OF JOHN LENNON

In the "do you remember where you were when you heard the news?" stakes, the shooting of John Lennon comes second only to the assassination of JFK or the events of 9/11. If you were alive when the murder of John Lennon was announced on the evening of December 8, 1980, you will undoubtedly remember it, wherever you were. As the news broke around the globe everyone was shocked. No one could understand why anyone would want to kill one of the members of the most beloved musical group of all time. Why would anyone want to murder an ex-Beatle? Why would anyone want to deny the world this true musical genius and very influential campaigner for peace?

The explanation offered in the press was that the gunman – Mark David Chapman – was a disturbed loner, obsessed with the Sixties star and convinced that Lennon was in league with the Devil. After a 60-day psychiatric evaluation that turned into a year and 60 days of absolute silence, Chapman pleaded guilty to the murder a matter of hours before his trial was scheduled to start.

It wasn't long before conspiracy theorists were supplementing the media's version of events with their own interpretations of what actually happened on the tragic night

above John Lennon and Yoko Ono. His radical politics could have made him a target.

that robbed the world of a cultural giant. In their eyes, the shooting was not simply the work of a madman, it was part of a huge political plot.

THE STRANGE PART

One of the usual reasons put forward for why people like Chapman murder celebrities is that they wish to become famous themselves. This obviously is not the case with Chapman. Since he committed the crime he has turned down more than 60 interviews and repeatedly said, "I do not want publicity." He has only given one major interview and that was merely to ask to be released after he failed to get parole in October 2003. His apparent calmness after his arrest was unusual. However, more significant is the fact that he managed to evade metal detectors at two major airports when transporting the murder weapon from Hawaii to New York – something bound to raise alarm bells with those favouring a conspiracy as an explanation for Lennon's death.

THE USUAL SUSPECTS

The FBI

The late FBI Director J Edgar Hoover had a pathological hatred of Lennon and had tried to persuade President Nixon's chief of staff to help him bust the musician and get him thrown out of the country. The FBI kept Lennon under close scrutiny throughout the Seventies and tried to thwart his attempts to gain US citizenship. Many of their files on him are still classified, some because they are linked to British Intelligence information on Lennon. If there was a conspiracy to kill the singer, it is not unreasonable to deduce that the FBI may have played a part in it.

Right-wing Activists/Military Industrial Complex

Reagan had recently been elected President and some felt that opposition to his aggressive foreign policy and plans to spend massive amounts of the budget on expanding the American military was bound to develop around veteran peace campaigner Lennon. In fear of him inspiring the youth to rebel, as he had done in the Sixties, right-wing activists and certain sections of the Military Industrial Complex plotted to silence him.

The CIA

Chapman had worked for defence companies with close links to the CIA. He also showed some evidence of having been hypnotized. In this light some have looked in the direction of the CIA's outlawed project to create programmed killers – MK-Ultra – for the real reason Chapman murdered his former hero.

THE UNUSUAL SUSPECTS

Satanic Forces

Lennon was shot outside the Dakota building – an apartment block that had provided the backdrop to Roman Polanski's film about the birth of the Antichrist, *Rosemary's Baby*. Beatles music and lyrics were used as elements in Charles Manson's warped reasoning that eventually led to the ritual killing of Roman Polanski's wife, Sharon Tate. David Mark Chapman believed that Lennon was, in fact, the Antichrist. These spooky synchronicities have been enough to produce wild claims that the shooting was the result of machinations carried out by satanic forces or members of a satanic cult that caused Chapman to be possessed.

Christian Fundamentalists

Mark David Chapman was not the only one who thought Lennon was the Antichrist. Ever since Lennon's "bigger than God" quote, certain American fundamentalists believed the ex-Beatle was a dark force dedicated to corrupting the youth of America by spreading a gospel of love, drugs and rock 'n' roll. With Lennon's return to the spotlight after a self-imposed period as a househusband, it may be that they decided to silence him once and for all.

MOST CONVINCING EVIDENCE

The strength of the fight put up by the FBI against those using the Freedom of Information Act (FIA) to try to force the agency to make public its files on the singer is suspicious. So too is the fact that even now not all of the material on the files has been disclosed. Given that the FBI claim the reason their files cannot be made public is to protect national security, previously paranoid-sounding claims made by conspiracy buffs may have more veracity than it is comfortable to believe.

MOST MYSTERIOUS FACT

Conspiracy theorists who believe that Paul McCartney is dead and has been replaced with a lookalike, examine The Beatles' lyrics and album covers in search of clues. In a similar way, fringe researchers into the mystery surrounding Lennon's death have also found significance in certain publicity photos and songs. In the booklet that came with the original *Magical Mystery Tour* album in the States, there is a picture of John and a sign next to him stating: "The best way to go is by MD&C." Given these are the initials of Mark David Chapman, some have seen this as either a strange example of synchronicity or a massive clue signposting an astonishing conspiracy.

SCEPTICALLY SPEAKING

The proposed conspiracy theories all go out of their way to overlook the obvious fact that America's lax attitude to gun control laws and a mentally-disturbed man who had an obsession with Lennon are enough of a dangerous combination to provide all the explanation you could ever possibly need.

PAUL McCARTNEY

When you are one of the most famous musicians in the world and your name is known to anyone who has ever listened to pop music, you cannot be too surprised when strange rumours spring up around you – it is the nature of modern celebrity.

In the latter half of the Sixties a rumour spread through the media, and consequently the rest of the Beatle-loving world, that Paul McCartney was actually dead and that an impostor, named William Campbell, was put in his place.

The alleged conspiracy was first exposed to the public by Detroit disc jockey Russ Gibb. He advised his listeners to seek for clues in the band's music, even if it entailed playing the record backwards. One such "clue" is allegedly featured in the "Number nine, number nine" lyric from "Revolution 9" on The Beatles' "White Album", which apparently becomes "turn me on dead man" when played backwards.

The rumour grew faster than Yoko Ono's hair. Millions of Beatles fans, and those who wanted a new hobby, spent hours of their time looking for new clues which revealed that Paul was dead. People were looking for evidence of a conspiracy in everything remotely related to The Beatles. Every clue confirmed what the many suspected – Paul McCartney was dead and there was a huge conspiracy to conceal this fact.

THE STRANGE PART

On the classic *Sergeant Pepper's Lonely Hearts' Club Band* album, Paul is wearing an arm patch with the initials OPD – commonly recognized as an acronym for Officially Pronounced Dead.

THE USUAL SUSPECTS

The Beatles

Conspiracy theorists of a more sceptical bent have concluded that there are in fact many clues to Paul's death scattered throughout the musical output of The Beatles, but that they have been placed there by The Beatles as a metaphysical hoax. They believe that Paul died spiritually and was re-born in the ways of the Maharishi. This spiritual rebirth and his old self dying became an in-joke among the group and they placed obscure references to it on their album covers and in the lyrics of their songs.

The Record Company

Mass hysteria was created by the rumour that Paul was dead. People fanatically searched for clues and evidence and went to ridiculous lengths to find them. More than one conspiracy theorist has suggested that it was all a hoax cooked up by the record company to help sustain interest in The Beatles. If this is correct, it certainly qualifies as one of the most fascinating publicity stunts of all time. Even those who feel the conspiracy theory is a hoax still love hearing the clues.

The CIA

Many people claim that the CIA wanted to bring an end to The Beatles' powerful influence on the world. They may have seen The Beatles and their massive, almost religious, following as a threat to society, which had already witnessed the outrage that John Lennon's comments on The Beatles being "more popular than Jesus Christ" had created. The Beatles were undoubtedly musical and social gods in the Sixties and may have been seen as a threat to the established order by the Agency. Their attempt to destroy The Beatles by murdering Paul was not completely successful as the other three Beatles enrolled the services of William Campbell, the winner of a Paul McCartney lookalike contest.

THE UNUSUAL SUSPECTS

Elvis Presley

A less grounded theory is that Elvis Presley employed the CIA to murder Paul. It has been claimed that Presley had been jealous and threatened by The Beatles' success from the day that The Beatles first set foot in the United States. He was the King of Rock 'n' Roll and no one was going to take that title away from him. So maybe he went to the extreme measure of sanctioning Paul McCartney's assassination. Elvis was popular amongst the highest politicians in the American government, and had extremely powerful contacts. Therefore, if he had been behind McCartney's alleged death, it would be unlikely that he would face any Jailhouse Rock for his crime.

The Devil

Another possible explanation was first proposed by the American academic Professor Glazier, who suggested that the Devil killed Paul as repayment for a bargain he had struck with McCartney for The Beatles' immense success in the world. Obviously rock stars were not the only horny beasts running around during the Sixties. Paul is said to have suffered the same fate as Brian Jones of the Rolling Stones, who also paid the price of success.

MOST CONVINCING EVIDENCE

The cover of the *Abbey Road* album was declared as evidence of Paul's death by Fred LaBour in *The Michigan Daily*. He claimed that The Beatles were depicted as a type of funeral group who were leaving the cemetery. John, dressed in white, represented a minister. George, a gravedigger, and Ringo was an undertaker. Paul, of course, was the corpse, who was barefoot and out of step with the others, suggesting an impostor was present.

right Is this the real Paul McCartney, or an impostor named William Campbell?

MOST MYSTERIOUS FACT

Among the many lyrics that could have been related to Paul's death, one in particular stands out. In the song "Glass Onion", John Lennon sings the words "The Walrus was Paul". It has been claimed that "Walrus" means "Corpse" in Greek.

SCEPTICALLY SPEAKING

The quality of the so-called clues is exceptionally dubious. The *Abbey Road* album cover features the licence plate 28 IF – which some have interpreted as being Paul's age if he had lived – but if Paul was still alive, he would have been 27, not 28. Many of the records that were played backwards sounded so strange and vague that almost any phrase could have fitted with the sound. It is all a case of looking so hard for something that you are guaranteed to find it. No impostor would have been able to duplicate McCartney's exceptional musical talent, though some conspiracy theorists argue that Paul's solo career is the ultimate proof of their claims.

MARILYN MONROE – DEATH OF A GODDESS

On May 19, 1962, President John F Kennedy enjoyed a very public birthday celebration at New York's famous Madison Square Garden. At the celebrity-studded bash, more than 15,000 people saw Marilyn Monroe sing "Happy Birthday" to JFK in breathless, sexual whispers that have entered into pop-culture legend.

Just a few months later on August 4, 1962, the 36-year-old woman, born as Norma Jean Mortenson, was dead – found naked amid her silk sheets, an empty bottle of powerful barbiturates on her dressing table. Marilyn Monroe was a true Hollywood legend and probably the world's first global sex symbol, yet behind the legend is a tragic story of a tortured soul; an alcoholic who had been abused by all of the famous, powerful men in her life. Everything pointed towards the fact that the star had taken her own life.

On the other hand, some have always felt that Marilyn's suicide was just a little too neat and convenient, especially for a range of interested parties such as JFK, Robert F Kennedy, the Mafia, the CIA and the FBI – who all had good reasons for wanting her to be kept permanently silent. The best way for a murder to go undiscovered is for it to look like an accident or a suicide. Conspiracy theorists have never believed Marilyn Monroe deliberately or accidentally took her own life. Remarkably, one thing that almost all those who believe Monroe was murdered agree on, is that if she was killed, it was probably done whilst she was held down with pillows and injected in the foot with barbiturates.

THE STRANGE PART

It became well known in the years following her death that Marilyn had been the mistress of both John and Bobby Kennedy and that the CIA and FBI were keeping her under surveillance, both as a possible threat to national security and as a risk to the President's reputation. Given the level of their involvement in monitoring the star and the clear suggestion that evidence about her last few days of life had been tampered with or covered up, a plot to murder Marilyn is not entirely without credibility.

THE USUAL SUSPECTS

The CIA

The CIA was keeping Marilyn under surveillance because her time as JFK's mistress meant that she had knowledge that made her a potential threat to national security.

left Marilyn Monroe singing to President Kennedy at Madison Square Garden in 1962.

left Peter Lawford (centre) and Robert Kennedy (right) were among the last people to see Monroe alive.

Whether this concerned the CIA's use of the Mafia to try and eliminate Castro and blackmail other heads of state is unknown, but the CIA's interest in the blonde bombshell is as certain as is its agents' ability to carry out a discrete murder.

The Mafia

Having shared her bed with the President JFK, the Attorney-General RFK and various high-powered members of the Mafia – including the mighty Sam Giancana – Monroe knew things that could have destroyed the most powerful people in the US. When her usefulness to the Mafia had run its course with the end of her affair with Robert F Kennedy, they may have felt she was a dangerous loose cannon that needed silencing.

The FBI

Marilyn had been attempting to blackmail RFK into continuing their affair and may have been attempting a more audacious blackmail of JFK – threatening to expose the fact that he had only become President with the vote-fixing aid of the Chicago mob. FBI boss J Edgar Hoover was no friend of the Kennedy family, but as a self-styled patriot may have been happy to solve their problem with Monroe, to save the nation from scandal. Once he had arranged for Marilyn's death, he could control the upstart Kennedy brothers, forcing them to allow him to remain as head of the Bureau that had effectively become his own private police force.

THE UNUSUAL SUSPECTS

The Catholic Church

One organization that the Kennedy clan trusted completely and which had links to the CIA and the mob was the Catholic Church. JFK was the United States' first Catholic President and the Church was keen to ensure that nothing threatened its man in the White House. Some have suggested that the desire to protect him even went as far as arranging for the death of his troublesome former mistress.

Men In Black

If the prospect of the original men in black – Catholic priests – is not unusual enough, there are some who have suggested that Monroe was eliminated by the actual Men In Black who are charged with keeping the lid on the UFO conspiracy. If JFK knew the truth about extra-terrestrial life, he might have told Marilyn and thereby set in chain the series of events that led up to her death when she became uncontrollable and liable to reveal the secrets he had shared with her

MOST CONVINCING EVIDENCE

In recent years, legal documents dating from 1960 have come to light. These documents seem to prove that the Kennedy family promised to give Marilyn Monroe $600,000 in a trust fund for her mother, Gladys Baker, if Marilyn kept quiet about what she knew of the links between JFK and Mafia boss Sam Giancana. After the star died, it appears as if this pledge was broken and all references to it were covered up. These documents quickly became the subject of a hotly fought court action in the United States. Debate about their authenticity still rages. However, tests on the paper, ink and signatures have all suggested that the documents are valid. If this is the case, they are the strongest evidence to come to light that the Kennedy clan may have had a hand in the star's death.

MOST MYSTERIOUS FACT

There are a lot of rumours, and more than a dash of good circumstantial evidence, to suggest that among the last visitors Marilyn received at her home were Bobby Kennedy and Hollywood actor Peter Lawford – who was married to Pat Kennedy Lawford and was therefore part of the Kennedy clan. By all accounts, Lawford and Kennedy were accompanied by an enigmatic third man who was dressed in black and carried a medical-style bag. The identity of this mysterious figure could be the vital clue that needs to be solved if anyone is to unravel the truth behind Monroe's death.

SCEPTICALLY SPEAKING

It is easy to connect a lot of disparate dots in a revealing manner when it comes to the death of Marilyn Monroe. Affairs with the highest officials in the land, FBI files and links to the Mafia are all suggestive but do not necessarily mean that there was a conspiracy. By August 1962, Monroe was a psychologically damaged alcoholic: neither an accidental drug overdose nor a deliberate act of suicide would necessarily have been out of character for Marilyn at that stage of her life. The screen goddess always had a legendary quality about her during life and the conspiracy theories may just be an extension of the inevitable Hollywood myth-making process that doesn't stop just because the star concerned does.

JIM MORRISON – DEATH OR DISAPPEARANCE?

Lizard King, Rock God, shamanic spirit of the Sixties. Without doubt one of the biggest personalities of the music scene of his time, Jim Morrison always had a mythical quality about him. This appears to have done nothing but grow since his death in a Paris apartment on July 4, 1971. In fact, many conspiracy theorists feel his death is the greatest myth of Morrison's life; some believe it would take more than heart failure to rob the world of such a larger-than-life character.

After nearly five years of fame, Jim took a break from The Doors after they had fulfilled their contractual obligation to Elektra Records by delivering the seminal album *LA Woman*. They may have been a little disgruntled that he left during the mixing stages of the LP, but this was not the end of the group and they fully expected him to return from Paris.

Morrison was bored with life in LA and sought out Paris as it was a place to inspire him – a romantic city of art and poetry. He mentioned to some people his desire to purchase an old church in the south of France so he could renovate it and use it as a permanent base from which he would only venture back to the hustle of America when business demanded. He took with him his scrap books filled with poetry and ideas, reels from three of the films he was working on and plans to write a play.

He and his long-term girlfriend, Pamela Courson, quickly established a home for themselves in a Parisian apartment. Jim wrote, appeared as an extra in a play, drank vast quantities of alcohol and began to enjoy the freedom of not being recognized every time he stepped outside his door. He often expressed opinions during this time that he felt like he needed to change the direction of his life – it was clear that he wanted to get away from things and that he wanted to travel.

While years of drinking, drug-taking and other forms of physical self-abuse had made their mark on Morrison, his unexpected death – recorded as resulting from heart failure – took many by surprise. It also inspired doubts in others that he was actually dead, doubts that intensified when one or two curious facts ended up in the public domain.

THE STRANGE PART

No one who knew Jim really well, other than his girlfriend, actually saw him dead. Even after the official death certificate had been produced, some of his friends and even some members of his family doubted that he had really shuffled off this mortal coil.

THE USUAL SUSPECTS

Jim Morrison

It is rumoured that some people who had contractual arrangements with him in the music business immediately assumed that his death was staged in order to facilitate an easy release from some troublesome, binding contracts that he would have had to fulfil had he lived. Established facts also show that Morrison was enjoying the anonymity of his life in Paris and took great care to ensure that there were no new publicity pictures showing what he looked like after he left LA so he would not be disturbed. He talked of escaping his fame. Faking his death may have been the perfect way to achieve this aim.

Friends of Jim Morrison

Some suspect that the confusion over Morrison's death stems from the fact that they wanted to disguise that he died of a drug overdose. Chief conspirator in this intrigue would have been his partner, the late Pamela Courson, who was purported to have had his body removed from the infamous Parisian junkie joint The Rock 'n' Roll Circus to their apartment in order to avoid a scandal and police questioning. This might explain her actions after she "found" Jim unconscious in the bath – her first few telephone calls were to friends, not to the paramedics.

THE UNUSUAL SUSPECTS

The FBI

The FBI had kept Morrison under surveillance when he had been in the US. Files and memoranda to the then Director of the FBI – the infamous J Edgar Hoover – make mention of him trying to "provoke chaos". The Bureau certainly kept tags on those they thought capable of inciting rebellion or drug use among the young, and on people who were in contact with those thought to be subversive – two counts on which Morrison definitely qualified for attention. It should not come as too much of a surprise that some conspiracy theorists have conjectured that the FBI was involved in the strange circumstances surrounding Morrison's (alleged) death because they wished to ensure that Jim did not return to the USA and start provoking that chaos again.

Worldwide Witch Cult

Morrison had an intense interest in witchcraft and is said to have been an active participant in at least one witch cult. It is claimed by some conspiracy theorists, with an interesting grasp of the word "fact", that Morrison was abducted as part of a dark plot to obtain the living representation of Dionysus – Greek god of fertility and wine – for ritual sacrifice.

MOST CONVINCING EVIDENCE

Though it is easy to be jaded when hearing conspiracies such as these, there is some convincing evidence to suggest that all is not as it seems with the Morrison case. No autopsy was ever performed. People who knew him well – including band member Ray Manzarek – believed that he was still alive and

Morrison's own remarks that he wanted to escape the life of a rock star are all telling. However, the most convincing evidence is that more than a week after he had been "buried", Pamela Courson told a journalist working for United Press that Jim was staying at a special clinic outside Paris to convalesce from illness.

MOST MYSTERIOUS FACT

It is effectively impossible to exhume Morrison's body to prove he is actually dead. Apart from needing the family's approval, you also need the consent from seven French cardinals, who can each demand a right of veto and who are renowned for disagreeing on this type of matter. This is the case with all exhumations from the Père Lachaise cemetery, and Jim had speculated he might be buried there…

SCEPTICALLY SPEAKING

Towards the end of his life, Jim Morrison was an overweight, chain-smoking alcoholic who lived very dangerously by keeping up his intake of narcotics while also taking prescription medicines to combat his asthma. The death of someone in those circumstances is hardly surprising – it is pretty much inevitable.

IS THE KING STILL ALIVE?

The official version: Elvis died on August 16, 1977 from an overdose of drugs. He died sitting on the toilet, with his pants around his ankles, a bloated and burnt-out version of his former self and his body is now in residence at Graceland.

The conspiracy version has it that the death of the King of Rock 'n' Roll was an elaborate hoax on the public and that the original Hound Dog is still alive and being spotted by numerous people across the globe.

It has to be agreed that his death did come as a shock – 42 is an early age to die and Elvis did have a history of pulling off some rather bizarre and eccentric stunts. There are certainly some mysterious elements surrounding his alleged death.

THE STRANGE PART

A mere two hours after his death was announced, a man looking remarkably like Elvis bought a ticket for Buenos Aires using the name John Burrows. This was a pseudonym that the King himself had used quite a few times, notably on the occasion he flew to Washington to meet President Nixon. It was on the same visit to DC, that he went to the headquarters of the FBI, announced his desire to inform on fellow showbusiness performers and became an honorary member of the Bureau of Narcotics and Dangerous Drugs. It is alleged that John Burrows flew out of the USA on special State Department papers and this has fuelled speculation that Burrows was none other than Presley making his escape to a new life.

THE USUAL SUSPECTS

Elvis Presley

The hottest contender for the instigator of the conspiracy is none other than Elvis himself. The King definitely felt a prisoner of his own fame and was tired of riding in the trunks of cars to avoid detection and of not being able to get proper medical attention because any hospital he was in would be overwhelmed by fans. At 42, he was going downhill and was too proud to go out with a whimper. Elvis had already once faked his death by setting up deceptive shooting, so it is not impossible he staged a more final fake death.

The FBI

Elvis had recently lost a vast amount of money in bad deals with companies that had close links to the Mafia. There is a lot of speculation that the King decided to collaborate with the government to help expose gangsters. To ensure his protection, the FBI had to fake his death and provide him with a new life as part of a very unusual witness relocation programme.

THE UNUSUAL SUSPECTS

Burger Chain Companies

Could the faked death of Elvis be part of an innovative and radical marketing scam? It has been suggested that the frequent sighting of Elvis cooking fries in numerous backwoods burger joints – which then become very popular, acting as shrines and magnets for Elvis fans – is a joint plan between the King and the burger chain companies. Elvis gets to live a life free from the pressures of fame and is paid in cheeseburgers, while the fast food bosses get to increase business in their quieter establishments.

New World Order

Since Elvis allegedly bought the farm, it has become clear to many cultural observers that he is well on the way to becoming a religious figure. Books comparing him to Christ have hit the US best-seller lists, sightings of Elvis can be seen as similar to spiritual visions, and there is no denying that many fans have shrines to the King and describe visiting Graceland in terms of making a pilgrimage. If you are of a paranoid bent, you may want to consider the claims that the Elvis conspiracy was instigated by the New World Order as their attempt to lay the groundwork for a future new religion. Has Elvis been cryogenically frozen by the NWO to be revived as the globe's new messiah when it comes to power?

MJ-12

Every Elvis conspiracy is more than a little odd, but the suggested link between the King and Roswell – where in 1947 a UFO was alleged to have crashed and the military recovered alien bodies – is bizarre even by Elvis standards. It has been claimed that the military photographer who captured Elvis on film for US Marine publicity purposes was a man called Barret who just happened to be the US Army photographer brought in to record the dead alien's autopsies. Conspiracy buffs, with a love for the territory of deep weird, have it that the photographer sent Elvis a copy of those alien pictures with the fatal consequence that MJ-12 – the guys behind the UFO cover-up – had to silence the King.

MOST CONVINCING EVIDENCE

Aside from the frequently quoted fact that "Elvis" is an anagram of "lives", possibly the most convincing evidence surrounds the 900-pound coffin with a built-in air-chilling unit in which Elvis was buried. How did the Presley family manage to obtain a 900-pound, custom-made coffin ready for a funeral held on the day after his death, and still fail to follow the more basic request from Elvis, such as being buried next to his mother? In the days leading up to his alleged death, the King is said to have made odd nocturnal visits to several funeral homes. Why?

MOST MYSTERIOUS FACT

The King's name is spelled wrongly on his headstone. His full name was Elvis Aron Presley, but on his grave his middle name is spelled incorrectly with an additional 'a'. The unique spelling of Aron was an important Presley family tradition. When he was born, Aron was mis-spelled Aaron on his birth certificate and Elvis's father went to great lengths to correct the recording of his son's name. It seems very odd that Elvis's family would have allowed this error to occur on the King's tombstone.

SCEPTICALLY SPEAKING

The King is dead – get over it.

below Two conspiracy favourites – President Nixon and Elvis exchange a special handshake.

DEATH OF PRINCESS DI

above Grief swept the land in the wake of Diana's death.

The death of Princess Diana was an event that affected people across the planet. Britain grieved, the world grieved. Even people who had never devoted any real attention to the British Royal Family felt deep emotion at the tragic circumstances that robbed the world of someone who qualified as a global cultural icon.

At first it appeared to be nothing more than a simple tragic accident. Diana had enjoyed a romantic meal with her lover, Dodi Al Fayed, at the Ritz Hotel owned by his father, Mohammed Al Fayed. A little before midnight the couple left, accompanied by Diana's bodyguard – Trevor Rees-Jones. To escape 30 paparazzi parked outside, they went out via the back door. The chauffeur of their bulletproof Mercedes-Benz was Henri Paul, the Ritz Hotel's head of security.

The car sped away and a tourist captured the scene on video as an innocent-looking Citroen followed and the paparazzi, realizing they had been duped, began to give chase on their motorcycles. After a few minutes' pursuit, the Mercedes entered the Pont de l'Alma tunnel at high

speed and all we know is that Diana, Dodi and Henri failed to emerge from it with their lives. It took the French investigation several years to produce an official version of events. Not surprisingly, they supported the instant verdict from the world's media that it was a woeful auto accident caused by the combination of a drunk driver, pursuing paparazzi and a failure to wear seatbelts.

The first public suggestion that there was a conspiracy to kill Princess Diana surfaced on the BBC World Service a couple of days after the unfortunate events of August 31, 1997. In bizarre propagandist tones, the BBC made pains to deride a speech made by Libyan leader Colonel Moamar Qaddafi in which he claimed that the "accident" was a joint French and British conspiracy because they did not want Diana to marry a Muslim man. Conspiracy theories began circulating on the night of her death, most of them speculating on how strange it was that on the day she died, Diana had already told one major British national newspaper to prepare for an amazing announcement.

THE STRANGE PART

The Queen intervened to clear Diana's former butler, Paul Burrell, when he was on trial at the Old Bailey just before he was about to take the stand and possibly reveal a number of uncomfortable facts about the Princess in November 2002. It later emerged that after Diana's death, the Queen had spoken at length to Burrell. Using dialogue that would not have been out of place in *The X-Files*, she warned Burrell to be careful, saying, "There are powers at work in this country which we have no knowledge about." The warning led Burrell to wait until October 2003 to make public the fact that Diana had written him a note ten months before she died. It stated: "This particular phase of my life is the most dangerous. 'X' is planning an accident in my car, brake failure and serious head injuries in order to make the path clear for Charles to marry". The Princess' startling prescience has heightened the belief she was a victim of a conspiracy, not a tragic accident.

THE USUAL SUSPECTS

MI6

Sworn to protect the British crown, it is alleged that a renegade faction within MI6 took it upon itself to rid the Royal Family of the one woman who looked capable of destroying the monarchy by exposing the hypocrisy of the Windsors. That she may have been pregnant, about to convert to Islam and marry the son of establishment bogeyman Mohammed Al Fayed may have been the final factors that made them decide she must die.

Military Industrial Complex

Diana had waged a one-woman war against the evils of landmines, in doing so risking her personal safety and earning strident political criticism in the UK as a "loose cannon". While the Military Industrial Complex makes more money from disposing of landmines than it does selling them, it may have feared the possibility of Diana turning her attention to the arms industry in general. Clearly, it would have been in their best interests to wipe out someone who could have turned into the world's most powerful peace campaigner.

Also suspected: the CIA; Mossad; Islamic Fundamentalists; Saddam Hussein; The Freemasons (she died under a bridge – an important Masonic symbol) and the IRA.

THE UNUSUAL SUSPECTS

The Committee

An alleged Anglo-American cabal of intelligence agency operatives from the USA and UK. Supposedly headquartered in Bristol, England, the Committee is apparently a tool of an even more clandestine group that wants the special relationship between the US and UK to become a union of both powers. Perhaps Diana's popularity, willingness to tackle the establishment on sensitive issues and possible pregnancy persuaded them she could be a dangerous opponent to their schemes.

Princess Diana

Another bizarre hypothesis is that Diana staged her own death so she and Dodi could live free from the glare of publicity. Not surprisingly, there's little hard evidence to support this piece of wishful thinking.

MOST CONVINCING EVIDENCE

Claims have been made that Henri Paul was three times over the legal alcohol limit. A second blood test ordered by his disbelieving family showed a level of carbon monoxide in his body that was not only lethal, but would have entered his bloodstream before he got into the car. The security video from the Ritz that night does not show him as a drunk, or reeling from carbon monoxide poisoning. The mystery of Henri Paul deepens further with the revelation that he deposited more than 164,000 francs into his bank account shortly before he died. When, in 2003, it was announced that British inquests were to be held into the deaths of Diana and Dodi, conspiracy theorists were dismayed to find out they would be held by Surrey Coroner Michael Burgess. As he was also the Coroner for the Royal Household, many doubted that the truth would emerge at the inquests. Even his replacement as coroner for the inquests by Dame Elizabeth Butler-Sloss, after strong protests over his impartiality, did nothing to raise some researcher's faith in the process, especially as Dame Elizabeth tried to carry out crucial hearings in private. In December 2006, the official, supposedly independent UK investigation by Lord Stevens, a former chief of the Metropolitan Police was forced to admit that the case is "far more complex than any of us thought".

MOST MYSTERIOUS FACT

The crash happened in the Pont de l'Alma tunnel that was built over a site used in the time of the Merovingian dynasty (between 500–751 AD) as a sacred ritual area. Some secret societies, such as the Prieur de Sion and the Templars, claim that the Merovingian and all true European royalty – including Diana Spencer's family – are connected to the pagan cult of Diana. It is odd that Britain's Queen of Hearts may have died on a former site of worship for the goddess whose name she was given.

SCEPTICALLY SPEAKING

Even if Diana was pregnant, that does not mean there was a conspiracy to kill her. Driving at high speed through Paris is dangerous enough without being pursued by a pack of motorcycle paparazzi. Add a barrage of camera flashes and passengers not wearing seatbelts and you no longer need a conspiracy to explain a fatal crash. Faced with such a tragedy, it is not surprising that some people cannot accept it as a mere random accident. The crash may be the perfect example of why some conspiracy theories come into being: if they didn't we'd have to face the banality and indiscriminate nature of death.

SID VICIOUS

When New York's finest entered Room 100 of the Chelsea Hotel on October 12, 1978, they discovered a horrific sight. Lying beneath the bathroom sink, clad only in her underwear and covered in blood, was Nancy Spungen. She was dead, killed by a single knife blow to her abdomen. Her boyfriend, himself in a drug-induced muddle, was Sid Vicious, bass player with the then notorious punk band, The Sex Pistols. He was charged with Spungen's murder and later released on $50.000 bail.

The romance between Vicious (born John Simon Ritchie) and Nancy Spungen was the stuff rock 'n' roll nightmares are made of. After being recruited by his best friend John Lydon – aka Johnny Rotten – to replace the existing bass player in his band, the Sex Pistols (named after Malcolm McLaren and Vivienne Westwood's London boutique, "Sex"), Vicious soon found himself at the epicentre of pop-culture phenomenon. The band was already notorious in England. Spearheading the UK punk movement, the Pistols had originally been put together by McLaren to specifically appeal to the disaffected youth of England. With songs calculated to infuriate all the wrong people (anyone over 30), The Pistols tore through England on the breaking wave of punk rock. With songs such as "Anarchy In The UK" and "God Save The Queen", coupled with outrageous outbursts on television and other media, they were nothing short of a slow-motion atom bomb about to shake the foundations of pop culture worldwide.

Which wasn't bad for Vicious, considering there was debate about whether he ever knew how to play the bass at all. Instead, he relied more on image: cutting himself with razor blades, spitting blood and even urinating while on stage. The anarchy poster boy, beloved by many newborn punk rockers, he proved irresistible to one fan, an American girl called Nancy Spungen, who came over to England with the express purpose of capturing the heart – or anything else – of a Pistol. She and Vicious met in 1977 and soon became lovers, careening into an affair riddled with drug abuse. Vicious' love of Spungen, coupled with Spungen's abrasive personality, became so intense that it began to tear the band apart. When the Pistols' ill-fated American tour ended abruptly, with lead singer Johnny Rotten returning to England in disgust, Vicious stayed with Spungen, finally ending up in New York's Chelsea Hotel. After Spungen's death, out of despair Vicious tried to commit suicide and carved his entire forearm with a knife. Somehow surviving that, he finally succumbed to a heroin overdose (with heroin brought for him by his mother, fearing that her son might get caught in a police sting) on February 2, 1979. He was only 21.

THE STRANGE PART

Theories have arisen over the possibility of a conspiracy concerning Vicious' death. There are dark hints that there was more at hand than the tragic deaths of two heroin-addicts, and even murmurs that Vicious may not have killed Spungen at all.

THE USUAL SUSPECTS
Unknown Residents of the Chelsea Hotel

Keeping in mind the drug-hazed state of Vicious and of Spungen before her death, it's entirely probable that someone other than Vicious may have killed Spungen. In his befuddled state of mind, he may not even have been aware of the murder. The perpetrators, worried about the truth coming out if Vicious' case went to trial, ensured his silence by making sure that Vicious' mother brought a lethally cut dose of heroin for her son.

Former Associates

Some conspiracy theorists feel that former friends and associates of Vicious may have had him supplied with a hit of lethal "hot" heroin. This was meant as an unusual act of mercy to spare him having to face the living hell of a long prison sentence served out in New York's most notorious jail, a place he would not have been vicious enough to survive.

THE UNUSUAL SUSPECTS
The CIA and FBI

Just as the murder of John Lennon may be attributed to a mutual desire by the CIA and FBI to remove any pop-culture figure that could possibly lead the population to revolt, Vicious might have been killed because he represented punk anarchy in all its glory. He had the potential to give American youth a role model that made the young Elvis look the model of respectability. Indeed, some theories suggest that Vicious could have been a simple trial run of a CIA or FBI rub-out programme before attention moved on to the more difficult task of removing Lennon. Both men died, coincidentally, in New York.

MOST CONVINCING EVIDENCE

However tormented and tortuous the relationship between Spungen and Vicious, it was painfully clear to all those around him that he needed her, perhaps more than anything or anyone else. Regardless of his state of intoxication, to kill her would seem completely out of character. In telephone conversations with Spungen's mother after Nancy's death, Vicious never made any comments about it at all. If he were as guilt-ridden over killing her as we would be led to believe, would he be able to hide his pain that well? In all other things, Vicious was not known as a paragon of restraint.

MOST MYSTERIOUS FACT
While Sid's mother was returning her son's ashes to England, John Lydon claims that she dropped the urn in Heathrow, scattering them across the airport floor. A significant proportion of them were sucked into the ventilation system.

SCEPTICALLY SPEAKING
Although it would be romantic to think that all the rock stars who die young do so because the "Powers That Be" want them dead, there are times when death is simply a tragic end to a tragic story. Sid Vicious was a young man with next to no musical talent, who was simply in the right place at the right time looking the right way. When McLaren created the Sex Pistols he wanted stars he could manipulate and he got that with Vicious. Unlike general perceptions of John Lennon and Jim Morrison, the idea that Vicious could ever be a threat to American society is ludicrous. He was the "It Boy" of the punk generation, and nothing more. If his death was to be chalked down to anything, it should be heroin, and the equally dangerous drug of media exposure.

left Love's young dream? Sid and Nancy were punk rock's highest profile couple.

SHARON TATE

The Sixties' dreams of peace and love were shattered forever on the night of August 9, 1969. For many, the following morning became a waking nightmare when news broke that Hollywood actress Sharon Tate and four of her friends had been found brutally murdered at the home of her husband, the film director Roman Polanski.

The scene inside the Polanski residence that confronted investigating police officers was truly horrific. The killings were particularly brutal with the victims being beaten and stabbed after being shot, and there were clear ritualistic elements to the affair. The slogans "Death to Pigs", "Rise" and "Healter Skelter" [sic] had been found written in the victims' own blood on the walls, and the word "War" had been carved into one of the victim's bodies by a fork that was left embedded in his corpse.

The fact that Tate was pregnant and two weeks away from giving birth at the time of her savage slaying merely added an extra note to the horror. When, on the following night, two more victims were murdered in what the media immediately assumed was a copycat ritual killing, a wave of panic gripped the whole of California and much of Middle America.

Given the concern that the social turmoil at the time was causing the establishment, it was not surprising the theory quickly took hold that the killings were of a politically-inspired nature. This perception was heightened by the fact that radical American terror group the Weathermen – who took their name from a line Bob Dylan's *Subterranean Homesick Blues* – had issued a statement declaring 1969 to be "the year of the fork". The Black Panthers or radical "hippies" were among the police's first potential suspects.

Whilst panic about the murders mounted, an unconnected police operation on August 12 raided the Barker Ranch in Death Valley in an attempt to smash open a major auto-theft ring that was operating from the property. Amongst the 26 people arrested was one Charles Manson – whom the police only found when they spotted his matted hair sticking out from beneath the closet in which he was hiding. The majority of those caught in the bust were young female drop-outs who formed the "Manson Family" and saw Charles in almost Messianic terms.

Over the next three months, thanks to an alleged confession to a cellmate by one of the Manson Family members – ex-stripper and Satanist Susan Atkins – and a tip-off by notorious California biker gang the Straight Satans, Manson became the authorities' top suspect. In their eyes, he went from an eccentric guru and auto-theft mastermind to the inspiration for his followers to kill Tate and her friends.

During December 1969, Prosecutor Vincent Bugliosi brought conspiracy indictments against Manson, who was described as a "Top Hippie". Bugliosi claimed that Manson thought the lyrics of The Beatles' *White Album* were written for him – especially the tracks "Piggies" and "Helter Skelter" – directing him to try and start the Apocalypse. The murder trial sought to prove that Manson's followers, including Susan Atkins, Linda Kasabian, Leslie Louise Van Houten, Patricia Krenwinkel and Charles "Tex" Watson, had committed the murders in an attempt to frame the Black Panthers and start a race war to herald the Apocalypse itself.

Bugliosi's prosecution was successful and, despite no evidence ever placing him anywhere near any of the murders, Manson remains in prison and is not due for another another parole hearing until 2007.

THE STRANGE PART

When Manson's base in the desert at the Barker Ranch was raided, police found a number of firearms including high calibre pistols and a sub-machine gun. If the Manson family had murdered Sharon Tate and her guests, why were they shot with a small calibre.22 (5.5mm) Hi Standard Longhorn revolver? Why use a gun most often used for sport and shooting vermin? Many weapons experts have raised an eyebrow over why a gun that is reputed to be deadly only in the hands of highly-trained shooters was used, when other usually more lethal guns were readily available. Did someone other than members of Manson family murder Sharon Tate and set Manson up to take the blame?

Manson was certainly known to the authorities and action could have been taken to tackle him earlier. A planned police raid on the Barker Ranch in the weeks prior to the murders was called off. Preston Guillory, a former deputy sheriff in the LA force told author Paul Krassner: "We were told not to arrest Manson or any of his followers ... the reason he was left on the street was because our department thought he was going to launch an attack on the Black Panthers."

above Mr. Self Destruct – Manson arrives at court with a swastika carved into his forehead, a clear indication of his mental state.

THE USUAL SUSPECTS

Richard Nixon

Given the use made of the fear generated by Tate's murder in his election campaign and the personal interest he took in the case during Manson's trial, many conspiracy theorists believe Tricky Dickie played a role in this case. They believe the killings were a plot he created to generate a moral panic that he could exploit to strengthen his strong law and order and anti-counter-culture election platform.

Satanists

There were a large number of active Satanist groups operating in California at the time of the murders. Given the ritual elements of the killings and Polanski's notorious film involving Satanism, *Rosemary's Baby*, many feel that it would make more sense to blame followers of the chief fallen angel rather than followers of a petty criminal and failed rock star. Tate herself had been linked to Satanism on film via her role in the movie *Eye of the Devil*.

The FBI

Both the CIA and FBI undertook many covert operations to try and implicate the Black Panthers in a range of publicly damaging criminal activities. In September of 1968, FBI Director J. Edgar Hoover described the Black Panthers as "The greatest threat to the internal security of the country." He authorized an illegal campaign to discredit them and cause gang warfare between the Panthers and other groups. It may be that the slaughterhouse at the Polanski residence was a result of one of their scams where the mud failed to stick to the intended target.

THE UNUSUAL SUSPECTS

The Process Church

The strange and secretive English religious group known as The Process Church of The Final Judgment, who believed that one of the paths to God is via following the example of Lucifer, had an influence on Manson. The group was co-founded by Robert "DeGrimston" Moore, who took the organisation to the USA. Manson once wrote for their LA magazine and Process Church members visited him whilst he was in prison. This leads some to believe they had a hand in the events surrounding Tate's death.

Hollywood Sex Cult

Victim and former boyfriend of Tate – Jay Sebring – was well-known for his interest in sado-masochistic sex orgies and dealing cocaine. Some conspiracy theorists have claimed celebrity members of a Hollywood sex cult ordered the killings to silence Sebring who may have threatened to expose their drug and sexual debauchery. Rumours of missing pornographic movies secretly filmed by Sebring circulated at the time and it is noteworthy that several of his close associates died in the months following the massacre.

Kenneth Anger

Polanski later admitted that in the months following the murders that he suspected various friends and associates of the killings. Even tough guy Steve McQueen was so worried that someone inside Hollywood was behind the murders that he packed a gun when he went to Jay Sebring's funeral. Some believe that someone was film director and occultist Kenneth Anger – whose former housemate and magical partner Bobby "Cupid" Beausoleil was later sentenced to life imprisonment for another killing undertaken on behalf of the Manson family. Anger had already notoriously cursed the Rolling Stones through ritual magic, and was linked to occultists angered by Polanksi's *Rosemary's Baby*.

MOST CONVINCING EVIDENCE

Manson's trial was so flawed in terms of legal process and natural justice that it is not hard to imagine him having had more chance of getting a fairer hearing at a Stalinist show trial in Soviet Russia than at the Los Angeles courthouse in 1970. Whilst the trial was still ongoing and before any verdict had been reached, President Nixon publicly stated, "Manson is guilty." The seeming absence of the usual concept of "innocent until proven guilty" – as articulated by the most powerful man in the USA at the time – has helped convince many conspiriologists that Manson was nothing more than an eccentric patsy in a baroque conspiracy.

MOST MYSTERIOUS FACT

Members of the Californian music community knew a different side to Manson. He had been taught to play guitar during an earlier spell in jail by Alvin "Creepy" Karpis, the sole survivor of the infamous Ma Barker Gang. Despite failing an audition to become a member of the TV-show-band The Monkees, it was due to his musical ability that he met The Beach Boys and lived for a time at the Malibu mansion of band member Dennis Wilson. Wilson referred to Manson as "the Wizard" and The Beach Boys bought one of Manson's compositions to use as a B-side. In 1994, rock musician Trent Reznor built the "Le Pig" studio in the house where Tate was murdered, recording the hit Nine Inch Nail album *The Downward Spiral* there.

SCEPTICALLY SPEAKING

When you have a whacked-out career criminal with Messianic delusions, living in the desert surrounded by a group of followers taking vast amounts of hallucinogenic drugs, almost any conspiracy theory is likely to make as much sense as the drug-addled nonsense that actually led to the killings.

DAVID ICKE

Few figures in the world of conspiracy theory research cause more polar extremes of reaction than David Icke. Like some kinds of food, it seems you either love or loathe him, and there does not seem to be any neutral ground.

Many sober, serious parapolitics investigators, who hate any mention of aliens, secret occult societies and long-disproved mega-conspiracies blaming all the world's ills on just one group, will froth at the mouth if he is mentioned. At the other end of the conspiracy spectrum, among those who have rejected most ideas relating to consensual reality, he is hailed as a hero. To this group, his talk of the late British Queen Mother being a form of humanoid reptilian existing at a higher dimensional level is a sign of bravery, and not that he should be confined to a lunatic asylum.

In my former role as a journalist, I have interviewed David Icke and formed my own views on him. Given Icke's profile in conspiracy circles, it also has been hard to miss his often apparently bizarre statements and interesting speculations. However, in 2004, something happened that changed my view of David Icke and his self-proclaimed role since 1990 to expose "who and what is really controlling the world."

Every researcher into parapolitics should have at least a couple of spooks – agents of the secret services – amongst their sources of information. While you have to expect a certain amount of disinformation, spooks are often able to provide interesting leads and help confirm the veracity of information. It was while drinking with a spook I first learned Icke was the victim of an odd rumour campaign. During the course of the meeting, my spook source outlined an outlandish conspiracy theory in which he claimed David Icke was working for MI5. The source claimed Icke was deliberately promoting fantastic assertions that the bloodlines of powerful families such as those of President Bush and Queen Elizabeth II were linked to reptilian humanoids to purposefully discredit the whole field of conspiracy research. By making such peculiar claims, his alleged paymasters hoped more straightforward areas of conspiracy investigation would be tainted with an air of the ludicrous in the eyes of the public.

At first I took this as a one-off comment. However, other authors had heard similar whispers. In fact, some conspiracy theorists had already begun publicly discussing claims of Icke's involvement with the British security services, making the reasonable point MI5 have a track record of infiltrating the conspiracy community. MI5 do this partly to keep track on certain rampant crypto-fascists within parapolitical research and partly because it is wise to monitor those trying to monitor you. As the CIA have shown over the years in

above The Lizard King – David Icke's books and lectures have won him thousands of believers for his ideas involving humanoid reptilians.

ufology, it can also often be useful to use a conspiracy theorist to discredit a subject and spread misleading rumours.

If there were a secretly orchestrated campaign to make David Icke look like a MI5 puppet, it would only be the latest instalment in a life that often looks like the unfolding of a surreal soap opera. David Icke had certainly made an incredible journey. His first career was as a professional footballer, keeping goal for Coventry City before a leg injury finished his playing days. He turned to journalism and eventually became a sports reporter and then anchorman for the BBC. At the height of his fame, he left television to become an activist for the Green Party. In 1990, Icke received a number of messages from a medium. By 1991 he had gone public with a number of his controversial views – such as his "I am a channel for the Christ spirit" – and became a subject of national public ridicule.

Although it is acknowledged by many researchers that Icke has unearthed some interesting facts to support some of his conspiracy ideas on areas such as 9/11, he has also often relied on material thoroughly disproved to have a basis in reality. He has repeated claims made by a man called Mark Phillips about the existence of a mind-control programme to produce child sexual slaves for senior US politicians. Needless to say, Mark Phillips has never been able to produce any objective proofs of his claims. It is hard to doubt that Icke's promotion of these views along with his talk of reptilian humanoids has cast a shadow of media derision over some elements of conspiracy research.

THE STRANGE PART

If David Icke were a mere lunatic who has wandered so far off the map of reality he is almost beyond ridicule, why would anyone bother to indulge in a campaign to undermine him? Surely his quoting of highly dubious sources and belief in the reality of hyper-dimensional reptilian humanoids raise enough obstacles to creditability? It is strange the slander about him being an agent of disinformation seems designed to cause most harm to his reputation with the thousands who buy his books and attend his public lectures. If Icke is a threat to no one and speaking rubbish, who would bother to try and further denigrate his reputation?

THE USUAL SUSPECTS

Reptilian Humanoids

Some conspiriologists back David Icke's ideas about the world being controlled by higher-dimensional reptilian humanoids working through the prominent families and secret societies. They claim any slander or attempt to smear Icke is the work of these reptilian humanoids working through their global network of human agents.

British Royal Family

Icke has made repeated claims that some members of British Royal Family whom we perceive as human, are in fact secretly lizard people. If you were in the position of power enjoyed by Queen Elizabeth II and were fed up with a former footballer calling you and your late mother lizards, what would you do? Get agents in your security services to try and discredit the miscreant perhaps?

MI5

Fed up with Icke accusing them of working on behalf of lizard paymasters and sticking his nose into their operations, MI5 may have spontaneously taken it upon themselves to start rumours about one thing they knew would hurt any conspiracy researcher – working for them.

THE UNUSUAL SUSPECTS

Left-wing Conspiriologists

Conspiracy researchers with a left-wing bias have regularly attacked Icke for bringing ridicule to the whole field of parapolitical research. They have also criticised his links to authors such as Eustace Mullins, who once wrote a book entitled *The Biological Jew*. A secret cabal of left-wing conspiriologists would certainly seem to have motivation for orchestrating a campaign against Icke.

Anti-Jewish Defamation Campaigners

Numerous anti-Jewish defamation groups have accused Icke of anti-Semitism. They have claimed when he talks about lizards, he is really talking about Jews. Icke has always rigorously denied their allegations and they have not impacted on his growing popularity. Could elements of anti-Jewish defamation groups have changed tactics in an attempt to discredit someone they view as dangerously anti-Semitic?

MOST CONVINCING EVIDENCE

In the years following Icke's public ridicule in 1991, he has recovered some of his reputation. He was the subject of the 2007 TV documentary *David Icke: Was He Right?* and The Waterboys's song *Sympathy For David Icke* was written in his honour. Icke has produced more than 20 books, attracting a worldwide following for his ideas. It was only after a growing number of people began to take seriously his pronouncements about 9/11 and the "War on Terror" being the result of a conspiracy, that rumours about him being an agent of disinformation began. It was also only at the point he was enjoying a new surge in popularity that he faced other obstacles to promoting his views, such as a legal fight for ownership of 16 books he had written.

MOST MYSTERIOUS FACT

Several conspiratorial predictions made by Icke have ended up looking like prophecy. In January 2001 he wrote, "Don't be surprised if the USA finds itself in another manipulated war during this administration. You will see monsters being created in the public mind to justify such action", also adding that "before 2002 the USA will suffer a major attack on a large city". He had already predicted in 1998: "There will a plan to start a Third World War by stimulating the Muslim world into a holy war against the West."

SCEPTICALLY SPEAKING

Stripped of its stranger trappings, David Icke's message seems to be we should wake up to the lies told by our leaders and defeat the ills of the world through love. It is easy to see how anyone preaching that humanity is systematically exploited, hypnotized by television and needs love to overthrow the illusions holding it prisoner could be seen as a dangerous radical by those in power. It would be far more suspicious if there were no trace of an anti-David Icke campaign – that really would smack of him being either totally irrelevant or acting on hidden orders. Besides, to be slandered by some conspiriologists and British spooks should be taken as huge badge of honour.

EXTRA-TERRESTRIALS

ALIEN ABDUCTIONS

One of the most prevalent conspiracy theories disturbing the sleep of millions today is that of alien abductions. All over the world, the lives of innocent men and women are apparently being disrupted by incidents of otherworldly kidnappings. Suddenly, they find themselves forcibly removed from their homes, transported to alien crafts or environments where they are horribly violated by creatures from beyond the stars. What makes these incidents all the more terrifying is the complete helplessness of the victims, who are completely at the mercy of these inscrutable aliens and their disturbing medical procedures.

Researchers into alien abductions have attempted to categorize the kidnappings, searching for common threads of experience among abductees. Among those categories are the basic physical abduction, where abductees talk of feeling tranquillized, then watching placidly as they are moved to an alien ship. They might be moved there by a smaller craft, by some form of tractor beam, or by some kind of inter-dimensional "gate". Some abductees report being moved directly through solid objects, such as the walls of a house.

Another popular form is the bio-energy extraction method: the abductees' bio-energy, or consciousness, is removed from their bodies by an alien technology that usually takes the form of a white to bluish-white beam of light surrounding and penetrating their bodies. The victim's consciousness is often inserted into another body before being returned to its original form.

There are also the telepathic lucid dream versions of abductions, which, while not being as physical in nature as a corporeal abduction, are no less damaging. In this kind of attack, abductees find themselves experiencing a lucid dream created by aliens, in which a normal dream disintegrates and is replaced by telepathic messages or visual images. As in the bio-extraction scenario, a beam of whitish energy emanating from the ceiling above them is sometimes seen by awakening victims.

above The Greys: The aliens that are most commonly alleged to abduct humans.

While abductions have been reported throughout history, there seems to be an increase in frequency of late. It's almost as if the perpetrators – aliens, or whoever is responsible for these heinous crimes against humanity – are growing increasingly desperate.

THE STRANGE PART

Throughout the ages, abduction is one of the great themes of horror stories. Some even try to suggest links between abduction by fairies and abduction by little Grey men makes them one and the same. Maybe they are, but only in the sense that our collective minds updated our nightmares after watching Steven Spielberg's *Close Encounters of the Third Kind*.

THE USUAL SUSPECTS

The Greys

The Greys are the most common type of alien experienced in the abduction scenario. Small creatures with melon-shaped heads and huge, black, slanted eyes, they are at the root of many alien conspiracy theories. The current thoughts on their involvement in abductions are varied, from an optimistic hope that they are our descendants coming back in time to save the Earth from destruction, to a darker suspicion that they are extracting sperm and ova from humans to save their own race.

Under this hypothesis the Greys are a race of clones that has lost the ability to reproduce sexually; the Greys hope to create a hybrid between themselves and humans in order to survive.

The US Government

The Majestic 12 – also known as MJ-12 – is a powerful shadow group within the US government that may be working with the Greys, allowing them to continue their experiments in exchange for technology. This deal has allegedly helped give rise to weapons such as the B-2 stealth bomber and the F-117 stealth fighter. Many abductees recall seeing military personnel and installations, often without seeing aliens. (This poses the question of whether this arrangement is merely a matter of working in conjunction with the Greys, or whether the US government has its own agenda – perhaps mind control?) Using masterful disinformation tactics, this group discredits and ridicules any research into UFOs and indeed, anything else that may shed light on the mysterious Greys, thereby ensuring continued abduction work, continued misery for thousands, and continued technological payoffs for the US government.

THE UNUSUAL SUSPECTS

Dolphins

The Greys may be either future descendants of dolphins or genetic extrapolations of dolphins that travel back to our time for their own nefarious purposes. The similarities between Greys and dolphins, in skin texture, colour and their ability to emanate an ultrasonic blast to stun enemies (Greys use the "Stare" to subdue abductees, for example), bear consideration.

MOST CONVINCING EVIDENCE

Following abduction experiences, many victims have found themselves implanted with small metal devices, usually in the nasal cavities, but often found in other areas of the body. When these implants are successfully removed by surgeons, their origins become no less clear. The metal that is used in many of these devices is unknown to today's science, and their purpose remains an unsettling mystery. Are they tracking devices, or something more?

MOST MYSTERIOUS FACT

The commonality of experience among abduction victims, from descriptions of the Greys, procedures and implants, is disquieting. The meteoric rise of books, movies and reports of abductions hints that a greater truth is just lurking beneath the surface, ready to break through at any moment.

SCEPTICALLY SPEAKING

The same phenomenon occurred at the end of the nineteenth century. Although then, instead of alien abductions it was fairies. Chalk it up to end-of-the-century madness, coupled with pre-millennial paranoia.

CATTLE MUTILATIONS

For decades, cattle farmers around the world have been plagued by a problem, a problem that is as inexplicable as it is horrifying: the grisly puzzle of cattle mutilations. Representing more than just a simple financial loss associated with missing livestock, this exercise in abject cruelty may have a purpose, but like its perpetrators, that purpose remains cloaked in shadows.

While the majority of cattle mutilation cases occur in the United States, (particularly in New Mexico), the phenomenon has been reported in Puerto Rico, South America and Canada. Details of the mutilations may vary from case to case, but there are enough commonalities to suggest an orchestrated programme of sorts is underway. More often that not, the bodies of mutilated animals are found drained of blood. Missing organs have been removed with surgical precision, with the carcass often appearing to have been cauterized. The perpetrators show a particular interest in sensory organs such as the eyes, the reproductive and defecatory systems, and the anterior digestive tract.

As many as 10,000 cattle may have died in this manner, and as a result several theories have sprung up surrounding this disturbing trend. If dealing with predators, disease and rowdy young men in search of cow-tipping weren't enough, cattle ranchers now have to contend with an unknown sadistic force that comes and goes like an eviscerating thief in the night.

THE STRANGE PART

Usually, no marks around the bodies of the mutilated cattle are found, with the exception of a few tripod marks surrounding the bodies. Clamp marks have been found on some cattle, suggesting that the mutilation takes place somewhere other than the field in which they are found.

THE USUAL SUSPECTS

UFOs

The theory that aliens (such as the Greys) are seeking to find a way to save their race through bonding with our own gene pool, strays into the arena of cattle mutilation. The aliens could somehow be using cow blood and organs in their experiments, possibly because bovine parts are similar in chemistry to their own. More optimistic theories suggest the aliens are using cows to run random radiation tests in their efforts to save us all from nuclear annihilation. This is backed up by the reports of some human abductees, who claim to have seen cows being led onboard UFOs while they themselves were suffering experimentation. UFOs are often seen in the sky in the nights preceding cattle mutilations, and cattle have been known to become restless and stampede when a UFO is visible. This would seem to indicate that cows in general have had more experience with UFOs then they are letting on.

above The clinical precision and lack of blood renders some cattle mutilations practically inexplicable.

Black Helicopters

These mysterious craft have also been seen around cattle fields preceding mutilations, startling cattle with white hot searchlights. The presence of such craft would lend credence to the theory that the animals are airlifted away to be mutilated, with their dead bodies simply being dropped back into the field after the process is completed. The black helicopters are often associated with secret government programmes and the rise of the New World Order, and could possibly be using cattle to test powerful chemical weapons without hindrance of government guidelines.

Satanists

First thought to be responsible for the mutilations, Satanists were alleged to be using the cows as part of their profane ceremonies, so much so that they were investigated by law enforcement agencies. Nothing conclusive was ever found.

Also suspected: US military; major chemical companies.

THE UNUSUAL SUSPECTS

Natural Predators

Despite the precision of the mutilations, despite the lack of any footprints leading up to the bodies, wolves, coyotes or a so-far-undiscovered predator is thought to be responsible.

El Chupracabra

This mythical monster from Central America, referred to as "The Goat Eater", may be responsible for cattle attacks, perhaps in an effort to expand its palate.

Unknown Cattle Disease

An especially virulent, and as yet undiscovered, cattle ailment has also been blamed: a virus so powerful and quick that it can remove the organs and the blood in the space of a single night, and then completely vanish from any forensic detection.

MOST CONVINCING EVIDENCE

The neatness of the organ removal, coupled with the complete exsanguination of the bodies, points towards a high degree of technological sophistication, rather than to tooth and claw. Wounds are found to be cauterized, which could be the work of laser cutters. What is interesting is that such technology was not in use when the first cattle mutilations were reported, back in the early Seventies. The blood is also removed with such attention to detail that not one drop can be found around the bodies. This would seem to indicate either military or extra-terrestrial involvement, with the parties involved slipping up only occasionally by leaving clamp marks on the animals' legs.

MOST MYSTERIOUS FACT

After the bodies are returned to their fields, they are totally shunned by other animals. There is something so fundamentally wrong with the bodies that even carrion specialists, such as crows, vultures and the like, will not touch them.

SCEPTICALLY SPEAKING

Why would aliens need cow blood in their efforts to interbreed with humanity? Wouldn't it make more sense to kidnap gorillas or other members of the ape family? Surely the suspected government collaborators in the Trilateral Commission could get them a few rhesus monkeys from research facilities, no questions asked? Cattle mutilations could be nothing more than a twisted version of the crop circle phenomenon, with well-organized pranksters equipped with medical equipment and vacuum cleaners, killing cattle in the dead of night instead of tramping down wheat in circular designs in some poor unsuspecting farmer's field.

ALIENS IN HOLLYWOOD

Have extra-terrestrial forces taken an active interest in the world's entertainment industry? It would seem reasonable that if the aliens are here, and are planning at some point to come out of the closet, then it might be better to soften us up first by preparing us for the idea. The best way to get the idea of outer-space visitors seeded casually into the public consciousness is through the use of TV and film, in dramas and documentaries, and the best place to do that from is Hollywood, the heart of the world's film industry.

Over recent years there has been a glut of sci-fi films, TV shows and documentaries dealing with certain common themes. These include "Aliens who arrive without warning and try to take over the world", as in *Independence Day*, *Space: Above And Beyond* and *V*. These are the ones who appear out of nowhere all over the world and sooner or later, start killing people, only to be beaten off. Then you get the theme of "opposing aliens using Earth as part of their on-going battle", as in *The X-Files*, with its evil aliens trying to enslave humanity and the rebel aliens who are against this. Finally, there are the "aliens who are our friends next door", like *Men In Black*, *ET* or *Cocoon*, who arrive in limited numbers and prove to be, in general, rather friendly.

The message this is sending is clear: aliens who appear suddenly in massive numbers are evil, whereas the ones who approach subtly, in small numbers or isolated areas, are actually our friends. This is perfect propaganda for the Greys – the small, large-eyed, noseless aliens – who are here in small numbers, carrying out subtle research on us as part of their technology deal with the US government.

Once the public has been prepared sufficiently to be able to cope with the revelation of extra-terrestrial contact, the news will be broken over a period of years. The process will start with an official sighting of "something unexplainable", and end with a statement along the lines of "We've found them, here they are". In 1998, a panel of previously sceptical world scientists announced officially that some UFO sightings did provide evidence for aliens on earth, and NASA astronauts made a sighting of something unexplainable, so it could be that the process has already begun – but is it for the good or bad of humanity?

THE STRANGE PART

It could be that the major theme park and movie companies have a significant part to play in progress of this conspiracy. One of them was rumoured to be creating a space exhibit for touring around the US. This exhibit would focus on extra-terrestrial encounters and was to generate enormous publicity for the "fact" that Roswell happened and that there was a conspiracy between the US government and the Greys. Some feel that it would have been used to prepare the public for an impending announcement by the government on the reality of UFOs.

THE USUAL SUSPECTS

The Greys

These are the little critters so familiar to popular culture, with the roughly triangular heads, big oval eyes and little slit mouths. They get their name from the colour of their skin. They are here for research purposes, and have been in league with the US government ever since the Roswell crash. While the government still believes that they are interested in mutual advancement, they may well be after something far more sinister – such as humans for breeding purposes.

The US Government

Aliens may just be a way of diverting attention from the US government's own experiments into human biology and psychological manipulation. By implanting the myth of the Greys into the public consciousness, State scientists are able to get up to all sorts of unpleasant research without fear of the repercussions. Their ultimate goal is, of course, a weapon that will allow world domination.

THE UNUSUAL SUSPECTS

The Nordics

Another race of aliens, conforming strangely to the old Nazi vision of the Master Race – tall, muscular, human-like beings with short blond hair – may be behind the manipulation. The Nordics are aware that the Greys are working with the government for sinister purposes, and want to help humanity, so they are trying to portray the Greys as sinister. Hollywood is an ideological battlefield, with pro-Grey and pro-Nordic films slogging it out at the box office.

MOST CONVINCING EVIDENCE

As part of the publicity launch for a proposed venture where visitors to a theme park would have a chance to view a replica alien corpse, a former chairman of a major entertainment company appeared in a documentary that suggested that the US government had an alien craft in a secret research lab (care of Roswell, natch), that this had

above Hollywood has recently produced a range of films filled with alien invaders.

been covered up, and that soon we would all be meeting the aliens face to face. The chairman and his corporation must have been fairly certain of the accuracy of their information to go on record with these startling claims.

MOST MYSTERIOUS FACT

At a private preview screening of *ET* in the White House, President Reagan is reputed to have turned to Stephen Spielberg and said: "Only three people in this entire room know how Goddamn true to life this film is."

SCEPTICALLY SPEAKING

Dr Seth Shostak of SETI, the group searching for evidence of alien civilizations in the universe, was so irritated by the major entertainment corporation's allegedly unscientific and one-sided announcement of the "truth" in the promo video for a proposed venture, that he personally complained to the chairman of the company about how the corporation was misleading children. The cynical observer might also point out that as long as the public flock to sci-fi films and alien exhibits, profit-based organizations are going to do their very best to exploit them.

left Dr Seth Shostak of SETI.

UFOs OVER IRAQ

On December 16, 1998, tracer fire lit up the skies of Baghdad. The ongoing "tepid war" against Saddam Hussein, which had continued since the first Gulf War had failed to remove him from power in 1991, had erupted into one of its periodic phases. The Allied air strike on Iraq's capital city was part of Operation Desert Fox and, just like the first Gulf War, it was being shown live to millions of TV viewers around the world, thanks to CNN. However, that night CNN managed to capture more than the breaking news regarding Desert Fox, they also filmed a UFO hovering above Baghdad. Their footage even showed it moving away to avoid being hit by a stream of anti-aircraft fire.

At the time celebrated among the UFO community as a new piece of strong evidence to prove the existence of UFOs, the incident has taken on a much wider significance among certain conspiracy theorists. More and more have come to believe that there is a solid connection between UFOs seen over Iraq and America's decision to launch an invasion of Iraq in 2003. The constant patrolling and bombing of Iraqi installations by the UK and US airforces in the northern Iraq "No-Fly Zone" produced a wealth of UFO sightings by fighter pilots and a vast number of unexplained radar contacts, with craft moving much faster than any known terrestrial fight craft. It has even been reported that Allied Forces engaged in combat with a UFO in the first Gulf War thinking it was an Iraqi fighter jet. Reports also emerged that US aircraft had brought down a craft of unknown origin in Saudi Arabia in 1998. Residents in the area of the crash site – officially claimed to be that of a jet fighter – were ordered to leave the area while American military engineers recovered all the wreckage for further study. However, residents claim that before they were forced to leave, they were able to establish that the craft was round and did not have any engine or wings. They also reported that even large bits of the wreckage were as light as a feather.

These intriguing tales took an unexpected twist when Russian intelligence sources suggested that a UFO had crashed in Iraq and that Saddam was now engaged in a programme to try and reverse engineer alien technology. At first dismissed as entirely fanciful, a number of intriguing stories relating to this claim started to surface. Among them were reports that Saddam had given sanctuary to the craft's occupants, housing them at his most secure palace

above According to some reports, US pilots engaged in more battles with mysterious lights than Iraqi fighters.

right Were weapons of mass destruction the only things that US forces in Iraq were searching for?

– the citadel of Qalaat-e-Julundi. After the revolution that brought Saddam to power, the old Royal Family stronghold of Qalaat-e-Julundi became a palace for the new dictator. A vast underground bunker network was built under the existing building, already considered the most impenetrable place in Iraq as it stands on a hill surrounded by vertical precipices on three sides, plunging down to the Little Zab River. Soon after Saddam was alleged to have installed his guests there, people living in the Little Zab River Valley began to report strange lights in the sky, "dancing ghosts" seen only at night and a number of strange deaths.

Some of those struggling to believe in any of the official reasons put forward for the second Gulf War believe that the weapons of mass destruction argument was purely a cover story created to give a pretext to an invasion of Iraq. They consider that the real reason for vast military campaign was to prevent Saddam reverse-engineering the crashed alien spacecraft and developing a technological advantage over the US military just as the Americans had done over the Soviets with the Roswell crash in 1947.

THE STRANGE PART

After US forces rolled into Baghdad, a GI with the 3rd Brigade, 101st Airborne Division – who was fighting in the Little Zab Valley – photographed an oblong-shaped UFO. Locals who saw the UFO close to the holy city of Najaf believed that it, "had come from Allah's Gardens of Bliss to protect the Tomb of Ali". The mosque at Najaf stands over the grave of Ali, son-in-law of the prophet Mohammed. During the war it miraculously escaped damage from the 101st Airborne's howitzer barrage and heavy Allied

bombing raids on the area around Little Zab River Valley focussed on the citadel of Qalaat-e-Julundi.

THE USUAL SUSPECTS

MJ-12

The group thought to be behind the cover-up and subsequent reverse engineering of the UFO crash at Roswell are alleged to secretly control the Joint Chiefs of Staff. They may also have close links with the Bush family through George Bush Snr, going back to when he was director of the CIA. Having used the knowledge to ensure American supremacy since 1947, the prospect of being usurped by Saddam was unacceptable and they were forced to create a pretext for an invasion of Iraq so they could seize the crashed craft for themselves.

Reptilian Aliens

Reptilian beings from the Draco system are often accused of having entered into a secret alliance with parts of the world's ruling elite. Rumoured to be at war with the oft-sighted Greys, the Draconians may have instructed their allies in America's military and government to recover the Grey aliens being given shelter by Saddam. This was done under cover of war, rather than having to reveal themselves by a dramatic show of Draconian power in Iraq.

THE UNUSUAL SUSPECTS

The French Government

The French and Iraqi regimes enjoyed good relations and Saddam may have been negotiating with his friends in Paris to share UFO technology with them if they could prevent him from being removed from power by Bush.

This would have allowed the French to lead a European challenge for global power. Right up until the moment of war the French provided solid support for Iraq and US Secretary of State Colin Powell answered "yes", when asked if France would be punished for its actions.

MOST CONVINCING EVIDENCE

Bush's claims that there was, "No doubt that the Iraq regime continues to possess and conceal some of the most lethal weapons ever devised and that it threatens all mankind" were dubious, even before the post-war $500 million search of Iraq failed to find them. Though almost all of the Bush administration claims about Iraq weapons were disproved by UN inspectors, America still went to war, which suggests there must have been an ulterior motive for the military action.

MOST MYSTERIOUS FACT

Zecharia Sitchin, one of the few people in the world able to translate ancient Sumerian cuneiform, believes that ancient texts tell how the civilization of Sumeria (based in the area occupied by modern-day Iraq) was aided by an advanced race of beings. Called the Anunnaki (Sumerian for "those who came from Heaven to Earth"), their existence would mean that Saddam is not the first ruler in that area to have been helped by extra-terrestrials.

SCEPTICALLY SPEAKING

Expanding the power of America to ensure it controls the twenty-first century. The backfiring of Saddam's bluff that he had lethal weapons. A war fought on behalf of American oil companies. George Bush Jr trying to prove to his father that he could kick Iraqi ass better than George Snr could. Whatever the real explanation for the second Gulf War, surely crashed UFOs has got to be the least likely?

MEN IN BLACK (MIB)

I f you've seen a UFO and report it the police, you can expect many things: ridicule, questions concerning your alcohol consumption, odd looks from friends, and perhaps a call from the local newspaper looking for a bit of light news for the next day's edition. But even worse than the preceding events, you may receive a visit from the dreaded Men In Black.

The Men In Black have long been associated with UFO sightings and phenomena. They are reported to appear at the homes of some UFO witnesses shortly after they've reported their sighting to the police or media, threatening them to keep quiet. Any materials found relating to a UFO sighting are promptly confiscated. In some cases, they have even knocked on the doors of witnesses before they've told anyone else of what they have seen, seemingly knowing everything that has happened before the witnesses had a chance to sort it all out in their heads themselves. The Men In Black deliver their message in a variety of ways, from direct threats to roundabout hints, but their message always carries the same dark undertone: "Keep your mouth shut, or you'll regret it…"

The Men In Black are so called because of their sartorial colour of choice – black. Black suits, black hats and black sunglasses… this intimidating colour scheme extends to their cars – vintage models of Buicks, Cadillacs or Lincolns. They have been described as having complexions ranging from olive to grey to dark, with slightly slanted eyes, speaking in an almost computer-like monotone. Their age is difficult to determine, since all of them seem to be verging towards middle-aged. They move in a robot-like manner, and are perhaps best summed up in one word: "odd".

Despite their numerous appearances and incredible powers of intimidation, finding conclusive proof of the existence of the Men In Black is as slippery a task as acquiring evidence of the existence of the very UFOs they seek to protect.

THE STRANGE PART

The Men In Black definitely seem to be not of this world. Examples of this can be found in reports of MIBs disintegrating coins in their hands and inexplicably trying to sing to birds in trees. In one incident, a MIB sat down on a chair, which caused his trouser leg to rise up. There, apparently grafted to his leg, was a large green wire. In other cases, MIBs are seen crossing muddy fields, yet arrive without a single spot of mud on them. In the most vicious cold weather, they will show up wearing nothing but a thin coat, oblivious to the deadly chill.

THE USUAL SUSPECTS
Aliens

In an effort to keep their activities on Earth quiet, aliens would employ the Men In Black to suppress any media attention to their activities by intimidating eyewitnesses of UFOs into fearful silence. From their inhuman way of moving

above Hollywood's Men In Black, are they part of an insidious propaganda programme?

and mechanical way of speaking, the MIBs could be androids, programmed by the aliens involved in the sighting they are sent to suppress. Some people think that the Men In Black are aliens themselves, possibly Greys or another race, the Horlocks, (a reptilian race without souls). This would explain their remarkable strangeness around other human beings.

US Government

Working in conjunction with the aliens, the US government would utilize the MIBs and their attendant oddities to suppress reports of UFOs. The Men In Black would be actors instructed to be as odd and bizarre as possible, thus adding to the already confused and emotional state of eyewitnesses. The MIB would be untraceable agents, not linked to any known governmental institution, thus allowing the "Powers That Be" to keep their hands clean of any violation of human rights.

THE UNUSUAL SUSPECTS

The Planet Sirius

The symbol of the Eye of Horus has been linked with secret societies in allegiance with the planet Sirius. This same symbol has been seen on some MIBs, and some Men In Black have said they work for an organization called "The Nation of The Third Eye". The role they play in the plans of the denizens of Sirius is unclear.

UFO Eyewitnesses

If UFO sightings are nothing more than a complete mental breakdown of the witness involved, then the appearance of the MIB could be just a continuation of the hallucination, perhaps representing the witnesses' need for punishment and correction.

MOST CONVINCING EVIDENCE

The power of the Men In Black cannot be discounted. They have been responsible for the cancellation of *Space Review*, a magazine dedicated to studying flying saucers, and have even gone as far as gassing an eyewitness during a terrifying interrogation. It is possible that incontrovertible proof of alien existence does exist, whether it is photos, videos or actual aliens, but has been suppressed by the ruthless efficiency of the MIBs. Research has discovered that the lineage of the Men In Black may go back as far as the Elizabethan age.

MOST MYSTERIOUS FACT

The vintage automobiles of the MIBs are often illuminated from within by otherworldly greenish glows, and their clothing has a "shiny" alien texture to it that doesn't correspond to any known fabric on Earth.

SCEPTICALLY SPEAKING

If they were truly aliens, with the technology capable of enabling themselves to travel between the stars and capable of wiping out the memories of abductees, then why would they waste their time sending loonies in bad suits to knock on doors? Surely a good death ray would do the trick?

below The ancient Egyptian symbol the Eye of Horus has been seen worn by the MIB.

SECRET BASES ON THE MOON

The Moon has always held a fascination for humanity – both as a source of romantic inspiration for poets and as an astronomical curiosity for scientists. However, is it also a secret base for the Third Reich? Apparently so.

As early as 1942, the rumours go, the Nazis landed on the Moon with the aid of giant rocket saucers. These Nazi flying saucers are reported to have stood 45 metres high, contained 10 storeys of crew compartments, and had a diameter of 60 metres. Upon landing on the Moon, the Nazis quickly began building underground bases, solidifying their hold on the lunar surface while losing their grip on power in Europe below.

This colonization continued through the Forties, with the Nazis ferrying up more people, raw materials, and robots in their giant interplanetary Nazi saucers. After the end of the Second World War in 1945, the Germans continued their space efforts from their Neu Schwabenland base in Earth's south polar region. This colonization continues to this day, with the full knowledge and assistance of other world powers.

There are certainly convincing photographs, taken during the Second World War, showing Nazi-produced flying craft that look remarkably similar to the classic concept of a flying saucer. These craft – going under such fabulous names as the Vril Odin 7 and Haunebu II – were developed at secret bases similar to the famous rocket base Peenemunde. It is well known that German scientists, many of whom ended up as founder members of NASA after the War, had planned to turn Peenemunde into a space port and springboard for Moon colonization after what they thought would be inevitable Nazi victory against the Allies.

THE STRANGE PART

Where to begin? Two things give this rumour a degree of credence. The first is growing weight of scientific evidence that the Moon is not totally arid and that the frozen ice on it could be utilized by any colony. Second, video footage taken from a NASA space shuttle clearly shows an unidentified object leaving the surface of the Moon. While there may be a non-conspiratorial explanation, strange lights, inexplicable markings on the surface and even potential structures observed by astronomers on the lunar surface push the number of odd questions needing answers to a disconcerting level.

THE USUAL SUSPECTS

The Nazi Party of Germany
Perhaps sensing the inevitability of defeat by the Allies as early as 1940, the Nazis decided to move their base of operations to a lunar plane, thus ensuring the long-term success of the Third Reich. Knowing Hitler's love of the supernatural and the fantastic, this does not seem implausible – just typically far-fetched.

The Axis Powers of Japan and Italy
Germany kept close ties with its allies during the Second World War, sharing its advances in weaponry with Italy and Japan. Rocket designs of German origin were routinely tested in Italy's research facilities, and in July of 1945, at the end of the War, a German U-Boat reportedly delivered a new invention to Japanese research and development units: a spherical, wingless, flying machine. Working under German instructions, the Japanese constructed the device, without knowing how it worked. Once activated, it roared off into the sky in a burst of flame, never to be seen again. Shaken, the Japanese scientists decided to forget about the whole thing. However, in January, 1946, a Japanese-German team, numbering in the hundreds, flew to the Moon in another saucer, surviving a near crash landing.

THE UNUSUAL SUSPECTS

NASA
NASA may be lying about the truth of the Moon's atmosphere, in order to keep other countries from wanting to explore it as well, thus ensuring a monopoly on the Moon. The story goes that when the United States and Russia constructed their own moonbases in the Fifties, they were the guests of the Nazis when they landed.

Vril Society
A major mystical, secret order that was the source of much of the perverse ideology behind the early philosophies of the Nazi Party, the Vril Society claimed high-ranking members of Hitler's regime, major industrialists and powerful occultists among its ranks. It lent its name and money to the development of the mysterious Vril flying craft. It is known that some members believed the Aryan race developed from aliens who that landed in Sumeria around 4,500BC and were viewed as gods. Could Vril have been the power behind the establishment of Nazi moonbases?

Aliens
Some conspiriologists believe that the Nazis were in league with extra-terrestrials and that the many advances they made in genetics and rocket science can be traced to a helping hand from beyond the stars. Debate rages over exactly which type of alien was assisting Hitler, but the favourites are the Aryan-looking Nordics rather than the Greys. However, given the type of experimentation on humans the Greys seem to love, and the depraved medical research performed by some of the human monsters of

the Nazi regime, no one is ruling out an alliance with that particular branch of villainous space scum.

MOST CONVINCING EVIDENCE

The only proof of the American landing on the Moon comes from photographs published by NASA. However, over recent years these photos have been classed as fake because they are full of inconsistencies. Shadow lengths are at odds with the sun, the directions of shadows vary within pictures and there is plenty of evidence of the photos having been taken with the use of large sources of artificial light. If the photographs from NASA are not to be trusted, what else should we doubt?

MOST MYSTERIOUS FACT

There have not been any lunar landings – at least in the public's eyes – in over twenty years. Is this to distract the world's attentions from the colonies – Nazi, Russian and American, with populations estimated at over 40,000 – at work there?

SCEPTICALLY SPEAKING

The drives needed to power such huge saucers – listed by conspiracy theorists as "free energy tachyon drives" – cannot help but raise eyebrows. But with the reverse engineering associated with the salvaged technology from the Roswell crash and the lack of photos of the Moon's dark side, one can't help but wonder.

left A V2 rocket at the Peenemunde. Did the Nazis develop craft advanced enough to travel to the Moon?

THE RENDELSHAM LANDING – ENGLAND'S ROSWELL

There are mean-spirited cynics who will tell you that conspiracy theorists live only for the moment when they can rub their hands together and say, "I told you so." But in the annals of alien conspiracies, there is only one case where the conspiracy research can leap up like an overactive dog and shout, "I told you so, it is official – there was a conspiracy!" That case is Rendelsham.

On December 27, 1980, an Unidentified Flying Object landed in a clearing in Rendelsham Forest next to the joint USAF air bases of Bentwaters and Woodbridge near Ipswich, England. Deputy Base Commander Lieutenant Colonel Charles Halt and several of his men witnessed the landing. It was tracked by British military radar and left behind physical evidence. Twelve years later, a British Parliamentary Watchdog ruled that the UK government had attempted to cover up all of the above facts. In 2002, Parliamentary Ombudsman Ann Abraham ruled that the UK Ministry of Defence had refused to divulge full details of the Rendelsham witness accounts and conspired to prevent knowledge of the event ever becoming known.

The incident is regarded as one of the most important ever UFO sightings and has become known as the "English Roswell". Possibly, it is just coincidence that both cases involve the US military and happened close to highly sensitive military bases with links to top-secret arms of American nuclear defence structure. Alongside being the only alien conspiracy where a government attempt to cover up the facts has been proven and exposed, no other case has as many staggering eyewitness accounts by highly credible military professionals.

Shortly after midnight on Boxing Day, radar screens at RAF Watton in Norfolk showed the sudden appearance of an object near Rendelsham Forest. Given that the twin airbases leased to the USAF on the perimeter of the forest housed a vast stockpile of weapons, alarm intensified when the object suddenly disappeared before reappearing without warning on the radar of the Bentwaters base. While further radar confirmations of the strange craft were coming in from other tracking stations, three military policemen saw light in the trees outside the back gate of the airfield and set off, fearing a crash. In his report of that night Deputy Base Commander Lt Col Halt wrote, "They reported seeing a strange glowing object in the forest. Metallic in appearance and triangular in shape approximately two to three metres across the base and 2m high. It illuminated the entire forest with a white light. The object itself has a pulsating red light on top and a bank of blue lights underneath. The object was hovering or on legs. As the patrolmen approached it manoeuvred through the trees and disappeared. At this time animals on a nearby farm went into a frenzy."

The next night Lt Col Halt joined a patrol that found three depressions on the forest floor where the object had been sighted. Radiation readings of ten times the normal level were discovered and as they were investigating the craft returned. Several years after the incident, Halt released an 18-minute audiocassette made on the night of the encounter. It makes chilling listening, especially the moment when another officer on the patrol sees the craft and shouts, "Look at the colours! Shit!" The tape also records the panic-stricken men as they see a beam from the craft disabling electrical devices in the area for a time and other military personnel in the area recording the event with both still and video cameras.

Given the impeccable witnesses and multiple types of physical evidence, you might think the public would at last be told that things that were unidentifiable and flew really did exist. However, in the years that followed, both the American and British military did everything in their power to cover up the Rendelsham Forest incident. It even seemed as if other shadowy elements were also involved in a conspiracy to enforce silence – discrediting, scaring and threatening anyone witnessing the case, or who had knowledge of it. In 1983 conspiracy researchers got their first major break when a copy of a memo written by Lt Col Halt to the British Ministry of Defence was released under the Freedom of Information Act. With the first part of the puzzle out in the open, the battle to reveal the truth really began.

below A UFO sighting linked to US nuclear bombers, no wonder it is a conspiracy.

THE STRANGE PART

As more and more of the US military witnesses to the landing on the second night were identified, one USAF security patrolman, Larry Warren, even went public with an account claiming that he saw three "aeronaut entities" communicating with senior officers. The next morning, he and colleagues were checked for radiation exposure and instructed to sign statements, which merely mentioned seeing "unusual lights". The statements were arranged by members of the National Security Agency and warned them not to discuss what they had seen.

THE USUAL SUSPECTS

The NSA

The US National Security Agency had a strong presence at the bases and played a key role in attempting to keep the landing secret. The NSA have an alleged contact and humans-for-advanced-technology exchange programme with the Greys and Rendelsham was purely a routine business meeting that was accidentally witnessed by Lt Col Halt and his men.

Project Phoenix

An ultra-secret programme run by America's Defence Advanced Research Projects Agency. One element of Project Phoenix may be dealing with advanced microwave, laser and hologram weapons meant to create totally convincing illusions to baffle and demoralize the enemy. Rendelsham may have been an experiment to test the credulity of crack troops as well as assessing the impact on morale amongst elite warriors of these weapons.

THE UNUSUAL SUSPECTS

Parallel Earth Travellers

In medieval times, in an area close to Rendelsham, two mysterious green-skinned children were found, causing some to speculate that this part of Suffolk is home to a gateway to a parallel Earth. The visitors to Rendelsham may not have been extra-terrestrial visitors but instead, extra-dimensional. Either they took a wrong turning or were on a scouting mission to our Earth.

Zeta Reticalans

Grey humanoid aliens from Zeta Reticula were scouting the US bases as elements of the American military are in a secret alliance with reptilian aliens from the Sirius system. Their craft got into trouble and they were forced to land to make repairs behind enemy lines. However, luckily for the Zeta Reticalans, the soldiers at Rendelsham did not know they were at war and therefore let space reptile sworn enemies slip away.

MOST CONVINCING EVIDENCE

Despite the fact that it was tracked by radar, left impressions in the ground and massive radiation readings, the military and others later tried to claim that the event was purely down to the evolving beam of the Orford Ness lighthouse, five miles away. The depressions in the earth were merely rabbit diggings and the radiation was of natural levels. Many witnesses were sacked, defamed, harassed, stalked and threatened by the authorities as well as military intelligence agents and shadowy "men in black" – all of which is a bit over the top if the soldiers and civilians had just mistaken a lighthouse!

MOST MYSTERIOUS FACT

Author and society gossip columnist Georgina Bruni turned conspiracy researcher on the subject of Rendelsham and wrote a classic book on the case. At a social event in 1997, she seized her chance to ask former British prime minister Margaret Thatcher about the landing. Thatcher was annoyed at being questioned about Rendelsham and railed at Bruni, "You can't tell the people."

SCEPTICALLY SPEAKING

Hands up all those who are surprised that the UK government and the US military conspired to keep quiet about something strange landing close to an air force base housing enough nuclear to turn all of Europe into a radioactive wasteland?

ROSWELL

It was July 3, 1947 when W W "Mac" Brazel saddled his horse and rode out to check his sheep on his sprawling New Mexico ranch. There had been a thunderstorm the night before, and Brazel felt concerned for his animals' safety. But as he rode, he came across bits of strange wreckage strewn across the land. He also discovered what appeared to be a wreck of some sort. A huge gouge had been dug into the earth, running for hundreds of feet. Mystified, Brazel retrieved a piece of the strange material that littered the ground, and showed it to a neighbour. Wondering if he was holding something from a government project or possibly a UFO, he drove into nearby Roswell to tell his story to the local sheriff, George Wilcox, and by doing so, launched one of the most enduring nesting grounds for conspiracies in the twentieth century.

The truth about the incident at Roswell has remained hidden behind government subterfuge and the unreliability of ageing eyewitnesses. What is undisputed is that Wilcox dutifully reported the wreckage to Intelligence Officer Major Jesse Marcel of the 509th Bomb Squad. For the next few days, the site was closed off as the US Army Air Force removed the wreckage. On July 8, 1947, a press release prepared by the USAAF reported the debris was from a "flying disc". The following day, however, the government quickly retracted the story, stating firmly that the mysterious debris was not from a flying saucer, but merely the wreckage of a crashed weather balloon.

And there the story ended, or so the US government hoped. But strange stories began to grow, gaining strength by the unusual silence from military and government leaders. Among these stories were tales that it was indeed a crashed flying saucer, that the government was covering it up; that there were actual alien bodies aboard the ship, and even that some of the aliens had survived. More than fifty years have passed since the incident at Roswell. Conspiracy theories have flourished, generating much media attention and providing an eternal burr beneath the skin of the government. Eventually the US Air Force released a report

above Modern day inhabitants of Roswell have turned their town into a tourist spot.

inset US President Harry Truman.

– The Roswell Report: Case Closed – on June 24, 1994, in a vain attempt to shut the lid on perhaps the greatest Pandora's Box the conspiracy world has ever known.

Not surprisingly, it failed.

THE STRANGE PART

During the clean up of debris, Glenn Dennis, a mortician working in a Roswell funeral home, answered a few phone calls from the morgue at the local airfield. The Mortuary Officer there was looking for information on how to best preserve bodies that had been outside for a few days without suffering further contamination of the bodies' tissues. He also requested small, hermetically sealed coffins.

THE USUAL SUSPECTS

The US Government

A crashed UFO would have been a major technological windfall for the US government, and it would have wanted to keep such a find as secret as possible. Some people feel that the Roswell crash led the military into trying to decipher the mystery of the downed craft, reverse-engineering the alien technology to derive new weapons and anti-gravity capabilities. President Truman allegedly visited the crash site, and may even have spoken to surviving aliens. Shortly afterwards, Truman instigated the removal of all of the UFO crash material, including that found at Roswell, into the keeping of an anonymous multinational syndicate that now controls all UFO technology.

The US government has even been accused of torturing the alien survivors of Roswell, if not killing them outright, according to a secret policy of dealing with extra-terrestrials.

Other, less fantastic theories place the blame on to the military, testing secret planes built using Albert Einstein's withdrawn work on gravity field theory.

The Greys

There's no shortage of theories that state the Greys are using mankind to perfect genetic manipulations in order to save their own race. Alarmed that mankind had graduated to using nuclear weapons in 1945 (in much the same way we would if we discovered a pet hamster with an Uzi), the Greys reportedly began reconnaissance missions around military bases. This could have been the case at Roswell, where two ships may have collided, or the reconnaissance craft could simply have been struck by lightning.

THE UNUSUAL SUSPECTS

The Soviets

During the raging Cold War paranoia, it was suspected that the Soviets might have perfected their offensive missile capability with pilfered Nazi technology. The Roswell debris could have been the remains of a failed missile attack.

Hollow Earth Mole Men

There is a theory that the middle of the Earth is a hollow space containing land masses, a sun and oceans. According to that theory, the race living there might have been alarmed, much like the Greys, at the rise of nuclear testing by the creatures living on the surface of the planet. Flying out of the huge polar holes that lead to the hollow part of the Earth, these "Mole Men" may have crashed their ship on a reconnaissance mission.

MOST CONVINCING EVIDENCE

The need for the Air Force to release a "final report" implies a guilty conscience. If there was really nothing to Roswell, why go to the trouble, expense and possible ridicule of commissioning and publishing a report? The sudden leap forward in technology that followed the Roswell crash, especially the invention of transistors, is suspicious.

MOST MYSTERIOUS FACT

After driving out to the airfield hospital, the Roswell mortician Glenn Dennis saw several bits of wreckage carved with strange engravings. Speaking to a nurse there, she explained about the bodies, going so far as to draw him pictures on a prescription pad. A few days later, she was mysteriously assigned to a post in England, and then seemed, apparently, to drop off the face of the Earth.

SCEPTICALLY SPEAKING

The wild variations in the accounts of several "eyewitnesses" and the pure schlock of such gems as the purported Roswell alien autopsy video give this potentially devastating event all the appeal of a trailer park fun fair. It has become alien conspiracies equivalent of Elvis sightings.

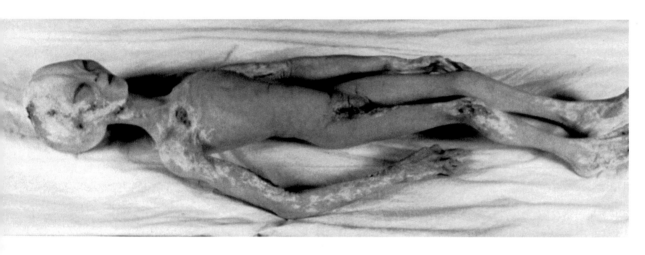

left Is this what the Roswell "aliens" looked like?

SPACE SABOTAGE

Travelling to the stars has always been a daunting task, but is it being made more difficult than it need be? Is someone – or something – doing its best to keep mankind on Earth, by sabotaging space flight after space flight? The problem has become so widespread that NASA has jokingly referred to this enigmatic and often deadly force as the "Great Galactic Ghoul". But is it the subject for levity, or something far more terrifying?

The high incidence rate of spaceflight accidents, disappearances and technological foul-ups would have crippled any other endeavour that didn't have the benefit of government funding. From simple faults such as wires burning out in satellite systems to the tragedy of the *Challenger* explosion, the Great Galactic Ghoul shows no national

preference – both Russian and American space programmes have been plagued by its disruptive hand.

Recent examples include the fiasco surrounding the Hubble telescope. Once in space, the much-vaunted telescopes was found to be far from perfect, thus making its pictures far more blurred than expected. An expensive repair mission was needed, but the Hubble pictures are still being discounted as more a triumph of selective filters, designed to hide the telescope's imperfections, than the groundbreaking shots the project's supporters claim them to be.

Another example was the *Mars Explorer* mission of 1993, which was launched to take closer pictures of the mysterious Cydonia Region of Mars. Just as the craft was entering Martian orbit, it suddenly stopped functioning. Other failures include: the Soviet *Koralb 11* (blew up); *Sputnik 24* (blew up): NASA's *Mariner 3* (missed Mars): *Mariner 8* (fell into Atlantic); the *Apollo 13* mission; and the fiery deaths of the astronauts in the Space Shuttle. The list goes on and on, and is either a testament to staggering incompetence or evidence of an ongoing act of sabotage, perhaps even on a galactic scale.

THE STRANGE PART

Missions to Mars fare the worst when it comes to sabotage. One of the most disturbing was the fate of the Russian Phobos probes. Launched in 1988, the Russians sent the two probes to investigate Phobos, the smaller of Mars' two moons. The Russians were interested in the irregular orbital patterns, which led many to believe Phobos was either an artificial construction or perhaps hollow. The first probe was somehow lost on the journey from Earth. *Phobos 2* made it to Mars and on its way to the small moon took photographs of a cylindrical-shaped shadow on the surface of Phobos. Shortly after that, the probe was destroyed. Its final picture, beamed back to Russia, has been declared too sensitive to release to the public. On the night that final picture was sent, orthodox Russian priests were asked to go to the Phobos 2 Control Centre in Moscow to discuss the pictures received.

THE USUAL SUSPECTS

NASA

As horrible as it sounds, especially with human lives being lost in some accidents, it is possible that a secret contingent within NASA could be sabotaging missions in order to satisfy elements in the US government that do not want the space programme to discover the alien presence surrounding Earth. Corresponding dissidents would, of course, exist in the Russian space programme.

Competing Contractors

The financial windfall associated with landing a lucrative government contract would prove irresistible to many businessmen. The best way to succeed in the cut-throat tendering process would be to discredit fellow competitors, using whatever means available, including sabotage. The power of the dollar, especially one from a government source, would easily overcome the sanctity of human lives in the eyes of many.

Also suspected: the FBI; MJ-12; sheer human incompetence.

UNUSUAL SUSPECTS

The Greys

For reasons of their own, it would be in the best interests of the Greys to keep Earth isolated from the rest of the Universe. If the Greys are rebellious slaves escaping from their masters and using human genetic material to reproduce and save themselves from the degradation of their cloned bodies, it simply would not do to have mankind drawing the attention of other alien races, particularly those masters.

Martians

The surprising number of incidents involving Mars missions goes beyond pure coincidence. The Monuments on Mars indicate that there was – or may still be – life on Mars, life that may wish to be left alone or that will make its presence known in its own good time. The breakdowns, disappearances and erratic behaviour of craft around the Red Planet has led some

above A high number of expensive space explorations launches end in a disastrous manner.

NASA employees to joke about a Great Galactic Ghoul living in between the asteroid belt and Mars. Perhaps this Ghoul is nothing more than a disgruntled Martian.

MOST CONVINCING EVIDENCE

Before the launch of the *Mars Observer* on September 25, 1992, NASA technicians examined its outer housing for a routine check. Inside, they were shocked to find the probe filled with garbage. This garbage included metal filings, dirt, paper, fibres and plaster of Paris. Even though Hurricane Andrew had blown through the area, it was impossible for debris of this kind to have entered the probe driven by the force of the storm alone...

Maybe it is not so surprising that of the 35 attempts to reach the planet, only 12 have succeeded. Of these, nine were attempts to land on the surface, but only three survived. The rest crashed or exploded in orbit. Even the successful ones had problems. Sojourner, which was launched in 1997, could only manage to move a few dozen metres from its landing zone.

MOST MYSTERIOUS FACT

In July, 1998, the *Galileo* spacecraft was passing Europa, one of Jupiter's moons, when it suddenly stopped transmitting information. It has long been speculated that Europa, along with Mars, may be able to sustain life.

SCEPTICALLY SPEAKING

We are a race that has trouble programming our VCRs. Is it any wonder our spaceships keep blowing up?

REVERSE ENGINEERING

Have you ever felt that the world was moving too fast? Have you ever wondered at the amazing technological leaps mankind seems to have made in such a relatively short amount of time? Have you ever felt a pang of uneasiness when you consider that humanity went from barely being able to fly a crude airplane to walking on the Moon in under seventy years?

The unprecedented way humanity's level of technology has increased in the twentieth century is simply baffling and may be a sign of one of the most pervasive conspiracies of all time. While the scientific community pats itself on the back and ascribes such progress to the diligence and ingenuity of its members, a look at the "innovations" of the last few decades seem to owe more to "intervention" than ingenuity.

In fact, many theorists feel that the true force behind the current technological juggernaut is not elbow grease and endless nights burning the midnight oil, but alien assistance. For reasons unknown to the general public, governments worldwide are reverse-engineering alien technology – that is, taking apart alien artifacts to discover what makes them work, then applying that knowledge to their own ends. This knowledge is putting us light years ahead of where we should be technologically and, perhaps, even culturally. Like children playing with fire, we are not mature enough to handle it, and are in serious danger of getting burnt.

THE STRANGE PART

Most of the major leaps in technology occur after 1947 – from more powerful computers to the Apollo lunar missions. It was in 1947, coincidentally enough, that the US government allegedly salvaged a crashed UFO from Roswell, New Mexico.

THE USUAL SUSPECTS

The US Government

It has long been theorized that a UFO (or UFOs) crashed near Roswell and Corona in New Mexico in 1947, and that the US government quickly made off with the remains. Caught in the Cold War with the USSR, the US was desperate for any military advantage, and so began the slow process of reverse-engineering the alien technology found aboard the crashed flying saucers. Much of this reverse engineering is thought to occur at the infamous Area 51, a secret military testing site in New Mexico.

The Greys

In exchange for being allowed to kidnap and experiment on humans with impunity, one theory has the US government – and possibly other governments – agreeing to look the other way in exchange for alien technology. This would explain why incidents of abduction and UFO sightings are treated with ridicule by government authorities as they try to divert attention from what is truly going on – the sale of humanity for capital gain.

THE UNUSUAL SUSPECTS

Time Travellers

Time travellers could be bringing technology in the hope that leaving their futuristic gadgetry with us could change circumstances in their time, altering it to their advantage. Other theories state that the US government has experimented with short-range time travel, and is bringing back technology from our own future. Similar theories lay the blame on dimensional travel, with advanced tech coming from more advanced versions of our own present day.

Benevolent Aliens

In preparation for an invasion force coming to Earth, benevolent aliens have provided world powers with the technology to defend themselves, as evidenced in the Star Wars satellites. The advances seen by the everyday populace – cell phones, microwaves, home computers – are merely lucrative spin-offs generated by reverse engineering of this technology and are a bonus for the government contractors that undertake secret defence work.

MOST CONVINCING EVIDENCE

Perhaps the most incriminating bit of technology, that ushered in the current wave of progress, was the transistor.

This has been rumoured to be a direct result of reverse-engineering work on the crashed ship at Roswell. Other more sinister applications of this alien science could be the US military's weaponry, including the B-2 stealth bomber.

MOST MYSTERIOUS FACT

Curious citizens who have reported seeing strange lights that resemble UFOs around Area 51 – and an NBC News crew that filmed something odd in the sky in 1992 – have had to contend with armed forces harassing them and confiscating cameras and video equipment. Some people have even been chased by black helicopters, which are often seen around areas of suspected alien activity.

SCEPTICALLY SPEAKING

One problem with the reverse-engineering theory is that it assumes humans are brilliant. If we went back in time and handed Mr Cro-Magnon a Pentium laptop, a remote-control garage-opener, and a Thigh Master, the reverse-engineering theory would have us believe that he'd be founding MagnonSoft in ten years. Sadly, he'd probably grunt at the items and then drop them on someone's head. Well, maybe he'd keep the Thigh Master.

left Has alien technology played a role in advancing US military craft?

MURDERED OR MISSING

3

AMELIA EARHART

She was the golden girl of the aviation set, a media celebrity, and an inspiration to women everywhere. Amelia Earhart strode into the male-dominated world of flying, setting new flight records for women, with a noble mix of courage and grace. Beloved by an America torn apart by the ravages of the Depression, Earhart was a national hero. Her sudden disappearance while trying to fly around the world in 1937 shocked the nation.

Amelia Earhart was born July 24, 1897, in Atchison, Kansas. Coming from a wealthy family, Earhart studied to be a nurse's aid in Toronto, and worked as a Voluntary Aid Detachment nurse in a military hospital during World War I. In 1920, she moved out to California with her family. It was there she attended an aerial meet, and her love of flying was born. Quickly learning to fly, Earhart set a women's altitude record of 14,000 feet two years later, and as the years passed, her reputation as a pilot flourished.

In 1928, New York publisher George Putnam, asked her to become the first woman to cross the Atlantic on the "Friendship" flight between Great Britain and America. She agreed, setting another yet another record. She was tagged with the name "Lady Lindy", after the first pilot to cross the Atlantic, Charles Lindbergh. Earhart disliked this name, because she had merely been a passenger on the "Friendship" flight.

As if to prove herself even more, Earhart continued to set new records. In 1928, she flew across America, travelling from the Atlantic to the Pacific coast. In 1931, she set an altitude record of 14,000 feet in an autogiro. A year later, in 1932, Earhart flew across the Atlantic alone, landing in Ireland. She became the darling of the lecture tours, and was honoured by President Hoover and by Congress, becoming the first woman to receive the Distinguished Flying Cross. But her greatest challenge still lay before her – a flight around the world.

above Amelia Earhart takes off from Newfoundland.

On June 1, 1937, Earhart flew out of Miami, Florida in her Electra aeroplane to circumnavigate the globe. Accompanied only by her navigator, Fred Noonan, she set out first for Puerto Rico. From South America, they flew to Africa, then to the Red Sea. By June 29, they were in New Guinea, ready for the long flight across the Pacific. They were almost home. They left New Guinea at 0:00 GMT, with the US Coast Guard ship *Itasca* positioned off Howland Island, near Hawaii, to provide radio contact.

They never arrived. Earhart sent a message to the *Itasca* at 7:42am, saying that they were unable to see the ship, and that their gas was running low. A brief message came through at 8:45am, then silence. The people of America, listening at their radios, was stunned. A shaken President Roosevelt sent out a military search party consisting of 66 aircraft and nine ships, but nothing was found. On July 18, 1937, the search was reluctantly called off. Amelia Earhart and Fred Noonan were gone.

THE STRANGE PART

In an uncharacteristic loss of control, Earhart made an error while trying to lift off from an airfield near Pearl Harbor. The undercarriage collapsed, severely damaging the plane. In what could be construed as an omen, it was the same plane she disappeared in over the Pacific.

THE USUAL SUSPECTS

Amelia Earhart

It was known that Earhart had suffered dysentery during the flight, perhaps impairing her judgement, causing her to crash. It could also have been suicide – Earhart may have been burnt out by the constant attention and expectations of the media. Or she could have simply chosen to disappear, setting up a new life after away from the public eye. Some theories have her going to an isolated island to live peacefully with native fishermen.

The Nazi Party

It has been suggested that Earhart was on a secret mission for President Roosevelt to monitor Nazi activities around the globe. Shot down or captured by the Germans, this would explain the sizable military force Roosevelt sent out to rescue her in an attempt, perhaps, to retrieve sensitive American information or useful data on the Nazis.

THE UNUSUAL SUSPECTS

Temporal Rift

Earhart may have flown into a temporal rift, which is what the Bermuda Triangle is rumoured to be. This would explain the trouble with radio contact between the plane and *Itasca*, and her confusion. Perhaps her plane is simply lost in the past or the future.

The Japanese

Along the lines of the Nazi Party theory, this theory sees the Japanese capturing Earhart, coercing her to take to the airwaves as the dreaded "Tokyo Rose", the female propaganda machine that was a deadly scourge to GI morale during World War II.

The US Government

If Earhart was an American spy, perhaps she discovered something disturbing about her employers. In retaliation, the Air Force would have shot down her plane, then valiantly mounted a search party for public relations purposes, while ensuring that no evidence remained.

Also suspected: UFOs; sea monsters.

MOST CONVINCING EVIDENCE

Despite the largest military search for civilians ever mounted, no wreckage or material from Earhart's plane was found at the time, suggesting that either Earhart was off course (with her formidable flying skills, this is doubtful), or the plane never crashed. None of the bones found since the disappearance have turned out to belong to her. Even recent evidence unearthed by The International Group for Historic Aircraft Recovery, suggesting her plane was at Gardner Island, failed to conclusively solve the mystery, due to the absence of bones that failed a genetic match with Amelia.

MOST MYSTERIOUS FACT

For a week after Earhart's disappearance, several radio operators on ships and aircraft heard a distress signal coming from the vicinity of Gardner Island. It's possible Earhart may have landed there, but mysteriously nothing was ever found. Sixty years later searchers believed they might have found items of Earhart's clothing, which rather begs the question: why wasn't this noticed before?

SCEPTICALLY SPEAKING

A light plane hitting the ocean at roughly 80 miles an hour would be like a car hitting a cement abutment at the same speed. Add scavengers like sharks and other hungry fish. End of mystery.

On April 4, 1968, as evening was setting over Memphis, King was shot as he stood on the second-floor balcony of the Motel Lorraine. The threat to the status quo was eliminated. James Earl Ray, a local criminal, was arrested for the murder, and was accused of shooting King from the bathroom of a nearby boarding house. Doubts, though, began to arise as to whether or not Ray was the true assassin.

THE STRANGE PART

James Earl Ray, who apparently had little money, somehow managed to become a world traveller following King's assassination. With his newfound wealth, he flew to Canada, England, and then Portugal. When he was arrested in London's Heathrow Airport he was preparing to fly to Belgium.

THE USUAL SUSPECTS

The FBI

It was no secret that the head of the FBI, J Edgar Hoover, thought King was one of the most dangerous men in America. In its attempts to remove King from his position of power, the FBI secretly taped King's alleged extramarital activities and used the tapes in the hope of convincing King to avoid public embarrassment by committing suicide. When that failed to work, there was only one alternative…

The CIA

Another theory suggests that King's assassins were provided by the CIA, disguised as Memphis police. Ray was framed for the crime; government agents carried out the actual killing. This would seem to be substantiated by the fact that when Ray was arrested, he was carrying several pieces of fake ID and more than one passport – documents rumoured to be the work of a CIA identities specialist.

The Ku Klux Klan

King represented everything that the Klan hates. He was a man who refuted their stereotypes of blacks and threatened their narrow view of the world. By killing King, especially in the American South, the Klan would send a message to the black community graphically illustrating what happens to blacks who rise above their Klan-appointed station in life.

THE UNUSUAL SUSPECTS

The Memphis Police

Memphis was not particularly friendly to King, and the violent end to the demonstration in March 1968 did not endear him to the city, let alone to the police force. It has been rumoured that CIA agents posed as policemen and killed King, they may not have had to – the police could have had their own grudge against the civil rights leader, racially motivated or otherwise. It's interesting to note that the office of the Director of the Memphis Police Force was heavily populated by members of the military shortly before the killing.

Inside Members of King's Party

It has been suggested that the conspiracy to kill King extended into his own camp. Rumours have persisted that more than one of his close followers was a spy for the police or FBI and may have helped throw pursuers off the scent of the true killers by pointing to the boarding house window after King was shot.

The Mob

The Mafia was allegedly approached by the FBI to kill King, and offered a million dollars to do the job. The Mob refused, mysteriously citing the "screw-ups" the FBI caused directly after the Kennedy killing, but they may have had second thoughts if the plot was sweetened.

MOST CONVINCING EVIDENCE

It is not just the conspiracy community that believes Ray was innocent. Members of the King family supported claims of innocence and when Ray died in prison in Tennessee in 1998, they were invited to attend the funeral. The service was even conducted by the Reverend James Lawson, the former pastor of Centenary United who had invited Dr. King to speak to striking sanitation workers in Memphis in 1968, during which visit he was shot. Maybe they were swayed by the fact that despite the large number of death threats directed at the civil rights leader, Memphis police quietly withdrew the expected police protection surrounding King one day before he was assassinated.

MOST MYSTERIOUS FACT

The only witness to claim he actually saw Ray at the boarding house after the shooting was Charles Stephens; other witnesses claimed that Stephens was too drunk to have seen anything. His wife refuted her husband's story, insistently claiming the man she saw in the boarding house was not Ray. The authorities went with her husband's story. For her troubles, Mrs Stephens was committed to a mental institution.

SCEPTICALLY SPEAKING

Of all the political assassinations in the Sixties, all with disturbingly clear government ties, the murder of Martin Luther King has to vie with RFK's for the title of being the most arrogant. It is staggering that it took the FBI over 15 days to publicly announce that a bundle, thrown by the assassin, belonged to James Earl Ray. Perhaps they should have announced they were giving him a "head start" as well.

DEATH OF A DREAM – ASSASSINATION OF RFK

Around midnight on June 5, 1968 there was magic in the air at the plush Ambassador Hotel in Los Angeles. Glamorous, charismatic and idealistic, Senator Robert F Kennedy had just won the California primary for the Democratic nomination for President. It looked like he was going to fulfil the dreams of many Americans and go all the way to the White House – just like his brother, John F Kennedy, had done before him.

Riding on the applause and congratulations of hotel workers, supporters and watching members of the public, RFK was being escorted by his security team through the hotel's pantry when his charge toward the presidency came to a tragic halt in a hail of gunfire. The hopes of many Americans lay dead on the tiled floor of the pantry.

After a fierce struggle that saw a small man, seemingly possessed of super-human strength, hold his own against several security guards, the apparent gunman – Sirhan Bashira Sirhan – was wrestled to the floor. His eyes were said to be enormously peaceful and the suddenly tranquil assailant was arrested. At the police station Sirhan claimed to have no memory of what had happened and showed all the symptoms of having been hypnotized.

The Los Angeles Police Department investigation into the murder quickly concluded that Sirhan was just another nut – a lone assassin in the mould of Lee Harvey Oswald. The courts agreed, Sirhan was convicted and thrown in jail. As far as officialdom was concerned, the tragic matter was over. As for the conspiracy theorists, the shooting of RFK is a case that definitely deserves to be looked at again.

THE STRANGE PART

At first glance the RFK case seems open and shut: there is no denying it, Sirhan was arrested with a gun in his hand at the scene. However, that is where all simplicity in this case ends. Sirhan was in the wrong position and out of range, and could not have shot Robert Kennedy. The Senator was shot from behind, but all witnesses place Sirhan in front of him in a face-to-face position. All witnesses placed Sirhan's gun as being between one and five feet from Senator Kennedy, but the autopsy findings clearly establish that the Senator was shot from a weapon held between less than one inch and no more than three inches away from his body.

THE USUAL SUSPECTS

The CIA

If, as many people suspect, the CIA had a hand in the assassination of Robert Kennedy's brother, then they would certainly have a significant reason to fear Robert becoming President. If RFK reached the White House, he

above RFK – close to winning the Presidency and minutes from death.

would probably launch an investigation into his brother's death – an investigation that could have proved the Warren Commission was nothing more than a cleverly constructed cover-up and that the President John F Kennedy had been removed in what amounted to a military coup.

Mafia

When his brother was President, Robert Kennedy had been Attorney General and led a successful war against the Mafia. Their attempts to blackmail him over his affair with Marilyn Monroe may have failed and they could have decided that if RFK gained power there would be no way to prevent him from continuing his war against them even more effectively. In this situation, the traditional Mafia solution involves bullets and hitmen.

Military Industrial Complex

Kennedy had pledged to end the war in Vietnam if he became President. Given the vast amounts of money that the

American misadventure in South East Asia was generating for the Military Industrial Complex, it is certain that its members would have done anything in their power to stop his election to the White House.

THE UNUSUAL SUSPECTS

MJ-12

Also known as Majestic 12, this ultra-secret cabal of scientists, senior members of the intelligence community, and of the military is understood by some to be the force behind the conspiracy to suppress the truth about UFOs and aliens. Already suspected of putting an end to JFK, MJ-12 might have killed RFK to prevent him from exposing their dealings with the alien Greys when he became President.

Neo-Nazis

Some conspiracy theorists feel that Robert Kennedy's ability to appeal both to black and to white voters would have allowed him to heal the racial divide in America and forge a nation free of discrimination and hatred. Obviously, this is not the type of place those who cherish the Nazi philosophy want to live in, so it speculated that a cabal of neo-Nazis used their connections inside the US intelligence community to carry out the execution of the enemy they feared most.

MOST CONVINCING EVIDENCE

Bullet holes in a door frame at the crime scene, which are documented in FBI photographs, clearly show that more bullets were fired than could have come from the gun Sirhan is meant to have used to kill Kennedy. The police never disclosed that these bullets existed, even though the removal of the spent bullets by LAPD investigators was witnessed by other police personnel. The door frame in question was then destroyed by order of the court directly after Sirhan's trial concluded.

MOST MYSTERIOUS FACT

According to the psychological evaluation presented in

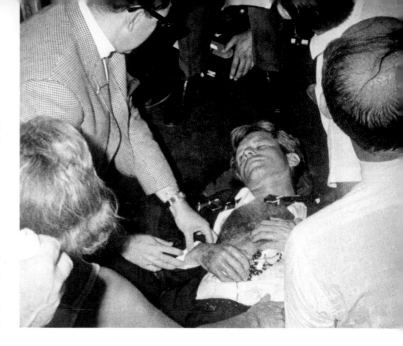

above Oh no, not again. Another Kennedy is killed.

court, Sirhan was definitely under a form of hypnosis at the time of the killing. Officially, this state was described in court as self-hypnosis, but others have doubted this. Claims have been made that the late hypnosis expert, William Bryan, boasted that he had hypnotized Sirhan. This might not amount to much if it was not for the fact that in Sirhan's diaries, which are filled full of strange automatic writing, one name is scratched into the paper over and over – DiSalvo. It might not be a coincidence that Bryan's most famous hypnotic subject was the alleged "Boston Strangler" – Albert DiSalvo.

SCEPTICALLY SPEAKING

The RFK conspiracy is probably one of the hardest to be sceptical over, but it would be dangerous to underestimate what a determined lunatic can achieve when he has easy access to a powerful handgun. Especially when scandalously bad security allows that same armed lunatic to be given a perfect opportunity to shoot someone famous.

CHANDRA LEVY

When the skeletal remains of missing former Washington intern Chandra Levy were found in a Washington DC park in May 2002, almost 13 months after she vanished without a trace, a missing person case became a murder investigation and a political scandal developed into a full-blown conspiracy theory. When she came to Washington to begin an internship at the Federal Bureau of Prisons in September 2000 Levy was just 22. Within weeks, friends had introduced her to Democratic Congressman Gary Condit, who represented her home district in California. It was a fateful meeting, as the two quickly became secret lovers.

Condit, a member of the US Congress since 1989, was married and the father of two adult children. A major political player in

above Former Congressman Gary Condit – an affair with Chandra cost him his career.

above Chandra Levy had wanted to be a spy from an early age.

Washington, he had founded a voting coalition of conservative and moderate congressmen. He also sat on several committees connected to espionage agencies and acted as an overseer of the CIA, through his work as a member of the House Permanent Select Committee on Intelligence. However, it was not just through her intimate relationship with Condit that Levy had access to information for which some conspiriologists would happily exchange various body parts. Her role at the Federal Bureau of Prisons involved making access arrangements for the press to view the execution of Timothy McVeigh, the man convicted of the Oklahoma Bombing. (To many conspiracy cynics, he is known as Lee Harvey McVeigh, due to their belief that he was merely a patsy.) Levy had access to sensitive Bureau and Department of Justice records relating to the condemned prisoner.

On Monday April 23, 2001, Levy was somewhat surprisingly released from her internship. A mere week later, she was seen alive for the last time when she called in to cancel her membership of the Washington Sports Club. When her worried parents contacted the police on Saturday May 5, 2001, they searched her apartment and found suitcases packed and ready to leave but no trace of Levy. Officially declared missing, suspicion began to build on Condit and the nature of his relationship with Levy. Questioned by both the police and her parents, at first he denied having an affair. When inconsistencies in his story surfaced, he eventually confessed to police that he was having a sexual relationship with Levy.

Over a year later, Levy was still missing and with his reputation in shreds, Condit was ousted from his seat in the Democratic primary by Dennis Cardoza, a former member of his own staff. However, the eventual discovery of Levy's body did not even begin to answer any of the questions her family, the police and conspiracy theorists had as to why she had gone missing in the first place.

THE STRANGE PART

Levy's skeleton was found by a man walking his dog in Rock Creek Park, in an area previously searched by the police and just 300 yards (274.30 metres) from a running path that she was known to have used. Police discovered Levy had looked at a website about the Klingle Mansion, a farmhouse built in 1823 and now used as park offices, on the day she disappeared, which made the park a major focus of the investigation. Given that it was not buried, how come it took almost 13 months to find her body?

THE USUAL SUSPECTS

The CIA

Given Condit's role in overseeing the CIA, many believe that it was something he discovered in this capacity that led to Levy's death. Her disappearance not only helped to remove him from any position of power over the Agency, it also served as a warning of the fate that might lay in store for him, if he shared his knowledge with anyone else.

The FBI

At the time of Chandra's disappearance, questions were mounting up with regard to the FBI and their investigation of Timothy McVeigh. A court battle over evidence that the FBI had concealed led to a delay in the planned date of his execution. Did Levy's work involving that execution lead her to discover something about McVeigh that may have made the FBI take a hand in arranging her fatal vanishing act?

THE REPUBLICAN PARTY

Even the former first lady Hillary Clinton talks about a "vast right-wing conspiracy" against successful Democrat politicians. So it is no surprise that there are those who believe that the whole Chandra Levy affair was a plot by a clique of renegade Republicans to unseat Condit and yet again drag the Democratic political establishment through the mud over sexual impropriety with young interns.

THE UNUSUAL SUSPECTS

Mossad

Ever since she had been a little girl, Levy had wanted to be a spy and she and other members of her family had strong connections with Israel. Some theorists believe that she had been recruited by Mossad – the Israeli secret service – to infiltrate to the highest possible levels in Washington, possibly to provide future blackmail on key politicians. If agents of the US or a country hostile to Israel had discovered this, it could certainly have been a motive for her death.

Members of Condit's Staff

Not every conspiracy needs to be about global politics. Often they can be local and personal. If that is the case with Chandra Levy, then it is easy to understand why some have already pointed the finger at members of Condit's own staff, who may have wanted to expose the Congressman for either personal or Democratic Party benefit.

MOST CONVINCING EVIDENCE

Given Condit's sensitive position as a member of the House Permanent Select Committee on Intelligence and the access he had to highly classified intelligence, one of the most surprising and suspicious elements of the Chandra Levy case is just how little interest the US secret services took in her disappearance. In most other countries, if an intern of the Federal Bureau of Prisons, who was connected to a politician with close links to foreign intelligence, disappeared, it would not just be the conspiracy theorists massing to try and find out what happened to her. The absence of serious investigation by the shadowy forces responsible for security of the State convinces many that a full-blown cover-up is involved. They believe the reason they are not looking is because they already know the answers – they just do not want anyone else to know.

MOST MYSTERIOUS FACT

The lead FBI investigator in the Chandra Levy case was Special Agent Bradley J Garrett, someone who had already come to the attention of some conspiracy researchers. Garrett had played a key role in the prosecution of Pakistan national Aimal Kasi, who was accused of murdering CIA agents in a car parked outside the Agency's HQ in Langley, Virginia. He had also investigated the suspicious death of another young female intern – Mary Caitrin Mahoney – shot in what seemed like a professional hit in a Washington DC Starbucks. Being an FBI agent involved in *two* conspiracies with unresolved questions makes you either incredibly unlucky or highly suspicious in the eyes of conspiracy research, but *three*? Not even Fox Mulder from *The X-Files* was that unlucky.

SCEPTICALLY SPEAKING

An unknown random attacker murders a young woman; a married politician has a career-wrecking affair with an intern – sadly, these are hardly uncommon occurrences. Were it not for the coincidence that both headlines could be related to Chandra Levy, conspiracy theorists would have their work cut out finding anything to worry about. Give it up, boys! Washington DC is convoluted and murky enough without having to invent new twists and turns through the cesspool.

DAVID KELLY

A government scientist reveals to a journalist the truth about false evidence designed to make the public accept an unpopular war and is then found dead in suspicious circumstances. It sounds like the plot of a major Hollywood thriller. However, it happened in one of the most high-profile and intriguing conspiracies of recent times when the UK government's leading arms expert Dr David Kelly was found dead in a field near his home with his left wrist slashed.

Weeks before his death, Kelly was thrust into the media spotlight after being revealed as the man the government believed could be a source for a BBC report on Iraq. Although briefing journalists was part of his job, Kelly was shocked when he became a key public figure in the row between the government and the BBC over claims that Downing Street had "sexed up" a dossier concerning Iraq's weapons capability.

The Oxford-educated microbiologist was the scientific adviser to the government's proliferation and arms control secretariat. Kelly was also senior adviser on biological warfare for the UN in Iraq between 1994 and 1999. Nominated for a Nobel peace prize, he was renowned for being so bright "his brain could boil water". He had been the UN weapons inspector who had previously discovered Iraq's radioactive material and was so good at his job Saddam was reported to have said that he should be thrown out of the country.

Kelly found himself at the centre of a huge political scandal after government rules were breached and he was exposed as the source for the BBC story that questioned Prime Minister Blair's claims about Weapons of Mass Destruction. He was forced to give evidence in public to the Foreign Affairs Select Committee on July 15. Two days later, Dr Kelly left his home at 3pm, telling his wife he was going for one of his regular walks. When he failed to return home by 11.45pm, his family contacted the police.

The next morning the Thames Valley police made public his disappearance, shortly before they found a body in woodland on Harrowdown Hill, near his Oxfordshire home. As Blair struggled to answer questions about Kelly's death during a press conference in Japan, police and MI5 officers were sweeping through the germ warfare expert's house in search of "relevant documents".

Quickly reported as an apparent suicide, public speculation over the circumstances surrounding the death of Kelly and the media's focus on the case meant the government was forced to hold a judicial inquiry into the affair. Headed by Lord Hutton, the inquiry aimed to investigate the circumstances of his death and the allegation that the government doctored intelligence reports.

One of Russia's top scientists and a former colleague of Kelly, Professor Sergei Rybakov, immediately cast doubt on the alleged suicide. Rybakov asserted: "David was optimistic and never lost his cool even under extreme pressure. He was not capable of committing suicide."

Rybakov's claims gained weight when the inquiry found that four months before his death, Kelly had predicted that if the American and British invasion of Iraq went ahead, he would "probably be found dead in the woods". His chilling and accurate prediction was made in February 2003 during a conversation with David Broucher, British ambassador to the disarmament conference in Geneva.

THE STRANGE PART

Aside from prophesying his own death, not leaving a note to his beloved wife and being a member of the Ba'hai faith, which is opposed to suicide, there is the question of an email Dr Kelly sent before his death. At the Hutton inquiry it

below Dr David Kelly found himself caught in the global glare of the media.

find that there is a section of the conspiracy community that is convinced that Little Grey Men rather than human forces spirited Kramer away. After all, they reason, if Kramer had been able to pass on the secrets of his breakthrough, their superiority in the technology stakes would have been compromised.

MOST CONVINCING EVIDENCE

James A Traficant Jr, the Representative for Ohio, has made two attempts to get the FBI to investigate the case on the grounds that the nuclear technology knowledge that Kramer possessed make his disappearance a matter of national security. Usually it does not take a politician to point out to the FBI and the intelligence services that the disappearance of a major scientist with close ties to the defence industry is worthy of investigation – especially when he designed the guidance systems for the majority of America's nuclear missiles. It is significant that the authorities' interest in Kramer's disappearance has been minimal, verging on the negligent.

MOST MYSTERIOUS FACT

In the last few days before he vanished, Kramer told his wife Jennifer: "Honey, we are going to have to live behind walls. Honey, people are going to want to get at me." His paranoia seems to have been grounded in reality. It is reported by his father Raymond Kramer – a fellow scientist – that their laboratory was broken into more than once and that the intruders unsuccessfully attempted to breach the security of their computer system to gain access to data on Philip's "breakthrough".

SCEPTICALLY SPEAKING

By all accounts, in the weeks before he vanished, Kramer was a man under stress and short on sleep – two elements that may have plunged him into a state in which he could have wandered off without any memory of who he was. One or two black-hearted sceptics have commented that a man who is crazy enough to believe OJ is innocent is, without a doubt, sufficiently mentally troubled to attempt suicide.

LORD LUCAN

One of the most mysterious vanishing acts ever accomplished by a fugitive was the disappearance of Richard Bingham, the Seventh Earl of Lucan. "Lucky" Lucan was a member of the aristocracy and a professional gambler, a man with a well-known taste for the easy life. A popular socialite in well-to-do London circles, Lucan's expensive hobbies had left him heavily in debt. He had become estranged from his wife, and the couple were in the process of fighting a bitter custody struggle over their three children.

On the night of November 7, 1974, the 29-year-old nanny who looked after Lucan's children, Sandra Rivett, was brutally murdered in the family's home with a length of lead piping. When Lady Veronica Lucan went to investigate, she too was attacked and badly injured. The alarm was raised when she staggered into a pub close to the house, covered in blood, declaring that her husband had murdered the nanny.

Penniless and without his passport, that same night Lord Lucan left a letter saying that he was innocent. He borrowed a friend's car (the bloodstained vehicle was later retrieved at Newhaven Docks) and then vanished. The last sighting in the UK of the man himself had him some 18 miles away, in the town of Uckfield. Many find it significant that although his children eventually had Lucan declared financially dead,

his eldest son was not allowed to have him declared legally dead until the day after the hereditary peerage was abolished in 1999. If this had happened before, his son could have inherited his father's seat in the House of Lords.

THE STRANGE PART

Much like Elvis, Lucan is regularly sighted around the world. Reports have placed him walking on mountain slopes in Sicily and in permanent residence in Southern Africa. Scotland Yard still investigate supposed sightings of the Earl, and has had as many as 70 different sighting reports under investigation at once. If he is still alive and in hiding, Lucan would be in his seventies, having been penniless and on the run for a quarter of a century.

THE USUAL SUSPECTS

Lord Lucan – Dead

The most common theory is that the Earl is dead, having committed suicide in despair and remorse after bungling his attempt to kill his wife. He drove to the English coast, and then swam out into the English Channel to drown.

Lord Lucan – Alive

In this version, Lucan was helped out of the county by a rich friend – possibly the now-deceased Sir James Goldsmith – who flew him from the South of England to France in a private plane. The benefactor also provided money and clothing. Once within Europe, it would have been relatively simple to move around without a passport – border controls are often lax – and slowly make his way down to Botswana, where he now lives. Funded by people who would rather not see the peerage dragged into disrepute by a trial, he lives in modest comfort.

THE UNUSUAL SUSPECTS

Freemasons

While it is uncertain whether or not Lucan was a Freemason, many members of the nobility are part of the ancient fraternity. Uncertain of Lucan's guilt but desperate to prevent a hugely embarrassing trial, the Masons helped "Lucky" out of the country, and set him up with a peaceful life somewhere out of the way.

Meonia

Lucan may have been a member of the mysterious organization dedicated to preserving the bloodline of certain aristocratic British families and ensuring the continuation of Britain through mystic means. If one of their own was in trouble, the secret order would have seen it as their sacred duty to protect him from the threat of prison.

right Have you seen this man? Lord Lucan is still missing.

below Despite claims, the hippy known as Jungle Barry was not the Seventh Earl of Lucan.

MOST CONVINCING EVIDENCE

Even though his children eventually managed to have Lucan declared legally dead, the English police were far from convinced. In interviews conducted by author David Southwell in 1999, some detectives at Scotland Yard announced a suspicion that Lucan is living in Botswana in Southern Africa and that frequent trips made by his children to the area have been observed. Lack of funds made an investigation difficult to carry out. Lucan's children, however, dismissed the suggestion as absurd.

MOST MYSTERIOUS FACT

In 2003 a furore was caused when a photograph of an elderly man, claimed to be Lord Lucan, was published as part of the publicity for a book claiming that the missing Earl had died in Goa, India, in 1996. However, it later turned out that the photograph of a dishevelled man with a long beard bearing a resemblance to the 7th Earl of Lucan – taken in 1991 – was actually that of ancient hippie and one-time folk singer Barry Halpin. Also known as "Mountain" or "Jungle Barry", Halpin was a heavy-drinking, banjo-playing ardent socialist, who went to live in India because it was cheap, sunny and more spiritual than St Helens.

SCEPTICALLY SPEAKING

As the publicity around the mistaken Halpin photo showed, Lucan has become something of a popular tragic-heroic figure. He has even adorned the album cover of England pop band Black Box Recorder and been the subject of one of their songs. Given that his theoretical backers are now dead, if Lucan revealed himself today he could make a fortune and the publicity surrounding his case would make a trial almost impossible. If he returned and was exonerated of charges, there's little doubt he would become a genuine English folk hero. There's simply not enough scandal left to make hiding worthwhile any more.

LEE HARVEY OSWALD

The history books tell us that on November 22, 1963, in Dallas, Texas, Lee Harvey Oswald shot and killed John F Kennedy from a window in the Texas School Book Depository. The history books go on to recount that roughly 45 minutes later, Oswald then shot and killed Officer JD Tippit of the Dallas Police Force, and was later apprehended in a movie theatre. Two days later, Oswald was himself shot by Jack Ruby, apparently outraged at the murder of the President. According to the Warren Commission, which investigated the assassination, there the story ends – the late Oswald was the lone gunman, there was no conspiracy, case closed.

However, conspiracy theories continue to swirl around the incidents of that fateful day in Dallas, suggesting that the least probable theory is that Oswald acted alone. There also remains the mystery of Oswald himself. Even the most cursory of glances at him and his alleged activities around Dallas in the days preceding the assassination, is rife with inconsistencies and bizarre elements worthy of a conspiracy all on their own.

On October 26, 1957, Oswald joined the Marines in San Diego, California. While he was in the Marines he became enamoured of Russia and its politics. After a dishonourable discharge on September 13, 1960, he announced he was going to renounce his American citizenship and move to the USSR. He arrived in Moscow a little more than a month later. Travelling to Minsk, he married Marina, the daughter of a KGB colonel. The glorious life in Russia apparently soured and Oswald returned to the US with his wife in 1962. Back in the US, Oswald drifted from one job to another and was suspected of an assassination attempt on Major General Edwin Walker on April 10, 1963, in Dallas.

His political views got him arrested in New Orleans on August 9 that same year when he was involved in a fight with angry Cubans while passing out "Fair Play for Cubans" pamphlets. A friend of his wife – a Russian exile with CIA connections – arranged for him to get an interview back in Dallas at the Texas School Book Depository. Lying about his past, Oswald was hired on October 15, 1963. The rest, as the books tell us, is history. Or is it?

THE STRANGE PART

There are conflicting reports, of Oswald's activities before the Kennedy assassination. A Texas car salesman, Albert Guy Bogard, reported that Oswald took a car for a test-drive before the shooting, remarking about a large amount

above Bang! Bang! Hardly anyone believes Jack Ruby acted alone when he shot Lee Harvey Oswald.

of money he would be getting soon – yet Oswald never had a driver's licence. Another sighting has Oswald showing off at a Dallas area rifle range, expertly shooting the bull's-eyes in other patrons' targets – this, despite Oswald's inferior record as a marksman while in the Marines. Maybe these "Oswalds" were actors hired by the true parties behind the assassination to ensure the real Oswald would pay for the crime.

THE USUAL SUSPECTS

The Mafia

Jack Ruby originally claimed he shot Oswald to spare Jackie Kennedy the pain of a public trial. However, plenty of evidence abounds that Ruby was a member of the Mob. With several of the most believable conspiracy theories surrounding the assassination of JFK involving the Mafia, it probably is not coincidence that Ruby took out Oswald. Ruby killed Oswald to prevent the Mafia's role in the President's death being exposed.

The FBI and the CIA

Even before Oswald left for the USSR, he was under FBI scrutiny. The reason for his dishonourable discharge from the Marines – for wanting to be a Russian – was public knowledge, so the CIA would have the perfect fall guy: a lone assassin working for the dreaded Russians, which would play extremely well with the media.

THE UNUSUAL SUSPECTS

KGB

The KGB knew that if Oswald was ever brought before a court, his communist background and links to the KGB would emerge. If this happened, the Soviets would be suspected of organizing the Kennedy shooting, so they employed Ruby to ensure Oswald never went on trial.

MOST CONVINCING EVIDENCE

If Oswald had killed Kennedy for political reasons, then why did he never proudly take credit? Instead, he insisted until his death that he had been set up – hardly the actions of a fanatic. His murder by Jack Ruby – preventing the truth from ever coming to light – was far too convenient.

MOST MYSTERIOUS FACT

The CIA reportedly experimented with LSD on troops in Atsugi, Japan, as part of their mind-control tests in 1957. Oswald was serving with the Marines there at the time.

SCEPTICALLY SPEAKING

Of course Oswald shot Kennedy and therefore it is not impossible that an outraged American might want to take revenge. If you listen to some of the conspiracy theories about him you might also believe Oswald sank the Titanic and stole your newspaper this morning.

JEREMIAH DUGGAN

On March 27, 2003 Erica Duggan could not sleep. Her dreams had been unsettling, and she had woken in an agitated, unsettled state. Despite the fact that it was 4:30am, she went downstairs to make tea. She could not shake the sense of foreboding that had followed her back from her troubled slumber.

Within minutes the phone rang. She could hear the distressed voice of her son, Jeremiah – known to his family and friends as Jerry: "Mum, I'm in terrible trouble, deep trouble. I want to be out of this. You know this Nouvelle Solidarité, it's too much for me. I can't do this. I want out."

Before she could ask him any questions, the line went dead. As far as his mother knew, Jeremiah, a 22-year-old British student had taken a break from his studies in Paris to attend an anti-Iraq war meeting somewhere in Europe.

Seconds later the phone rang again. "Jerry where are you?"

"Wiesbaden."

"How do you spell that?"

"W. I. E. S..." The line went dead again.

Within 40 minutes of that call, Jeremiah Duggan was dead.

According to interviews later conducted by the police with motorists, Jeremiah Duggan had run out onto the Berliner Straße dual carriageway at a point 5 kilometres south of Wiesbaden. He had plunged straight into the path of an oncoming car and was knocked down. A second car then drove over him, killing him.

When the German police informed Erica Duggan that her son had died in a "plain suicide", she was immediately suspicious. It turned out that instead of attending a left-wing anti-war protest, Jerry had spent the final few days of his life attending events run by the Schiller Institute. In conspiracy research circles, the Schiller Institute is well known for being part of a network of organisations associated with Lyndon LaRouche Jr. – a wealthy economist and one of the most infamous conspiracy theorists in the world today.

A former Communist who had moved so far across the political spectrum that many believe he is now a right-winger, Lyndon LaRouche Jr. has led an interesting life. A perennial candidate for President of the United States, having run for the office eight times since 1976, he had also served six years in federal prison between 1988 and 1994 for fraud and tax evasion. His views had led him into losing lawsuits against those who described him as an "anti-Semite" and a "small-time Hitler". LaRouche had also had dealings with former German rocket scientists brought to the USA after the war by Operation Paperclip.

Duggan had been driven to the conference at the Schiller Institute by members of the of LaRouche Movement. However, what Jerry thought was just an anti-war conference proved to be something more when LaRouche talked about the Kennedy assassination. A member of the Schiller Institute told Erica that Jerry had stood up and declared, "I am a Jew", when he had heard a speaker claim the war was plotted by those whose Jewish ancestry prevented them joining the Nazi party.

After the conference, Duggan stayed on for seminars run by the LaRouche Movement "cadre schools". Before he rang his mother, he called his girlfriend Maya in Paris and told her, "I am under too much pressure. I don't know what the truth is any more, or what are lies. My arms and legs hurt. They are doing experiments on people using computers."

When Erica began trying find out how her son had died, a member of the management of the Schiller Institute told Erica Duggan: "We cannot take responsibility for the actions of individuals. We think your son has psychological problems." The Schiller Institute told German police that "Duggan was known to the Tavistock Institute in London, which is a mental institution." Jerry had attended the Tavistock Institute – renowned as a family therapy centre – 15 years before with his parents while they were divorcing.

Erica Duggan became even more convinced that something was amiss when it emerged that Schiller Institute officials had possession of Jerry's passport and could offer no justification as to why. Nor was there any logical reason why the markings of the vehicles on the road left by the cars supposed to have hit Jerry suggested much slower speeds than had been claimed they were going.

THE STRANGE PART

In 1974, followers of LaRouche claimed that a former member of his political group had been turned into a Manchurian-style assassin with orders to kill LaRouche. It was alleged that the agent had been brainwashed by British Intelligence through techniques developed at the Tavistock Institute. LaRouche has often articulated anti-British conspiracy theories. He has claimed Queen Elizabeth II is personally involved in a global drugs cartel and the British royal family have given orders to have him killed.

It is odd that Jeremiah was three things some followers of LaRouche often mention in the same breath as conspiracies – British, Jewish and linked to the Tavistock Institute. In 2006, Lyndon LaRouche himself suggested a conspiracy surrounded Jeremiah Duggan, claiming allegations linking the LaRouche Movement to his death were part of a "hoax" stemming from a campaign against him orchestrated by supporters of Tony Blair and US Vice President Dick Cheney. According to LaRouche, it was "such an obvious fabrication that no further comment is necessary." .

THE USUAL SUSPECTS

Elements Within the Larouche Movement

Unsurprisingly, given the circumstances surrounding his death, many researchers investigating Duggan's demise have concluded he died due to a conspiracy perpetuated by elements within the LaRouche Movement. Among the motives alleged by these researchers is that Jerry may have discovered something incriminating about the group.

Queen Elizabeth II

Some conspiracy theorist followers of LaRouche have claimed Duggan was killed on the personal orders of Queen Elizabeth II as part of a plot to discredit the LaRouche movement. They believe the murder was arranged by a cabal of Anglo-American intelligence agents called The Committee that secretly reports to the House of Windsor.

THE UNUSUAL SUSPECTS

Green Nazis

Lyndon LaRouche is a constant critic of the "man-made global warming" hypothesis. Some of his followers claim that the whole story of Jeremiah Duggan's death is a mere hoax created by high-placed Green Nazis to smear his name and limit his chances of exposing their lies on the subject.

Anti-Space Faction

Given LaRouche's support of former Nazi rocket scientists, his advocation of terraforming the planet Venus, the Strategic Defence Initiative and plans to colonize Mars, it is claimed by some conspiriologists that there is an anti-space faction of the global power elite targeting LaRouche. In this version of the conspiracy, they hatched Duggan's death to frame the LaRouche movement, in order to prevent it from exposing their ongoing campaign of sabotaging space missions.

Zionist Forces

Lyndon LaRouche Jr. has often been accused of holding anti-Semitic views by organisations such as the Anti-Defamation League and the Simon Wiesenthal Center. Some far-right conspiracy theorists have tried to suggest that secretive Zionist forces used Duggan and then his death to try and provide proof of their claims that the LaRouche movement has extreme anti-Semitic elements within it.

MOST CONVINCING EVIDENCE

In March 2007, solicitors working on behalf of Erica Duggan released two new independent forensic evidence reports undertaken by leading pathologists. Their findings contradict claims that Jerry's death was a simple suicide. The reports show that no traces of skin, blood or clothing were found either on the cars that hit Duggan or on the road. There were also no tyre-marks or other signs to show that the body had ever come into contact with the cars. Jerry's head injuries were consistent with being beaten and "exclude any

above Erica Duggan with a picture of her son Jeremiah Duggan. She refuses to accept that her son's death was suicide.

possibility that the injuries to his head occurred because a motor vehicle ran over the body".

MOST MYSTERIOUS FACT

Ostensibly the Tavistock Institute of Human Relations is nothing other than an organisation carrying out educational, research and consultancy work in applied psychology. However, claims made by LaRouche's followers have given it mythic status with some conspiriologists. Formed in 1946 by English mental health experts, it is regularly accused of trying to bring about the moral, spiritual and economic decline of the United States. It is alleged to have done this through everything from being behind the creation of The Beatles and the Process Church of the Final Judgment, to the brainwashing of top US politicians.

SCEPTICALLY SPEAKING

More than one heartless sceptic has remarked that anyone mad enough to go to a Schiller Institute conference is possibly disturbed enough to top themselves. However, even the most-blinkered sceptic would find it is hard to deny the forensic evidence is suggestive of some form of conspiracy.

ALEXANDER LITVINENKO

The explosive conclusions of some conspiracies produce flashbulb moments – the white magnesium flare leaving its violent after-image burned into global cultural memory. It is commonplace for those alive in the 1960s to talk of remembering where they were when they heard the news of the assassination of JFK. Among my generation, it's the point at which you heard the news that John Lennon had been shot that delivers total clarity of recall. For those in their teens, it is September 11, 2001.

It was the final dying moments of another conspiracy with a strangely personal connection to me that means I recall 24 November 2006. I had enjoyed a fantastic night out, drinking Bellinis at the Heights Bar high above London, watching 100,000 lights shine below me, transforming London into fairyland. I arrived home just before midnight and in auto-pilot mode switched on BBC News 24 to hear: "At 9:23pm Alexander Litvinenko died."

Suddenly I was a mess of empathy for his wife and son, anger towards his killers and a heightened sense of my own mortality. Although from the moment of his death, the world would come to know him mainly by the tabloid title of *"the radioactive Russian spy"*, to me Alexander Litvinenko was a fellow author of conspiracy books. He was also a generous source of information for some of the material in my book *The History of Organized Crime* that dealt with the Organizatsia and the links between Russian politicians and criminal networks. Alexander Litvinenko was not your usual conspiracy theorist. Before coming to live in England as a political exile from his Russian homeland, Litvinenko had been a Lieutenant-Colonel in the Federal Security Service of the Russian Federation (FSB), the successor organization to the Soviet KGB. On November 17, 1998, after more than 12 years loyal service in the KGB and FSB, Litvinenko took to a platform with four other senior FSB officers. The five men publicly declared that they had been ordered to assassinate Boris Berezovsky, a Russian businessman who then held the government post of Secretary of the Security Council and was close to President Boris Yeltsin. They claimed their orders had come from the top of the security service. At the time the head of the FSB was the future Russian President, Vladimir Putin.

After he made this claim, Litvinenko was dismissed from the FSB. The following year he was arrested on charges of having beaten up citizens and stolen explosives while carrying out anti-terrorist duties. After serving a brutal month in prison, the authorities released him on condition that he remained in Russia. With the help of old FSB contacts and friends of Boris Berezovsky, Litvinenko was able to flee to Istanbul on forged passports with his wife and young son. He eventually arrived at London's Heathrow airport where he applied for political asylum.

Once safely settled in Britain, Litvinenko began to make further conspiratorial claims about the role of the FSB in Russian politics. Some of his claims – such as those in his book *Blowing Up Russia* – were backed up by hard evidence. He was able to show members of the FSB carried out some of the wave of apartment bombings that killed more than 300 people in Moscow and other Russian cities in 1999. The bombing had originally been blamed on Chechen terrorists, but Litvinenko believed the FSB had carried them out to justify a new war in the disputed territory of Chechnya and help bring Putin to power.

Some of Litvinenko's other claims were harder to prove. He asserted two of the terrorists behind the Moscow theatre siege in 2002 were FSB operatives and leading al-Qaeda terror chiefs, such as Ayman al-Zawahiri, had been trained by and were still linked to the FSB. Some considered him a hero for announcing a FSB dimension to the July bombings in London in 2005. Others thought him a madman for maintaining that Vladimir Putin had ordered the killing of journalists who tried to expose his alleged paedophilia. However, no-one doubted that he was an expert on the workings of the FSB and links between the security services and elements of the Russian Mafiya.

On November 1 2006, Litvinenko suddenly became ill and was hospitalised. It emerged that he had been poisoned with the rare and highly toxic radionuclide polonium-210. Litvinenko told police that he had met three ex-KGB agents on the day he fell ill, drinking tea with them at the Millennium

below 'The beating wings of the angel of death' – Litvinenko's own words to describe the conspiracy that finally silenced him.

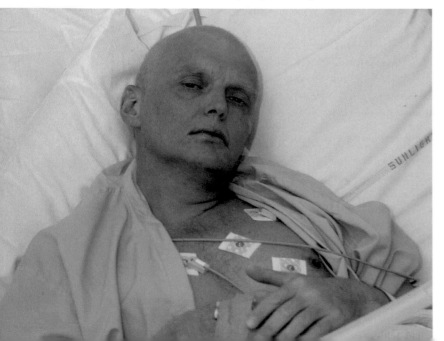

Hotel. He had then dined at the Itsu sushi restaurant in Piccadilly with Italian contact Mario Scaramella.

When it became clear that his death from radiation poisoning was imminent, Litvinenko converted to Islam and allegedly drafted a statement in which he blamed President Putin for the conspiracy to silence him through the "beating wings of the angel of death".

THE STRANGE PART

Why use polonium-210? As it can only be produced in minute quantities inside nuclear reactors, it is an expensive and difficult substance to obtain. It is also a ridiculously ostentatious way to murder someone. Polonium-210 even leaves a radioactive trail, which detectives can follow easily across continents via contaminated vehicles, such as passenger jets. It seems that whoever planned Litvinenko's murder was happy for him to suffer the type of strange, lingering death guaranteed to attract global media attention and leave a radioactive trail pointing back towards Russia.

THE USUAL SUSPECTS

Vladimir Putin

Alexander Litvinenko and many of those close to him believed that Vladimir Putin had personally ordered his death. Was Putin trying to make an example out of Litvinenko – one of his most virulent critics – his extravagant and cruel death a marker to deter others from speaking out against him?

Boris Berezovsky

Given the amount of spectacularly bad press Litvinenko's death and the claims of Putin's involvement brought the Russian president, the Kremlin has claimed that Litvinenko was killed by those trying to undermine Putin. Some FSB agents suggest that it was one of Litvinenko's closest friends and Putin's most powerful political enemies – Boris Berezovsky – who arranged the murder.

Renegade Vityaz Elements

Vityaz – Russian for "knight" – is a special unit of the Russian army created to fight terrorism and rebel insurgents. Litvinenko had often criticised its activities fighting a "dirty war" in the Chechnya, and Vityaz members used photos of him in marksmanship training. Fiercely loyal to Putin, some believe that renegade Vityaz co-operated with FSB agents in a plan to wipe out Litvinenko without their bosses having any knowledge of it, thereby giving them plausible deniability over events.

THE UNUSUAL SUSPECTS

Alexander Litvinenko

One offensive idea articulated by some Russian pro-Putin conspiracy theorists is that Alexander Litvinenko conspired with dissident FSB agents and exiled anti-Putin political activist to stage his own death. He used polonium-210 knowing it would help garner massive press attention and give him a global platform to denounce Putin.

The Organizatsia

Litvinenko was an expert on the links between the Russian Mafiya, high-placed politicians and the security services. During his time as a FSB agent and exiled conspiracy theorist, he had earned the hatred of the Solntsevo crime syndicate, the most powerful group within Russian organized crime. It is believed by some the Organizatsia had him silenced to protect their powerful friends in Putin's regime.

MOST CONVINCING EVIDENCE

A conspiracy, as defined in the dictionary way of "secret agreement between two or more people to perform an unlawful act", was clearly needed to orchestrate such an operatic death for Alexander Litvinenko. In addition, the aftermath unfolded almost as exactly predicted by conspiriologists in two ways. First, the FSB launched a major campaign to discredit Litvinenko, even suggesting a PR firm had been involved in drafting his final statement. Second, Boris Berezovsky exploited his friend's death for political potential, using it as a justification when he announced plans to stage a "second Russian revolution".

MOST MYSTERIOUS FACT

Andrei Lugovoi, a millionaire security consultant and former FSB agent dined with Litvinenko on the day he was poisoned. In May 2007, the UK tried to extradite him from Russia for the murder. Lugovoi has vehemently denied allegations made by the UK police and Berezovsky that he was involved in the poisoning, claiming it was actually the work of MI6. Lugovoi had previously been the head of security for ORT – a TV network owned at the time by Berezovsky – and the KGB bodyguard of former Russian Prime Minister Yegor Gaidar. In November 2006, Gaidar was poisoned in Ireland while on a book promotion tour.

SCEPTICALLY SPEAKING

It is impossible to deny that there was a conspiracy to kill Alexander Litvinenko. It is also clearly a conspiracy instigated by someone whose wealth, power or professional contacts made securing polonium-210 easy and who had no regard for ruining relations between Britain and Russia. However, knowing a conspiracy exists does not mean that any researcher, or even the authorities charged with trying to seek justice for its victims, have any concrete idea of who was behind it. It is easy to spot the pawns in a game of chess, but not always the hidden hand moving them. I personally think I know who ordered Litveneko's death, but there is no way the lawyers will let me tell you.

BOB WOOLMER

The Cricket World Cup is the premier global event in men's one-day international cricket. While it might not mean much to readers from the United States, where cricket is almost unknown, the tournament is the globe's third largest sporting event. With 16 competing cricketing nations playing in 51 matches, the 2007 World Cup held in the West Indies was televized in more than 200 countries with an audience of 2.2 billion viewers.

Like all great sporting tournaments it threw up some surprising results. Yet when highly-favoured Pakistan were knocked out of the tournament by Ireland – a predominantly amateur side – on St. Patrick's Day, many suspected a fix. For a country as obsessed by cricket as Pakistan, the defeat was a national tragedy. In Pakistani cities, effigies of the Pakistan cricket captain, Inzamam-ul-Haq, and the side's English-born coach, Bob Woolmer, were burnt in mass protests.

The day after the defeat, Bob Woolmer's semi-naked body was discovered in his bathroom at the Jamaica Pegasus Hotel in Kingston. Despite some of his colleagues on the Pakistani cricket team revealing he had been suffering from medical difficulties during the tournament and Woolmer's son initially putting the death down to stress, conspiracy theories were soon being shared by cricket fans the world over.

This was not too surprising. Outside of Hollywood, no other part of the global entertainment industry generates such a continuous stream of conspiracy theories as sport. One reason for this is that almost every major professional sporting activity is now part of a multi-billion dollar industry. Possibly the biggest reasons conspiracy theories abound in sport is due to the vast emotional commitment some fans place in their favourite sporting teams. Just as some conspiracy theories spring up when music fans cannot face up to the fact that their favourite recording artist has died in a random accident, many sports supporters cannot accept that their side have lost as a result of bad luck or the superior skill of their opponents.

Looking at Arsenal – the English football team I support – provides a good example of how the conspiracy process in sports works. Due to the fact it has Queen Elizabeth II, John Lydon (AKA former Sex Pistol Johnny Rotten), and Osama Bin Laden among its supporters, all sorts of conspiratorial nonsense has been written about the club. This is heightened by the fact its former ground, Highbury, was known to include Masonic symbolism within its construction.

News stories about sponsorship of the club by Emirates Airline and its possible takeover by an American billionaire have been pored over by some deluded conspiracy theorists. Such regular elements of sporting business have even been cited as "proof" of the hidden hand of al-Qaeda or the Grand United Lodge of England behind the club. When the Queen had to withdraw from a planned visit of Arsenal's new Emirates Stadium and the ground was tested for radiation as part of the investigation into the poisoning of Alexander Litvinenko, the febrile imaginations of certain conspiriologists went into meltdown.

These types of conspiracy phenomena can be seen across all types of sport. Conspiracies abound with many fans believing secret cabals are fixing matches, events and shaping the career of players from behind the scenes. Proof of genuine criminal conspiracies in sport often comes to light – from corrupt referees and officials to betting syndicates trying to fix matches. However, no conspiracy theory in sport has ever taken such an unexpected and dramatic turn as the events surrounding the death of Bob Woolmer.

Early suggestions of murder made by conspiriologists after the discovery of Woolmer's body were seen at the time as ridiculous speculation. However, they were seemingly confirmed when the Jamaican police announced they were treating the death as "suspicious". Four days after Woolmer's death, the top Jamaican detective investigating the case made the shocking announcement that "Bob Woolmer was murdered. He was killed by manual strangulation."

Suddenly cricket fans stopped focusing on the remaining matches of the World Cup. The question on their minds was no longer who would lift the ultimate prize in international cricketing. All anyone wanted to know was who was behind the death of Bob Woolmer. By the time the Jamaican police decided, three months after Woolmer's death, that he had died from natural causes, many fans and the majority of conspiracy theorists failed to believe the new official explanation.

THE STRANGE PART

Bob Woolmer had been one of the most widely respected men in international cricket. Before the nightmare defeat of his team at the hands of the Irish, Bob Woolmer allegedly enjoyed good relations with officials and players in the Pakistan team. He had no known enemies within the cricketing world or outside it.

The Jamaican police originally dismissed theft as a motive for his death, as nothing was taken from his room. They also refuted the idea that an opportunist Pakistan fan could have bypassed the sophisticated security at the hotel. Yet if Woolmer was murdered, someone had a reason for wanting him dead.

THE USUAL SUSPECTS
Betting Syndicate

The most common conspiracy theory surrounding the motive for Bob Woolmer's death is that he was about to resign as

Pakistan coach and go public with information on match-fixing within the game. The Pakistan cricket side had a history of involvement with match-fixing and suspicion had arisen over the team's shock loss to Ireland. In 1999, Hanif "Cadbury" Kodvavi, the bookmaker at the heart of the last big match-fixing scandal involving Pakistan had been found dead in Johannesburg. The fact he had been shot 67 times and then hacked to pieces proved criminal betting syndicates involved in cricket corruption are ruthless when it comes to silencing those who threaten to divulge details of their operations.

Tablighi Jamaat

According to former Pakistan cricket team media manager, PJ Mir, Woolmer had come into conflict with members of his squad for being "More interested in praying than playing." It is alleged some Pakistan players and officials were members of Tablighi Jamaat – a Muslim missionary movement. Individuals linked to Tablighi Jamaat have been charged with planning terror attacks. Many view the organization as containing a cadre of violent extremists who may have plotted to kill Woolmer because of what they perceived as anti-Islamic bias in the way he ran the squad.

THE UNUSUAL SUSPECTS

ISI

In Pakistan, cricket is a national obsession. Many in the country blamed Woolmer for their side's disastrous World Cup performance and saw him as having shamed their country. Some conspiriologists suggest disgruntled fans with links to the Inter-Services Intelligence (ISI), Pakistan's most powerful security agency, killed the cricketing coach. They believe the ISA was happy to allow murderous fans access to their resources and specialist knowledge of assassination to gain revenge for their loss of national sporting pride.

D-Company

In 2000, South African star cricketer Hanse Cronje was exposed as working on behalf of an Indian betting syndicate to help fix matches. Woolmer had been the South African coach and knew Cronje well. Many believe the syndicate Cronje was involved with was linked to Dawood Ibrahim and his criminal network known as D-company. The most feared criminal group operating in India, the CIA regards D-Company as a "global terrorist organization" with links to al-Qaeda. If Woolmer had been planning to go public on information linked to match-fixing during his time as South African coach, it may have been expedient for D-Company to murder him.

MOST CONVINCING EVIDENCE

It takes great strength to strangle a man with your hands – especially if your victim is large like Bob Woolmer. When

above The light eternal – shocked Pakistani cricket fans lit candles forBob Woolmer during a prayer ceremony for him.

police found signs of illness in Woolmer's bathroom, but no signs of a struggle, they suspected he had first been poisoned to subdue him. The initial toxicology report suggested Woolmer could have ingested some form of poison, a fact that causes conspiriologists to disbelieve the later police belief that Woolmer had died of natural causes. If he was murdered, the use of poison and the evading of the hotel's security systems, including electronic door locks that record every attempted entry into a room, rule out a spontaneous killing.

MOST MYSTERIOUS FACT

In 2002, two years after receiving a lifetime ban from cricket for his role in match-fixing on behalf of an Indian betting syndicate, disgraced South African cricket star Hanse Cronje died in a plane crash in which he was the only passenger. Cricket coach and former South African international cricketer Clive Rice knew both Cronje and Woolmer. He has gone on record as saying, "I am convinced the crash wasn't an accident." Rice is not the only person who has publicly declared there may be a link between Cronje's death and the murder of Woolmer.

SCEPTICALLY SPEAKING

Conspiracy theories flourish in sport because its most passionate supporters need someone to blame when they cannot accept a result going against them. The simplest motivation for the killing of Woolmer is one related to the distraught, inconsolable rage of someone associated with the sport that felt let down. Fan is short for fanatic for a reason.

HISTORICAL

THE GUNPOWDER PLOT

Remember remember the fifth of November – gunpowder, treason and plot." It seems as if every schoolchild grows up having to learn the famous phrase, but few of them ever see beyond the fireworks and bonfires and think of it is as the most famous political conspiracy in English history.

Given that the Gunpowder Plot was exposed before it was successfully completed, there is a tendency to view it as a failed conspiracy – one that has been fully investigated, resolved and consigned to the pages of dusty history books. However, some conspiriologists have nagging doubts over the whole matter and feel that the Gunpowder Plot we are taught about as children is only the visible tip of a much larger conspiracy.

The bare facts of the Plot are well known. Guy Fawkes was caught red-handed in a cellar underneath the Houses of Parliament the night before King James was due to preside over the State Opening of Parliament. His fellow conspirators

were soon hunted down. Those who did not die resisting arrest were tried, found guilty of treason and sentenced to death. Within a week of their trial they had all been hanged, drawn and quartered.

The accepted theory – usually the one you need to be deeply suspicious of – is that a small group of Catholic fanatics, working alone, planned to kill King James I, hoping in the confusion after his death that they would be able to put a Catholic on the throne of England. However, for many conspiracy buffs, those who were exposed and punished as conspirators were little more than the fall-guys for the true plotters whose aims may have had very little to do with restoring Catholicism to Britain.

THE STRANGE PART

One of the most significant aspects of the Gunpowder Plot is the spectacular nature of its failure. It seems incredible that

any group of conspirators – especially a group as amateurish as the one led by Guy Fawkes – could have gained access to a cellar under the Houses of Parliament, smuggled in several tons of explosive undetected and then have been magically caught almost in the act of lighting the fuse. Incredible – unless there was another unseen level to the conspiracy.

THE USUAL SUSPECTS

Robert Cecil, Earl of Salisbury

Cecil was England's spymaster and his speciality was uncovering plots – or, as some suspect, uncovering plots that he had set up in an attempt to frame enemies of the state and make himself look good. Cecil had met Guy Fawkes' main co-conspirator Robert Catesby previously, when he had uncovered the Essex plot and spared Catesby from execution. Conspiriologists believe that Catesby was recruited by Cecil as a double-agent to operate a plot that would be uncovered at the last minute, boosting not only Cecil's prestige but allowing for a ruthless crackdown on Catholics.

The English Nobility

When James was crowned King of England in 1603 he united two countries that had been at war far more often than they had been at peace. It is inconceivable that this unification could happen without upsetting plenty of people – as soon as James arrived in London he began appointing Scottish nobles to positions of power. Among the displaced English nobles were members of the mystical order known as Meonia – including Sir Walter Raleigh – who were known to have links with some Gunpowder Plot conspirators, including Robert Catesby and Thomas Wyntour.

THE UNUSUAL SUSPECTS

The Tobacco Lobby

Sir Walter Raleigh had first introduced tobacco from the New World a generation earlier and the fashion for smoking it had spread like wildfire throughout England – making some merchants who dealt in tobacco very rich indeed. One of the few men who had not succumbed to the demon weed was James I, who published his famous rant *A Counterblast To Tobacco*. There was a rumour that the King was intending to introduce a series of punitive taxes on tobacco to raise some much-needed cash. If these had been introduced they would have seriously damaged the financial interests of several powerful people in England and Virginia, so the Gunpowder Plot may have been one of the first times that big business decided to flex its muscles.

The Scottish Nobility

James I of England was also James VI of Scotland, and Scotland, at this point in history, was as torn apart with plots and treason as any soap opera plot could ever become. Plots, conspiracies and assassinations were commonplace and one of the most favoured ways of disposing of an enemy or rival was death by explosion. James I's father had been killed by this method and the King himself had ordered the destruction of his enemies be carried out with explosives. James had plenty of enemies in his home country who wanted him out of the way and would not have minded the Catholics taking the blame.

MOST CONVINCING EVIDENCE

Two of the other major plots exposed during James I's reign that led to the downfall of Sir Walter Raleigh – the Main Plot and the Bye Plot – shared certain common elements with the Gunpowder Plot. They both failed, they were both uncovered at the last minute thanks to Cecil, and they both left the establishment and the King stronger and more firmly in place.

MOST MYSTERIOUS FACT

On December 28, 1604, King James I attended the society wedding of the Earl of Montgomery to Robert Cecil's niece. Bizarrely, among the other guests attending this glittering social function was Guy Fawkes. If Guy Fawkes was the Catholic fanatic painted by many historians, with a burning desire to murder James I, then why did he not simply bring a knife to the wedding and attempt a more straightforward assassination? It seems more than a little strange that three of the key figures of the Gunpowder Plot were attending the same wedding.

SCEPTICALLY SPEAKING

Sometimes the official explanation is not only obvious but also correct. Catholic countries, such as France and Spain, certainly had an interest in destabilizing England and were known to work via underground networks of priests to ferment unrest. Maybe this is one conspiracy that really is as simple as it seems.

above Did Arthurian romances contain hidden messages about the true nature of the Holy Grail?

THE HOLY GRAIL

The legends of King Arthur and the Holy Grail, the cup that Christ drank from at the Last Supper, were largely set into their current forms in the fourteenth century, a time when French and German romantic poets were busy writing epic sagas based on common stories.

King Arthur and his round table of holy knights are a historical pastiche that misses the truth – the kind of plate armour that Arthur's knights are associated with was not invented until centuries after his time. Similarly, the idea of a glowing golden chalice humming with the divine power to heal the land and raise the dead, is actually a complete distraction from the true Grail.

The idea of the Holy Grail comes from a deliberate misinterpretation of the root term "Sangreal" on the part of the Catholic Church. Splitting the term into "San Greal", and from there to "San Graal", or "Saint Grail", the derivation of the idea of the Holy Grail is plain. However, if the word is split into "Sang Real", the true Latin meaning becomes clear – the Blood Royal. The Holy Grail is nothing more and nothing less than the royal line of descent founded by Jesus Christ.

Jesus was not born of a virgin, but in the normal manner. He was rescued from the cross by friends and was married to Mary Magdalene. They had three children, a daughter and two sons, and they settled in France in exile, far from the reach of the Romans. When Joseph of Arimathea arrived in England, legend says that he brought the Grail with him, rather than a cup, and he brought his neWphew Justus, Jesus's oldest son. Over the years, the exiled Hebrew royal family bred with local nobles, and the line became the Merovingian Kings of France. Even King Arthur's name is likely to be a nickname – Artos means the Bear. The real Arthur was a warlord related to the Merovingians – the Bear King, inheritor of the Blood Royal.

Through the centuries, the Holy Grail – the Blood of Christ – passed through the Merovingians to the Templars and the Crusaders, and into some of the royal bloodlines of Feudal Europe from the French Stuarts to the Scottish Sinclairs and certain noble houses of Greece and Italy. Interestingly, the Grail heritage is not part of the Germanic House of Saxe-Coburg-Gotha, reputedly now known as the Windsors, the royal family of Great Britain...

THE STRANGE PART

It is alleged that the name Britain comes from the term B'rith-ain, or The Land of the Covenant. Furthermore, the idea of Merrie England is in fact derived from St Mary the Gypsy, Mary Jacob, who came to Europe with Mary Magdalene. She had a widespread cult in early Europe, and is best known in the form of Maid Marian and the Merrie Men of Robin Hood. These little known "facts" only go to show the extent of the Holy Bloodline in Britain.

THE USUAL SUSPECTS

Meonia

The secret mystical order charged with protecting the fate of the British Isles knew all about the truth behind the Grail and manipulated history and Royal dynasties accordingly. It is open to conjecture if the organization had any involvement with Princess Diana's marriage into the Windsor clan – though Diana did have ancestral links to the Meonia organization.

Priory of Sion

This French version of Meonia is a more surreal organization. If they exist, they are almost certainly closely involved in the Holy Grail conspiracy.

The Catholic Church

There is no doubt that the Church has the most to lose if the Holy Grail ever became widely recognized as the line of Christ. By encouraging the romantic interpretations of the Holy Grail, and by constantly suggesting the idea of Jesus' birth and death being holy miracles, they safeguard their authority as derived from Godly favour. If it were ever known that the Christian faith was founded on a priestly hijacking of the power of the Hebrew kings, it would end in disaster for the Church.

THE UNUSUAL SUSPECTS

The Atlanteans

It has been suggested that Jesus was not of the line of David at all, but actually the descendant of the high priests of Atlantis. Jesus' revolutionary messages of love and acceptance for fellow humans is a direct throwback to his Atlantean teachings. His bloodline is holy because the people of Atlantis were genetically and spiritually advanced to a level never attained before or since, and the people who retain that heritage are still gifted with unusual powers and intelligence – *Homo Superior*. Frightened by the implications, jealous *Homo Sapiens* priests and rulers killed Jesus, and the knowledge that the Holy Grail is the *Homo Superior* mutation has been suppressed ever since.

MOST CONVINCING EVIDENCE

The long bloodlines in the Bible are there to prove Jesus' lineage as a royal descendant of David. The book of Matthew actually gives a line of descent from David the King down to Jacob being the father of Joseph, husband of Mary. The title of Christ denotes Jesus' royal status, and we should think of him properly as King Jesus. The whole concept of immaculate conception and divine succession was invented by the Catholic Church in the fourth century to justify their power, stealing the authority of the royal line for themselves, by the "Grace of God".

MOST MYSTERIOUS FACT

Although the House of Windsor does not share in the Grail heritage, Princess Diana was supposedly descended from the royal House of Stewart. Although it is generally said that Queen Elizabeth II is royal and Diana married into the family, in fact the truth was just the opposite; it was Diana who was descended from Jesus Christ.

SCEPTICALLY SPEAKING

If the Holy Grail is the *Homo Superior* mutation, and if it was passed into the royal families of Europe, there would be thousands of people worldwide with the gene, and any actual differences would have been noticed by medical science.

HITLER

Nobody is in any doubt that Adolf Hitler, leader of the Nazi party, was one of the most evil and dangerous men to have come to power in all of human history. The legacy of death and suffering that he left behind him is staggering. Approximately six million Jews were slaughtered, primarily in death camps, as part of his "Final Solution" – almost two thirds of their world population. It is also important to remember he murdered a large proportion of Europe's population of gypsies, Seventh Day Adventists, Jehovah's Witnesses and Socialists.

During World War II, some sixty million soldiers were mobilized across Europe, the Americas, Russia and the Far East. Almost a third of them were killed. The total death toll for the war has been estimated around 52 million people – 18 million soldiers, 16 million civilians killed in military action, and 18 million people murdered in the death camps. Hitler lurked behind all this death, the lynch-pin of the entire war. These facts are horrific enough that surely no conspiracy can compete – but there are suggestions that Hitler's ultimate goal was not to unite Europe under his rule at all, but simply to cause widespread death and destruction to appease his Satanic masters.

The Brotherhood of Death is the name given to a rumoured world-wide coalition of primarily Satanic organizations. Each organization has, as its logo, the skull and two crossed bones, the emblem we most commonly associate with pirates. The German branch of the Brotherhood of Death was allegedly the *Thule Gesellschaft*, or Thule Society. Centred on a semi-mythical land from ancient times, the legend of Thule shares certain features with that of Atlantis. The land of Thule is supposed to have been the cradle of the Aryan race.

In 1919, disgusted by the way that the German government had "thrown away" World War I, Hitler joined the Thule Society, which at that time was led by Dietrich Eckhardt. When the Brotherhood of Death began their ambitious plan to reshape society in a more controllable form, their end goal was the surveillance and monitoring of an increasingly isolated and malleable population. Europe was identified as a potential flash-point for a useful war. Germany, having just lost a major war, was ripe for destabilization, and Hitler, whom Eckhardt believed to be the Antichrist, was chosen as the obvious leader to initiate the gigantic conflict and death required. This would scar the human psyche so deeply that people would become paranoid and withdrawn, and once isolated they could be manipulated into giving up autonomy to the Brotherhood and its evil masters.

The Brotherhood of Death believed firmly that contact with ancient powers of spiritual evil – the Devil – was not only attainable but very desirable, and that by following the dictates of their master, they could achieve great earthly power. They used sexual perversions and practices to fuel their magical operations, which made their spells and rituals phenomenally powerful and opened channels of communication to the forces of evil.

By tapping the power of evil, the Thule Society was able to manipulate the consciousness of the German people and bring the Nazi party to prominence. By appealing to the basic human psychological programmes of hatred, fear and greed, the Nazi party was able to divert the current of evil into the minds of usually decent people, and foster the political climate that led to Hitler's rise. Once he was in power, it was frighteningly simple to steer the world into a gigantic war, with the death camps providing the incredible amounts of magical energy needed to change human consciousness for ever.

THE STRANGE PART

Eckhardt's final act was said to be Hitler's initiation through an astonishingly sadistic black magic ritual that left the Nazi leader impotent. From then on, Hitler was forced to seek sexual fulfilment through sadomasochistic release, and it was this blow that forced him into becoming the greatest monster we have seen this century.

THE USUAL SUSPECTS
Satan

If ancient powers of spiritual evil are behind the Brotherhood of Death and the *Thule Gesellschaft*, then that rather implies the Devil. Given the Devil's well-known propensity for misdirection, it seems likely that in the event that his plans succeed, the Brotherhood will lose out along with everyone else.

Bavarian Illuminati

This age-old German secret society is often thought to control everyone from the Mafia to the Knights Templar. The Illuminati were the power behind many occult orders in pre-war Germany and may have been Hitler's ultimate puppet-master. It is recorded that Heinrich Himmler was closely involved with societies linked to the Illuminati.

THE UNUSUAL SUSPECTS
The Elders of Zion

The least credible and perhaps most offensive theory is that the Elders of Zion were responsible for the actions of the Nazi party. By causing a massive depopulation of Jews, the England-based group would have less difficulty in claiming

above Adolf Hitler, Chancellor of Germany, is welcomed by supporters at Nuremberg in 1933.

to be the inheritors of Moses' wisdom. The horrors of the Holocaust would also breed sympathy for all causes even tangentially related to Judaism.

MOST CONVINCING EVIDENCE

On his deathbed, Dietrich Eckhardt is said to have announced: "Follow Hitler; he will dance, but it is I who have called the tune. I have initiated him into the Secret Doctrine, opened his centres of vision, and given him the means to communicate with the powers." Given that society continues to get more fragmented, violent and subjugated by television, despite the fact that it is in no one's interests, not even those of the world governments, the Brotherhood of Death could be said to be doing a particularly effective job.

MOST MYSTERIOUS FACT

The USA too has a society with the logo of the Brotherhood of Death – Yale's Skull and Bones society, rumoured to have been started in the 1800s as a US lodge of a German university-based society. President George Bush Snr belonged to this group, as did many important figures in American society and political circles.

SCEPTICALLY SPEAKING

To dismiss the Holocaust and the evils of the Nazi empire as a simple tool for generating magical energy seems somewhat offensive to those who died. In addition, the circumstances surrounding the rise of the Nazi Party are well understood in sociological terms – tragic, but hardly mysterious.

THE MAN IN THE IRON MASK

The mystery of the Man in the Iron Mask has been a focal point for doe-eyed romantics and for serious historians since the seventeenth century, generating countless theories about the identity of the masked prisoner. The interest continues even to this day, hence the recent film, *The Man In The Iron Mask*, starring teen heartthrob Leonardo DiCaprio. But the world is still no closer to discovering who this tragic figure was and, as the years pass, the chances of discovering his (or her) true identity continue to fade.

Little is known about the prisoner. What little information that exists in French official documents paints a deliberately sketchy picture: he was arrested in 1669, and was imprisoned first in Pignerol, a fortress high in the French Alps. He was transferred in 1681 to Exiles, which lay close to Pignerol, and in 1687 he was moved yet again to the southern French coastal island of Saint Marguerite. His stay on the island lasted 11 years until he was sent to the Bastille in Paris. Finally, the prisoner died in 1703, an undoubtedly welcome release.

Throughout his entire imprisonment, there were reportedly only two instances of witnesses who were not prison officials actually seeing the prisoner. During his move from Exiles to Saint Marguerite, the prisoner was seen wearing a steel mask. With the move to the Bastille, this cumbersome disguise was replaced with a more humane mask of black velvet. It has also been discovered, through official correspondence between a government minister and Saint Mars (the prisoner's jailer) that the prisoner was not to be allowed to communicate with anyone, by spoken or by written word. If he did, he was to be executed on the spot.

What terrible secret could this man have possessed that demanded such secrecy? Historians have wondered why he was even kept alive: if the knowledge he held was of such danger to the King and government, wouldn't it have been politically safer simply to kill him? And why such a concern over people seeing his face? Did he resemble someone well-known to the French populace, which would have to make him very famous indeed, bearing in mind the primitive state of print media during the seventeenth century? Once again, simply killing him – an option not in disuse in the French court of the time – would have made more sense.

The mystery of the Man in the Iron Mask is as unfathomable now as it was three hundred years ago. What is known is that a man paid a horrible price for an alleged crime – or deadly secret – that history can only guess at.

THE STRANGE PART

Saint Mars, the man appointed to jail the mysterious prisoner, held that position from the first day of his incarceration until the prisoner breathed his last in 1703. With the turnstile approach to political appointments of the day, this constancy is intriguing.

THE USUAL SUSPECTS
Louis XIV

Many fingers point towards the King of France. The masked prisoner could have been the twin brother of Louis, rumoured to have been conceived at the same time but unfortunately born last. He didn't know his own true identity and, to clear up any messy succession issues,

Louis imprisoned his brother. Other theories suggest that he could have been an elder brother, the result of an extramarital affair of Louis' mother. Another theory states that the prisoner was a doctor who attended Louis XIII's autopsy and unfortunately discovered the late king incapable of siring children, thus endangering Louis XIV's right to the throne. Following the same thread, the prisoner could have been the true father of Louis XIV, recruited on account of Louis XIII's inability in the bedroom.

Count Antonio Matthioli

He may have been the prisoner, wearing the mask for the most pointless of reasons – because it was the fashionable thing to do in Italy at the time.

Louis Oldendorff

A Lorraine nobleman, Oldendorff was the leader of the Secret Order of the Temple. The rules of this society would not allow them to replace him while he still lived. After he died, another man was made to wear the mask, thus maintaining the illusion of Oldendorff's imprisonment, and keeping the Order from selecting a new leader.

Also suspected to be the prisoner: Richard Cromwell; the Duke of Monmouth; Vivien de Bulonde.

THE UNUSUAL SUSPECTS

Hidden Daughter of Louis XIII and Anne

Terrified of not having a son, the elder Louis may have hidden away his newborn daughter and replaced her with an infant boy changeling. When she grew up and discovered her identity, Louis XIV (the changeling) had her imprisoned.

Molière

As beloved as the playwright was both by the French public and by Louis XIV, Molière made many enemies because of his lack of religious beliefs and general disdain for the French establishment. He especially angered the Company of the Holy Sacrament, a strong and influential Catholic group. The theory follows that Molière's death was staged in 1673, with the playwright becoming the Man in the Iron Mask as punishment.

Nicholas Fouquet

Fouquet was allegedly imprisoned for discovering hidden knowledge that Christ didn't die on the cross, but survived, leading to a secret bloodline of direct ancestors.

MOST CONVINCING EVIDENCE

The fact that the prisoner wasn't simply killed indicates that there must have been a royal connection. Anyone else would have been garotted and left to an unmarked grave.

MOST MYSTERIOUS FACT

Despite the back-stabbing of French politics, the gains that could be made by revealing who this prisoner was, and the methodical examination of records, there is no indication of who the prisoner was. It was a universally kept secret, by all parties involved.

SCEPTICALLY SPEAKING

The identity of the Man in the Iron Mask is so well hidden one can surmise it's simply because he didn't exist at all. The vision of such a figure would go far towards quelling any dissidence to the King's rule. The prospect of lifelong imprisonment does that sort of thing…

left Whoever he or she was, the real prisoner in the mask died in the infamous Bastille in 1703.

inset England's finest playwright, spy and bar brawler – Christopher Marlowe.

right Occultist and spymaster Dr John Dee may have been behind Marlowe's murder for reason of state security.

THE MURDER OF CHRISTOPHER MARLOWE

Fate can play cruel tricks on the gifted and Christopher Marlowe (1564–93) was undoubtedly gifted. At one time he was England's leading playwright, thanks to such works as *Doctor Faustus*. If the hand of history had dealt more kindly with him it is unlikely that this giant of the Elizabethan theatre would ever have been overshadowed by that relative upstart Shakespeare.

Marlowe was much more than just a talented writer. In his short but tempestuous life he experienced both wealth and poverty, was tried and briefly imprisoned and managed to kill a man in a brawl. Marlowe met an untimely end when he was stabbed in the eye in a Deptford tavern. The official story is that he was killed as the result of an argument over an unpaid bill, but conspiracy theorists never pay too much attention to the official version. There is another side to Marlowe. He was a spy.

England in the sixteenth century was a turbulent place. The country was troubled by enemies at home and abroad. The defeat of the Spanish Armada had ended the King of Spain's plans for a purely military conquest of the country, so he turned to espionage and began attacking England by more subtle means. The internal threat centred on religion. For many years there had been conflict between Protestants and Catholics, with prominent figures on both sides dying at the stake. Although the official attitude in 1593 was toleration, there was an active and dangerous Catholic underground with strong links to foreign powers.

To counter these threats it was necessary for the English crown to operate an efficient counter-espionage system. Elizabeth I's spymaster was Francis Walshingham, who recruited Marlowe at Cambridge University (for generations afterwards Cambridge remained a fertile breeding ground for spies and double agents). Marlowe's public profile and wide network of connections made him a useful, if somewhat unreliable, agent. He infiltrated many secret societies and organizations while performing this role.

Given his secret life, his murder may not have been the simple affair it has been portrayed as. The question remains in many people's minds – was Marlowe killed to end the career of one of Elizabethan England's equivalents of James Bond?

THE STRANGE PART

Fierce argument rages over whether Marlowe was killed by England's enemies, by its defenders or by some other clandestine organization with a grudge against him. It is strange to say the least, that although he was stabbed in a crowded tavern, no witnesses ever came forward and no one was ever punished for the murder.

THE USUAL SUSPECTS

Dr John Dee

After Walshingham died in 1590, Britain's top spymaster was Dr John Dee. When not running England's cloak-and-dagger activity, Dee dabbled in astrology, necromancy, contacting angels and alchemy. The transmuting of base metals into gold is a neat way of explaining the funds that passed through his hands and were provided by various paymasters. The doctor was not over-troubled by scruples and if he felt that Marlowe had become a double-agent, would have had no problems having him silenced permanently.

Spanish Secret Agents

Marlowe may have been involved in an elaborate attempt to infiltrate the Catholic underground and thwart the plans of the Spanish spies who were working through it in England. By posing as a double-agent he may have been attempting to gain their confidence and secrets. If he was exposed, they would certainly have had reasons for wanting to take their revenge and prevent him from passing on any information he had obtained.

THE UNUSUAL SUSPECTS

William Shakespeare

The theatre can be a cut-throat business and in the days before copyright and Arts Council funding a great many bitter feuds developed between playwrights. Shakespeare was a member of the School of Night – a shadowy organization that included spies, writers and representatives of the aristocracy among its ranks – and certainly had the connections to arrange for the elimination of one of his main literary rivals.

The Masons

Among the many secret societies that were flourishing in Elizabethan England were the Freemasons. It has long been suspected that Marlowe drew on Masonic imagery in his plays and was almost certainly a member of the order. While being a Mason probably helped to advance his career as a playwright, it would also have given him access to insider information in his role of spy. Marlowe may have made the foolish mistake of breaking his oath of secrecy to the organization. His murder may have been the consequence of underestimating just how much Masons value silence.

MOST MYSTERIOUS FACT

The threat of having an eye plucked out if you betray your colleagues forms the part of the initiation oath into several secret orders – including the higher ranks of Templars and Freemasons – so it is more than a little odd that Marlowe was killed by a stabbing to the eye. The nature of his death may point towards it being a ritualistic murder.

MOST CONVINCING EVIDENCE

Marlowe's arrest, under the pretext that he had murdered a man, provides strong evidence to support the idea that he was a spy. Even though it was a trumped-up charge used to detain him, the fact that he had the power and influence to be acquitted quickly suggests that he had friends in high places – or that he bought his freedom by switching sides and becoming a double-agent.

SCEPTICALLY SPEAKING

Spies shun the light and when they assassinate people they do it in dark alleys and not crowded taverns. Failing to pay your bar bill or clear your gambling debts tends to cause offence even if you are a spy. Marlowe had a talent for getting himself into trouble and it's quite feasible that he could have got himself involved in a fatal fight thanks to an overuse of clever words and irony – a faux pas that is still punishable with physical violence in some South London pubs today.

WOLFGANG AMADEUS MOZART

Genius may bring its blessings, but it also brings its fair share of enemies. No one knew this more than the brilliant composer Wolfgang Amadeus Mozart. A child prodigy by the age of five, his musical gifts brought him more pain than joy. While his work is heralded today as the finest that classical music can offer, in his time he was openly reviled, with several of his contemporaries plotting his destruction. History may have given him fame but in his lifetime he knew no such comfort. Mozart, perhaps the greatest composer ever known, died penniless, his remains buried unceremoniously in a common grave in Vienna.

Born in Salzburg, Austria in January, 1756, Mozart quickly displayed his musical gifts: by the age of four, his father had arranged harpsichord lessons for him; by five, he was composing his own music; by the time he was six, his father took the young Mozart on a performance tour of Vienna and Munich. By the time he was 15, he was concertmaster of the Archbishop of Salzburg's orchestra. The future seemed to belong to the extremely gifted young man.

But there were personality conflicts between the Archbishop and Mozart – the fact that Mozart wasn't paid for three years may have been one reason. In 1781, he left the prestigious (but poorly paid) position and went to seek his fortune in Vienna. There, the poor relationship he had had with the Salzburg court continued with the Viennese composers. This became so bad that Mozart's father complained to Emperor Joseph II that the other composers were deliberately ensuring that a composition of his son's was not being performed.

Yet Mozart persevered, despite his difficulty in getting paid and his inability to spend money wisely. His marriage to Constanze Weber was fraught with financial difficulties and tragedy – of their six children, only two survived past childhood. Mozart was not a favourite with the Viennese court, and his work received lukewarm response from the public, if it was played at all. By 1790, Mozart's debts were staggering, and his health was extremely fragile. The following year, he was secretly commissioned, by a mysterious stranger, to compose a Requiem. After finishing writing *The Magic Flute*, Mozart threw himself obsessively into writing this mournful piece. But fate (or a force more sinister) intervened, and Wolfgang Amadeus Mozart died on December 5, 1791 in Vienna; the Requiem was unfinished and the stranger who commissioned it disappeared into the shadows of time. Mozart was only 35.

THE STRANGE PART

The identity of the stranger who commissioned Mozart's final work has never been revealed. Theories point to an anonymous

above Rock me Amadeus! Mozart was an unparalleled musical genius, Freemason and a man with many enemies.

woman in black or to a man dressed all in grey. No one ever came forward to admit to commissioning the Requiem. Mozart was obsessed with the piece, and many feel that this obsession drove him to illness and, finally, his deathbed.

THE USUAL SUSPECTS

Antonio Salieri

A court composer, it has been widely rumoured (and even cited as fact in the film *Amadeus*) that Salieri was terribly jealous of Mozart's gifts and upset by his ribald way of life. Salieri may have commissioned the deadly Requiem himself, knowing full well Mozart's fragile health and the cost the work would exact upon him. He may have felt that with Mozart dead his own work would receive the attention he felt it deserved.

Count von Walsegg zu Stuppach

The Count was an amateur musician who may have wanted more glory than his talent would allow. The theory runs that the Count disguised himself as the mysterious stranger, hoping to pass off the finished Requiem Mass as his own work. To ensure that Mozart would not dispute this, he planned to have Mozart poisoned.

Unknown Viennese Composers

Mozart's work easily outshone the work of his

contemporaries: Handel himself said that Mozart was the greatest composer that had ever lived. However, with Mozart's hit-and-miss approach to success, coupled with the cut-throat world of court commissions and appointments, perhaps someone simply decided to even the field a bit. If Mozart's health had been better and if he had learned to manage his life better, he would have been unstoppable.

THE UNUSUAL SUSPECTS

The Masons

Mozart was a Freemason, but his dissolute lifestyle may have been considered a liability they no longer wanted to suffer. It is also rumoured that they were none too happy with his Masonic-inspired opera *The Magic Flute* for giving away one too many secrets.

Disgruntled Black Magician in the Court of Emperor Joseph

A story survives of an army general in Joseph's court complaining about Mozart's lack of court decorum to the Emperor. The Emperor replied that he could get a general any time he wished, but he would never get another Mozart. This could have led to someone in the court using black magic to kill Mozart, leading to the confusion among doctors concerning his death.

MOST CONVINCING EVIDENCE

While "miliary fever" was diagnosed as the cause of Mozart's death, the truth was that the attending doctors were unsure why he died. He suffered a range of apparently unconnected complaints, from toothaches to lethargy, but nothing pointed conclusively to one cause of death or another. The official diagnosis of "miliary fever" was perhaps nothing more than a face-saving way for the doctors to say they simply didn't know.

MOST MYSTERIOUS FACT

Mozart was initiated into a Viennese Masonic Lodge at the age of 18, with his father joining shortly thereafter. Curiously, despite the connection, Mozart was denied membership to the Viennese Society of Musicians. Also interesting to note was that his last public performance was a cantata for the dedication of his Masonic Lodge's new temple.

SCEPTICALLY SPEAKING

Mozart was a sickly man almost from his birth, plagued with one ailment after another. The question isn't why he died when he died, but why he didn't succumb sooner. Modern physicians have suggested that Mozart died of uremia caused by kidney disease. As for jealous rivals killing him, why murder a man whose work was never played?

below A jealous rival of Mozart, Salieri was a powerful intriguer at the court of Emperor Joseph II.

left Grigori Yefimovich – AKA Rasputin, AKA The Mad Monk.

РАСПУТИ

RASPUTIN

The Russian royal family at the turn of the twentieth century was completely dominated by the charismatic power of a defrocked monk-turned-psychic-healer-and-fortune-teller Grigori Yefimovich, known as Rasputin. The former holy man possessed the power to maintain the health of the Tsar's son, Alexei, who was dangerously anaemic. The hold this gave him over the Russian royal family is well documented, and Rasputin used his influence to great personal gain.

That the "Mad Monk" greatly destabilized the Russian imperial government is a matter of historical fact. He used his influence to put his followers in positions of power and authority, demanded extortionate bribes in return for persuading the Tsarina Alexandra, the Empress, to favour certain courtiers, business people or plans of action, and charged great sums for dispensing his "healing" among the lesser nobility. He was already a national scandal by 1911, and by 1915 had become the Tsarina's chief advisor.

He also had a voracious sexual appetite, and would frequently demand sexual intercourse from both men and women as part of the payment for his services – often insisting that he sleep with the teenage child of a supplicant, if such were available. He also had no end of groupies available, partly because of his power, and partly because of his 13-inch erection. His exploits outraged the general public, but the royal family was totally under his spell. Reports from the time suggest that his powers of healing and precognition were both entirely genuine. Letters from Alexandra to Rasputin also hint that he was having an affair with her.

Finally, a cabal of Russian nobles decided Rasputin's influence was corrupting the state, and that he had to die. Led by Prince Feliks Yusupov, the cabal lured the healer to a private party hosted by Yusopov, where he was murdered, on December 30, 1916. It was too late to save the reputation of the royal family, and shortly afterwards the revolution swept away the old order.

THE STRANGE PART

The tale of Rasputin's death certainly lends credence to his healing powers. Arriving at the party, the holy man was placed in front of a banquet laced with enough cyanide to kill a dozen normal men. One conspirator, a medical doctor called Lazovert, prepared the poisoned food. Rasputin became suspicious that Yusupov was not eating When the monk failed to show any ill effects from his feast, the Prince panicked, and shot him at close range. He was also shot by Grand Duke Pavlovich, the Tsar's nephew. Enraged but still seemingly mobile, Rasputin chased Yusupov out of the house and into the courtyard, where a gang of conspirators beat him to a bloody pulp with hefty iron chains. Dr. Lazovert examined the monk, and declared him to be alive, so they wrapped him in the chains and dumped him in a hole cut into the ice of the River Neva.

THE USUAL SUSPECTS

Spiritual Avatar

Perhaps the most common theory is that Rasputin genuinely did possess the healing and precognitive powers that history has granted to him, including the ability to mesmerize women. He used these powers to gain his position of authority, and it was this that led to his being murdered. The powers were derived from the fact that Rasputin was in fact a spiritual avatar or genuine saint.

St Germain

Rasputin was in fact the immortal known to medieval Europe as the Count de St Germain, smoothing the way for the Russian revolution so that history could follow its proper course. When he found himself stuck in the water and unable to tunnel out, Rasputin/St Germain decided that the best course of action was to feign death and lie low. He was dug out of the Neva by the conspirators, and hastily buried. From a shallow grave, he found it relatively easy to tunnel out. His enemies were certain he was dead, so he was free to make his escape. Rumour suggests that St Germain may now be in Los Angeles, having spent the 1980s in Eastern Europe bringing Communism to an end.

THE UNUSUAL SUSPECTS

Alien Invader

Rasputin's unnatural vitality was not a result of psychic ability at all. The healer was actually an alien, a rogue member of a small exploration team who decided to indulge himself in a few years of orgiastic amusement. Because his physiology was different to ours, the assassination was almost ineffective. In the end, it was lack of exposure to direct sunlight that killed him, not the low temperature or lack of oxygen.

MOST CONVINCING EVIDENCE

Rasputin's frozen corpse was finally retrieved several miles down-river from where it had been dumped. He had shaken loose of his chains, and had been trying to claw his way out of the ice from the inside when he had finally succumbed – after having been totally submerged in freezing water for at least six hours.

MOST MYSTERIOUS FACT

Perhaps the oddest feat of Rasputin's survival is his capacity to consume such a huge dose of cyanide. Equally as strange, though, is an artefact that surfaced in Paris in the 1960s – Rasputin's mummified penis. One observer described it as "like a blackened banana, about a foot long". There is no record of any of the conspirators castrating their victim, however.

SCEPTICALLY SPEAKING

It is just about possible that the poison was old and ineffective, that the gunshots failed to hit any vital organs, that the beating was mostly surface damage, and even that the cold of the river Neva slowed tissue damage from oxygen starvation so much that Rasputin was able to revive for long enough to lock his fingers in the ice. But if he was so precognitive, why did he not foretell the danger of taking Yusupov up on his invitation?

JACK THE RIPPER

The mystery surrounding the Jack The Ripper murders in 1888 has fascinated and tantalized criminologists, conspiracy buffs and Hollywood producers for more than a hundred years. Theories and counter-theories have arisen, mutually exclusive "authentic" diaries, confessions and notebooks have been discovered and published. It is doubtful whether anyone will ever be able to provide a definite answer.

On Friday August 31, 1888, Polly Nichols was murdered. Her death was followed by that of Annie Chapman on Saturday, September 8, then by Catharine Eddowes and Elizabeth Stride on Sunday September 30, and Mary Kelly on Friday November 9. Their throats were cut and their bodies mutilated; the internal organs were often removed with surgical precision and carried away from the scene of the crime. Mary Kelly, who was three months pregnant, was found naked, with her clothes piled tidily on a chair nearby. It is also possible that there was an earlier victim – Martha Tabram, who was murdered on Tuesday, August 7. Elizabeth Stride may not have been killed by the Ripper. All six women were prostitutes in the East End of London. Some commentators add three more women to this total.

The Ripper used a fairly consistent modus operandi. When the victim lifted her skirts she was grabbed and throttled to unconsciousness, then laid on the ground. Once the woman was lying down, her throat was cut, and in most cases one of the victim's internal organs was removed, presumably as a trophy. The degree of precision exhibited in this procedure suggests that the Ripper had medical training; in one instance, a kidney was removed frontally, without damaging any of the other organs. This would require some skill in an operating theatre, and would be very hard indeed at night, in the dark, under the pressure of being in a public place with the corpse of someone you have just murdered.

Scotland Yard's files show that two notes were received by the Central News Agency from a person claiming to be the Ripper, one entitled "Dear Boss", and the other "from Hell". Both were strangely written, and took a boastfully gloating tone. Most researchers into the matter doubt that either were actually written by the murderer. A chunk of diseased kidney was also sent to a Whitechapel vigilance committee with a letter that claimed the organ was from Katharine Eddowes. While there was no way of knowing for certain, the damage to the kidney was consistent with the effects of the particular disease from which Eddowes suffered.

THE STRANGE PART

On the night of September 30, police officers found a piece of Catharine Eddowes' apron that the Ripper had used to wipe his knife. This was very close to a doorway over which the message "The Juwes are the men That Will not be blamed for nothing" had been written. Senior police officers felt this would spark anti-Semitic riots and erased the message. The odd phraseology and strange spelling has sparked suggestions that it was actually a Masonic message, and the police erased it to hide the fact.

THE USUAL SUSPECTS

Prince Albert Victor

The grandson of Queen Victoria, Prince Albert Victor (known as "Eddy") was a mentally subnormal youth, described by one royal commentator at the time as "a gleaming goldfish in a crystal bowl". Eddy seems likely to have been an occasional homosexual – a criminal offence in Britain at the time – and died in 1892. Rumours suggested the cause of death was syphilis. His madness is supposed to have been the spur that led him to murder prostitutes, and fear of scandal led to a conspiracy hushing up the Prince's guilt. An alternative theory suggests that he may have got one of the prostitutes pregnant. When she tried to blackmail the government, she and her friends were killed by royal

agents in a manner that would distract investigators from the real reason for the deaths.

Dr Francis Tumblety

An American doctor, Tumblety was strongly suspected by John Littlechild, head of the Secret Department at Scotland Yard during the investigations. The doctor fled back to the USA, and Scotland Yard sent detectives to interview him.

THE UNUSUAL SUSPECTS

Dr Roslyn D'onston Stephenson

A heavy-drinking occultist who went to the police with his own theory to explain the Ripper and his murders, the doctor ended up becoming a suspect himself in some theorists' eyes due to the discovery made by author Mabel Collins in 1890 while cohabiting with Stephenson. She claims to have found seven bloodstained ties used in the murders. This possible evidence ended up with England's most famous occultist Aleister Crowley after he obtained them from Mabel's lover, Victoria Cremers.

Interdimensional Invader

Victorian London was also plagued with another notorious Jack – Spring-Heeled Jack. This strange figure, wearing armour, cloak and a helmet, could allegedly jump over buildings. He was seen by hundreds of witnesses and hunted for by a vigilante force led by none other than England's most famous soldier Wellington. Some feel that Spring-Heeled Jack was an interdimensional invader and the true Ripper.

MOST CONVINCING EVIDENCE

In 1970, Dr. Thomas Stowell claimed to have found documents that showed Prince Albert's doctor William Gull was seen more than once in the Whitechapel area on the nights of the murders. They also detailed how policemen and a medium had visited Gull to make enquiries and that Gull had confessed. Stowell believed this was a brave attempt to protect the real Ripper – the insane, syphilitic Prince Albert Victor.

MOST MYSTERIOUS FACT

When Stowell's claim found widespread attention he tried to retract his evidence and denied that he had implicated Prince Albert. However, Stowell died before his retraction could be printed and his family immediately burnt his notes and papers before his claims could be verified. They also burnt all evidence relating to Stowell's career as a Freemason. It may be a coincidence, but he died on November 9, 1970, the anniversary of Mary Kelly's death.

SCEPTICALLY SPEAKING

Jack the Ripper has become an archetypal nightmare figure and moved beyond the realms of unexplained murderer into Legend of the Night. A whole myth-making industry has grown up around the case, which is served by distorting the facts and lengthening the shadows. Given this, it is not surprising that conspiracy theories continue to proliferate and yet still fail to find a truly convincing solution.

below Elizabeth Stride, third victim of Jack the Ripper.

inset What part did Prince Albert Victor play in the Ripper conspiracy?

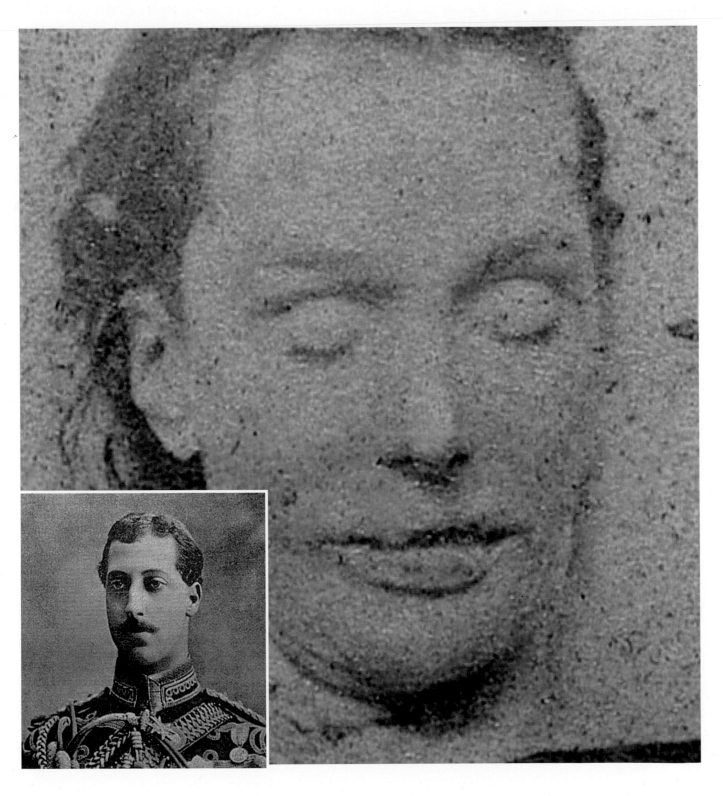

PLACES

ANTARCTICA

Desolate but beautiful, Antarctica is a dangerous environment and an environment in danger. It is a place of massive contrasts, but the greatest contrast that this mysterious continent may yield is that our perception of it as an uninhabited might not be true. Conspiracy theorists believe the truth about who lives in Antarctica is being hidden from the public.

The antennae of conspiracy enthusiasts have been twitching in anticipation of some strange truth being revealed ever since information began to leak out concerning the exploration of the continent by Nazis with links to mystical orders such as the *Thule Gesellschaft*, and Ahenerbe, the SS occult bureau.

When Admiral Byrd led a US military expedition force of more than 10,000 men to Antarctica in 1947 the mystery deepened. The force returned after just three months having suffered heavy losses on their mysterious mission. Even fifty years later, it is almost impossible to obtain any of the unclassified information concerning this inexplicable polar misadventure by the US military.

While debate rages over just who Admiral Byrd's men might have been fighting, most conspiracy theorists agree that underneath the ice of Antarctica is the remains of an advanced civilization destroyed by some great cataclysm. It is alleged that it is this fact that the Nazis stumbled upon and this fact that sinister forces are conspiring to keep secret from the rest of us.

THE STRANGE PART

Antarctica is governed by a treaty, signed by various powerful countries, that prevents any development or exploitation of its vast natural resources. Given that our governments do not generally have a good track record on defending the environment, this could be seen as a

above Antarctica – beautiful, remote and full of secrets.

Inset The Piri Reis Map drawn in 1513 clearly shows Antarctica before it was covered in ice, despite the fact that Antarctica wasn't officially discovered until 1818.

little curious. It has been suggested that the real purpose of the Antarctic Treaty is to eliminate the chance of any commercial organization stumbling on to the truth by digging through the two-mile thick crust of ice.

THE USUAL SUSPECTS

Nazis

In 1938, Nazi Germany made the most extensive survey of Antarctica to date, claimed it as their territory and renamed it Neuschwabenland. It is known that inner orders of the Nazi Party placed a special importance on Antarctica and that the Germans maintained a presence there throughout World War II. In 1946, German U-boats were spotted off the coast of Argentina heading towards the ice-bound continent. Conjecture has it that elements of the German High Command escaped justice to set up a base among the ruins of a lost Antarctic civilization.

The Jason Society

The Jason Society was, apparently, set up by President Nixon, in 1973. A secret organisation, its ultra-classified purpose was to run a project called "Secret Earth" and some claim that it is the group charged with exploiting the remnants of an advanced civilization found beneath Antarctica and in one or two other locations across the globe. Unlike many other groups behind conspiracies, it seems that the Jason Society may have a semi-benevolent purpose for keeping us all in the dark over Antarctica. It is suggested that the Society's aim is to discover enough about the vanished Elder Race to prevent us from sharing their fate.

Also suspected: MJ-12; Project Phoenix; the US National Security Council; the United Nations; and a cabal of Freemasons.

THE UNUSUAL SUSPECTS

Ancient Space Aliens

If there are ruins of an ancient culture buried deep in Antarctica's forbidding wastes, some argue that it is of an alien and not human nature. They feel that the conspiracy has developed to prevent widespread knowledge of alien involvement in Earth's history.

The Knights Templar

If civilization was established in Egypt by survivors fleeing Antarctica following the catastrophe that covered it in ice, their knowledge of their original homeland may have been preserved in certain secret traditions. The Knights Templar trace their lineage to ancient Egypt, so they may have inherited this information. If this is true, they may wish to control Antarctica and exploit the advanced technology below its surface in order to further their plans for world domination.

MOST CONVINCING EVIDENCE

The single most startling piece of evidence that gives some weight to the conspiracy theory concerning Antarctica is the Piri Reis Map – a genuine document that was drawn up in Constantinople in 1513. It clearly shows not only the western coast of Africa and the eastern coast of South America, but also the ice-free coast of a country called Queen Maud Land.

Antarctica was not discovered until 1818, and the astonishing accuracy of the map was not revealed until the Fifties when ground-penetrating radar technology allowed geologists to see the land beneath the ice for the first time. The map was drawn up from earlier charts, but no one is able to offer a convincing explanation of how it can possibly show what it does. Other similar charts exist, suggesting there may be some truth to the idea Antarctica could be have once been home to the civilization that has become popularly known as Atlantis.

MOST MYSTERIOUS FACT

In 1998, a vast earthquake was reported to have occurred in Antarctica measuring up to 8.1 on the Richter scale. This fact hit global news services, preparations were made and the entire east coast of Australia was put on alert – the authorities feared it could be hit by a huge tidal wave. Medical authorities, the police and the army called the alert off when the expected tsunami did not arrive. What makes all of this mysterious is that there are no plates at the South Pole and there is, therefore, no logical explanation as to what could have caused such a massive quake.

SCEPTICALLY SPEAKING

There is very little scientific evidence for Antarctica having been ice-free enough to support a civilization at any point during the last 15 million years. No archaeological evidence has so far been found to suggest an advanced culture ever existed on the continent.

THE BERMUDA TRIANGLE

The Bermuda Triangle – also known by the more intimidating name of the Devil's Triangle – is an area of the Atlantic Ocean that is generally accepted to fall within a triangle formed by Bermuda, Puerto Rico and Fort Lauderdale, Florida.

This mysterious area was first given its famous nickname by the writer Vincent H Gaddis in 1964. He wrote a magazine story entitled "The Deadly Bermuda Triangle" that drew upon centuries of seamen's legends concerning the Devil's Triangle and the many unexplainable disappearances of ships and planes that had occurred within its boundary.

The Triangle has been known as place of odd happenings ever since the fifteenth century when Christopher Columbus made an entry in his log concerning "a great flame of fire" that crashed into the ocean as his compass went wild and his crew saw strange lights in the sky. The area's notoriety was added to over the following years by a number of odd incidents – most notably with the disappearance of the crew of the *Mary Celeste* in 1872.

However, some of the oddest incidents that have enshrined the Triangle took place more recently. The most famous case is that of Flight 19 – which was featured in the film *Close Encounters of the Third Kind*. On December 5, 1945, five of the Navy's Avenger torpedo bombers on a routine practice mission vanished. A Martin Mariner, with a 22-man rescue crew, was sent out to find them – they also disappeared without trace. Added to this have the been the loss of more than 50 ships, such as the massive USS *Cyclops*, and the tanker SS *Marine Sulphur Queen*, which vanished in calm seas with her 39-man crew.

THE STRANGE PART

No wreckage from Flight 19 was ever recovered – despite a massive search – which suggests that something more than a mysterious five-plane crash or ditching into the sea is involved. The fact that absolutely no sign of any remains was spotted is typical of the disappearances said to occur in the Bermuda Triangle, where even massive ships vanish without a trace and without sending a distress call. Of course, conspiracy theorists believe that the authorities know that something mysterious is going on and have attempted to cover it up.

above The massive USS Cyclops, just one many ships that have disappeared in the so-called Devil's Triangle.

THE USUAL SUSPECTS

Aliens

Aliens top the list of those conjectured to be behind the disappearances in the Triangle and the need for the truth to be covered up. It is alleged that an alien race – probably those nasty little Greys – have an underwater base in the area of the Triangle. There are certainly plenty of reports of UFOs rising out of and diving into the ocean near Puerto Rico. As our unwelcome visitors have a thing about their privacy, they tend to dispose of anyone who crosses over into what they regard as their territory.

North American Air Defense Command

Extra-terrestrials are not the only ones alleged to have undersea bases in the Bermuda Triangle. Some conspiracy theorists hold to the idea that the North American Air Defense Command, also known by the acronym NORAD, has a vast submerged complex running ultra-secret technology that interferes with the signals that aeroplanes and boats rely on for navigation. If any plane or ship spots evidence of the NORAD base, they are meant to be "vanished" by the US military.

Also suspected: MJ-12; United Nations; and the ancient alien space deities Cthulhu and Yog-Sogoth.

THE UNUSUAL SUSPECTS

Chrononauts

Some feel it is not the Greys behind the missing pilots, sailors and passengers, but humans from the far future travelling back in time. The Chrononauts of this hypothesis take advantage of a gravitational time-space anomaly in the area to gather living evidence of the past. Of course, if anyone uncovers this fact, the Chrononauts can travel back into the past to change the timeline and prevent the evidence from being discovered.

Atlantean Ruins

Conjecture has been made that the Bermuda Triangle is situated above the sunken remnants of the ancient civilisation of Atlantis. The reason why so many ships and planes have vanished is that, buried among the supposed ruins of Atlantis, are huge crystals emitting powerful, random beams of energy. It is this energy that zaps unfortunate craft passing overhead. One or two even believe that some Atlanteans themselves remain below the waves and are actually responsible for the disappearances.

MOST CONVINCING EVIDENCE

Aside from the disappearance of more than fifty ships and twenty planes in the Triangle during the last century, and the fact that it is one of only two places on Earth where a magnetic compass does not point to true north, there is other evidence of strange goings on. Carolyn Casico, a licensed pilot, flew a charter flight to Turk Island in the Triangle. When she was seen flying over the island, Carolyn was heard over her radio saying: "I don't understand. This should be Grand Turk but there is nothing there. The shape is right but this island looks uninhabited." She circled the island a few times before heading out to sea and vanishing.

MOST MYSTERIOUS FACT

Before they vanished off the face of the Earth and into the limbo of the lost, the last message received from Flight 19 consisted of the letters "FT" repeated over and over again. No one has ever been able to make sense of what the pilots were trying to convey with their strange last words.

SCEPTICALLY SPEAKING

Storms, freak weather, tidal waves, explosive cargoes and poor navigators are all plausible reasons for many of the accidents behind the supposed mystery. Some sceptics argue the number of craft lost is not out of the ordinary, given the size of the area and amount of traffic passing through it. Added to all of this is the fact that many of the ships and planes said to have disappeared mysteriously in the Triangle were not in the Bermuda Triangle at all.

THE HOLLOW EARTH

There should be nothing more solid and dependable than the very surface of the Earth we walk upon, but many researchers in the conspiracy field believe that the interior of the Earth is populated by several bizarre groups. They feel that below a 1,000-mile-thick crust the Earth is hollow and illuminated by an inner sun.

It has long been felt that the entrance to the strange subterranean world of the hollow Earth is to be found at the poles. Everything, from the spectacular light displays known as Aurora Borealis and Aurora Australis – a side-effect of the inner sun – to gravitational and radio anomalies, has been cited in support of this idea. It is also known that some Eskimo tribes claim that they originated from much further north – from a warm land with perpetual daylight.

Some theorists believe that the hollow nature of Earth has been known by the initiates of some secret societies from the dawn of history. These organizations have been manipulating the scientific community and people in power so that the rest of us remain convinced that nothing lies below the Earth's surface other than rock, some patches of oil, and a molten core. It is a fact that the inner teachings of more than one secret society claim that the Earth is hollow, lit by a central sun, populated with an advanced race and connected to the outer Earth by a serious of tunnels. Have these secret societies been engaged in a plot to hoodwink us to the true nature of our planet?

THE STRANGE PART

Despite the full weight of the scientific community, the idea that the Earth is hollow and could be populated has never been totally quashed. Every few years another scientist breaks ranks and risks the wrath of academia and the end of his career by investigating the theory. The amount of scorn and ridicule these poor fellows are subjected to seems out of all proportion if the hollow Earth is only an invalid, crank idea.

THE USUAL SUSPECTS

Nazis

It is well known that many high-ranking Nazis totally believed in the fact that the Earth was hollow. It is recorded that, in the Thirties, Nazi expeditions were sent to Antarctica and Tibet to try and find a way to contact people living under the Earth. Indeed, Herman Goering even conducted rocket experiments based on the theory. Some people believe the theory that members of the *Thule Gesellschaft* and other Nazis escaped into the hollow Earth

at the end of the war and have established colonies there. Obviously, the authorities need to prevent this frightening information from becoming known to the public.

Aliens

Alien races, ranging from the well-known Greys to the less-exposed, Aryan-looking species nicknamed the Nordics, and the Orions (reptilians behind most of Earth's walking serpent legends) are all alleged to have bases in the Earth's interior. Our governments are reported to be aware of this, but are powerless to act against the extra terrestrials and so keep the rest of us ignorant of their presence.

THE UNUSUAL SUSPECTS

Terras

According to Dr Raymond Bernard – who acquired his PhD from New York University in 1932 – the Earth is hollow and its internal space is populated by the Terras. Members of this race of 12-foot-tall beings are purported to have descended from the original Atlanteans, to live on a diet of uncooked vegetables and to fly UFOs when they journey to the surface. Dr Bernard formed a colony in Ecuador for people who shared his beliefs that the authorities were suppressing the truth about the hollow Earth and the friendly Terras who want no more than to save humanity from an impending nuclear holocaust.

Deros

First identified in reports made by a decidedly odd fellow named Richard Shaver in the Forties, the Deros is one of several races that inhabit the hollow interior of the Earth. In Shaver's world view, the Deros are descended from the original alien inhabitants of the Earth who were forced to live underground by the consequences of a solar disaster that took place twelve thousand years ago. The Deros are masters of a superior technology that can control the minds of men and is used to enforce a conspiracy of silence about their subterranean world. Apart from a desire to prevent the truth concerning the hollow Earth coming out, the Deros also seem to have an unhealthy interest in surface-dwelling woman and sadistic sexual practices.

MOST CONVINCING EVIDENCE

Legends concerning underground kingdoms and the creatures that live within them have appeared as part of almost every culture over the last six thousand years, but it still seems odd – to say the least – that more than one government has invested funds in investigating the idea that the Earth is hollow. In the nineteenth century, the US government first sent American military hero Captain John Cleves Symes to the South Pole to find an entrance into the hollow Earth and establish a colony there. Before World

War II, it is known that Nazi Germany sent out more than one exploratory team in search of a way into the alleged world below. It is also rumoured that Admiral Byrd's mysterious military expedition to Antarctica in 1947 had more than a passing interest in the hollow Earth theory.

MOST MYSTERIOUS FACT

On November 25, 1912, American researcher and author Marshall B Gardner submitted an application to the United States Patent Office to obtain a patent on the theory that the Earth was hollow. Eighteen months later, after suitable bureaucratic delay, paperwork and investigation, the US government decided to grant Gardner the United States patent 1096102: The Hollow Earth Theory. This is probably the first time that a conspiracy theory was ever officially endorsed by a patent.

SCEPTICALLY SPEAKING

Short on anything resembling hard evidence and strong on the Too Bizarre To Believe factor, the hollow Earth conspiracy theory fails to stand up to the combined weight of established geology, history, cosmology and common-sense. If entrances to the hollow Earth existed, modern satellites would have spotted them.

MONTAUK POINT, NEW YORK

Many conspiracy theories earn the tag TBTB – Too Bizarre To Believe – and Montauk certainly has a strong claim to this label. Labyrinthine, truly mind-boggling and with an incredible scope, the Montauk machinations and weirdness were first brought to light by the pioneering work of journalist Peter Moon and two people who had been involved in the strange goings-on at Montauk – Preston Nichols and Alfred Bielek.

The conspiracy surrounds Camp Hero – officially, a deserted Air Force Station at Montauk Point on Long Island, New York State. Camp Hero was a US Army base established before World War II. It later became the Montauk Air Force base and was officially active until 1969. However, since then new telephone lines and high-capacity power lines have been installed and many witnesses have observed advanced military electronics equipment being tested in the area. Power usage for the derelict facility is measured with a gigawatt meter, which means it consumes enough power to run a small city.

Conspiracy theories suggest that the subterranean levels of this base continue to house a centre for research and experimentation into electromagnetic mind-control as well as manipulations of time and other dimensions. These experiments date back to 1943 and the infamous "Philadelphia Experiment" when Albert Einstein and Hungarian-born physicist Janus Eric Von Neumann worked on US government experiments that ripped holes in the fabric of reality during attempts to make a Navy vessel invisible to radar.

It is alleged that during the Philadelphia Experiment a battleship disappeared from sight and from our normal timeline. When it reappeared, the crew onboard had suffered devastating psychological damage and underwent terrible physical repercussions. Some sailors rematerialized in the hull of the ship or suffered third-degree burns. After the war, Montauk, and other associated bases and laboratories in the Long Island area continued research into what sounds like the most outlandish science fiction. When a US Congressional investigation into these secret projects decided to shut them down in the Sixties, it was not just the base that was underground. Montauk continued to run without governmental approval, receiving its funding from mysterious sources.

THE STRANGE PART

In 1984, the officially empty Montauk Air Force Base was given to New York State for use as public park land. Even though the property is under the care of the New York State Parks System, no part of it has ever been opened as a park. Significantly, the deeds transferring th e base to New York State make it explicit that the US government still holds all rights to any and all property beneath the surface. Given that plans from the US Army Corps of Engineers provide evidence of the existence of at least four levels of subterranean facilities beneath Camp Hero, maybe there is something to the conspiracy buff's claims of a massive underground centre conducting research at the borders of established science.

THE USUAL SUSPECTS

National Security Council

It is often alleged that Montauk is actually run by an inner cabal of the National Security Council of the US. All of the members of the cabal are also thought to be members of the Grand Orient Lodge of Egyptian Free-masonry who are using the advances made through research carried out at Montauk to further their ultimate aim of global domination.

Aleister Crowley

Possibly the most important occultist of the century, self-styled "wickedest man in the world" Crowley is known to have visited the Montauk area of Long Island shortly after the end of World War I in which he had been acting as an intelligence officer. Quite what his interest in Montauk was is open to speculation, but it is worth noting that his pupils included ground-breaking scientists such as Jack Parsons – the man behind NASA's Jet Propulsion Laboratories, and an associate of Janus Eric Von Neumann.

THE UNUSUAL SUSPECTS

Nazi Scientists

Nazi submarines were often spotted off Montauk during the war and many Nazi scientists went to work for the American military after the conflict finally ended. Montauk has had a large Aryan community since the Thirties and some conspiracy theorists believe that the experiments at Montauk were infiltrated and taken over by ex-Nazis, with a view to using the awesome powers that are being developed to further their own evil schemes.

Time Travellers

Given that many of the experiments at Montauk seem to involve time travel, some feel it is fair to assume that the real force behind the conspiracy are time travellers from the future.

above English occultist Aleister Crowley – self-styled 'most evil man in the world' – made mysterious visits to Montauk Point.

Stranded, in what is to them the past, they have taken over the experiments started by Einstein and Von Neumann in the hope that they can build a machine to take them back to their home time.

MOST CONVINCING EVIDENCE

For what is officially claimed to be merely a derelict military facility, within a designated state park, there seems to be a lot of security around Camp Hero. Picnicking women and children have been accosted and threatened at gunpoint by unidentified military personnel for venturing into its vicinity. Other people wandering through the park near to the supposedly abandoned Air Force Station have been told they have violated top-secret and restricted areas, and could be arrested. Non-uniformed armed guards from seemingly shadowy government and military agencies have a track record of performing some very unconstitutional activities in the area. If there is no conspiracy at Montauk why is this happening?

MOST MYSTERIOUS FACT
The land that the Montauk Air Force Base is built on – and possibly under – should, under the terms of American law, belong to the Montauk tribe of Native Americans who were the original inhabitants of the area. Despite huge amounts of evidence to the contrary, the US Federal Court has declared the Montauk tribe extinct in order to prevent the remainder of the tribe claiming the land. It should be noted that the Montauk Indians record numerous strange legends concerning the area, and can remember when the site of Camp Hero was actually home to an ancient and rather odd stone pyramid.

SCEPTICALLY SPEAKING
While there's plenty of fascinating conjecture, there's little independent, hard evidence to back up some of the wilder aspects of the Montauk conspiracy. It seems understandable that the US government – or dark forces within it – might test ultra-advanced technology at a secret base, but when there are places such as Area 51, there is no logical need to operate out of a base that's only 100 miles from New York City.

THE MYSTERY OF OAK ISLAND

Tiny Oak Island, located in Nova Scotia, Canada, has been called many things over the last two hundred years: the Money Pit; a cleverly protected trove of pirate treasure; and a deathtrap. In 1795, 16-year-old Daniel McGinnis was exploring the island when he discovered a depression beneath an ancient oak tree. Thinking that it looked as if someone had just dug a hole and refilled it, McGinnis enlisted the aid of two friends, and they began to dig, sure they were about to discover glittering piles of pirate treasure.

Four feet into the earth, they came across a layer of flagstones. At a depth of ten feet, they encountered a platform constructed of oak logs, embedded in the shaft walls. Another ten feet down, the boys encountered another oak platform, discovering yet another at a depth of thirty feet underground. Since the logs were impossible to remove, the boys abandoned the project.

With capital provided by Simeon Lynds, an affluent businessman who had enticed investors to finance a proper excavation of the pit, the boys returned in 1803. Digging deeper, they encountered more oak platforms, but also found something that was far more interesting: a large, flat stone with cryptic lettering etched across it. A later translation of this mysterious cipher yielded this message: "Forty feet below two million pounds are buried".

Moving past the stone, the excited workmen then ran into the problem that has plagued Oak Island excavations ever since: water. While the shaft had been dry up to this point, water began slowly seeping through the soil. It became so bad that the workers were removing two buckets of water for every bucket of earth. At a depth of 98 feet, the crew hit what sounded like yet another oak platform, but since the day was coming to an end, they stopped work. Returning to their work the next morning, the treasure hunters were horrified to find that the pit had filled up with water.

Undeterred, they dug another shaft 14 feet to the side of the water-filled Money Pit. Digging down 110 feet, they attempted to create a side tunnel towards the original shaft and reach the hoped-for treasure that way. Two feet away from their goal, however, water once again poured through the walls of the side tunnel. Soon, the new shaft was as waterlogged as the first. Lynds' team gave up shortly thereafter.

In 1849, another crew attempted the Money Pit, armed this time with a horse-powered mining drill. They discovered more layers of wood, and for the first time, layers of loose metal. They also discovered what looked like bits of an old watch chain. Sure that the Pit contained chests of treasure, they pushed forth, but were once again foiled by water pouring into the shaft. Curious as to where the water was coming from, the crew excavated the nearby beach, making a startling discovery. They found a system of five carefully constructed drains that fed water into a sump and then down a 500-foot tunnel directly into the Money Pit. Digging below the 90-foot mark broke a hydraulic seal in the Pit, causing water to run into it at a rate of 600 gallons a minute. Since the water was coming directly from the ocean, it was absolutely impossible to drain. Disheartened, the crew gave up.

Over the years, several expeditions have tried to pierce Oak Island's mystery, including such celebrities as Franklin Roosevelt, Errol Flynn and John Wayne. More mysteries were unveiled, including cement vaults, bits of cryptic parchment, and hidden caverns dug to the north of the original pit.

Six people have died trying to unlock the mystery of Oak Island, but to this day, she jealously guards her secrets.

THE STRANGE PART

In 1971, when a camera was sent down Borehole-10X, a shaft sunk to the north of the original Pit, it encountered a hideous sight in a newly discovered underwater cavern. Floating in the dark, silt-laden water was a human hand, apparently cut off at the wrist.

THE USUAL SUSPECTS

Captain William Kidd

The infamous pirate, Captain Kidd, apparently littered the world with hidden piles of treasure. Several stories of Kidd's treasure seem to point towards Oak Island.

The Spanish

One theory states that a damaged Spanish galleon, loaded with treasure, may have stopped off at Oak Island to effect repairs and store its cargo of treasure, safe from pirate attack, so that it could be picked up later on the voyage back to Spain.

Francis Bacon

Since no original manuscripts have been found of Shakespeare's plays, many argue that the Bard's dramas were written by none other than Francis Bacon. Bacon may have buried the incriminating plays on Oak Island, to be discovered in the future.

Also suspected: the Vikings; the French and/or the British colonial troops.

THE UNUSUAL SUSPECTS

The Inca and Maya

To avoid plundering by Europeans in the seventeenth and eighteenth centuries, the Inca and Maya, aided by compassionate Europeans, may have moved some treasures north to Oak Island.

The Knights Templar

Fleeing persecution in Europe, the Knights may have spirited away the Holy Grail to Oak Island for safekeeping. There are two pieces of evidence in support of this. First, a formation of rocks on the island, when connected by lines drawn on a map, form a giant Christian cross 250 metres long. Secondly, Henry Sinclair, a suspected Knight, arrived in the area in 1398.

MOST CONVINCING EVIDENCE

The ingenious engineering of drains and hydraulic seals seems to indicate something valuable is indeed buried there.

MOST MYSTERIOUS FACT

In 1970, an investment group called the Triton Alliance commissioned a geological study of Oak Island. That report has, mysteriously, never been made public.

SCEPTICALLY SPEAKING

Just how did the original architects of Oak Island plan to retrieve their treasure? Obviously they didn't. And why advertise it with engraved stones? Doesn't that defeat the purpose of hiding it in the first place?

left Is the treasure of notorious pirate Captain William Kidd at the heart of the Oak Island conspiracy?

DENVER, COLORADO

Denver International Airport is usually only noteworthy for being the most important airport in the US State of Colorado, so it seems a very unlikely setting for a globe-spanning conspiracy. However, in recent years many conspiriologists have been researching its possible mysteries, in the belief that solving them may help expose the existence of the New World Order, the destruction of the Earth by comet impact, and the true nature of the MJ-12 organization. So far they have only provided concrete evidence that the airport also houses a massive and mysterious underground complex.

Certainly, the airport has a wealth of occult and conspiratorial symbolism within its design: its runways seem to form swastika patterns, and its numerous murals are truly mind-boggling – one shows the destruction of city and forest while a small girl holds a Mayan Tablet predicting the end of the world. The most bizarre is an image of the mystical Nazi symbol of the Black Sun, which is in the floor of the airport's Great Hall. Any conspiracy theorist with knowledge of Freemasonry can tell you that "The Great Hall" is an important Masonic term – which may help explain why the Hall also features a Masonic Capstone.

Some feel it is very significant that Air Force Space Command is stationed at the Schriever Air Force Base close to Denver International Airport. Among the publicly acknowledged duties of Air Force Space Command is the control of the Milstar satellite communications system, which links mobile ground forces, ships, submarines and aircraft together to create a unified fighting force of incredible power. It is also responsible for other satellites that orbit the earth at altitudes of more than 23,000 miles and communicate on super-high frequencies. It is possible that this satellite network will allow forces across the world to be controlled effectively in the event of either a nuclear war or a global catastrophe.

Air Force Space Command also runs the Defense Support Program satellites, which are a key part of North America's early warning system. However, instead of purely detecting missile launches, space launches and nuclear detonations, Space Command may also provide early warning of UFOs and comets approaching Earth. It is rumoured that Denver was chosen as the base for Space Command because computer models show that its position and high altitude make it the perfect area to create safe underground buildings capable of resisting any type of disaster.

THE STRANGE PART

There was a lot of opposition to the building of the Denver International Airport from people in the locality. Officials high up in the Clinton administration became heavily involved in the project and they seem to have used their influence to ensure that the airport was built. Furthermore, the CIA may have stuck its nose in – Rodney Stitch, the author of *Defrauding America*, has claimed to have access to a tape showing a CIA agent paying the mayor of Denver to get the airport built. Why was this top-level pressure applied to build the airport and its underground bunker system?

THE USUAL SUSPECTS

The New World Order

Even before the bizarre details of the construction of Denver International Airport began to surface, rumours in the conspiracy field suggested that when the New World Order was established America would be split into two administrative divisions – the Eastern Sector and the Western Sector. The control centre for the Eastern Sector was to be based in Atlanta and the Western Sector's control centre would be located in Denver. To conspiriologists, this just makes the wording "New World Airport Commission" on the Masonic capstone of the airport even more ominous.

The Freemasons

It is hard to doubt that Denver International Airport is heavy with Masonic imagery, which leads some conspiracy researchers to believe that the obvious answer to the mysteries must lie with the Freemasons. As the Masons in America have a long history of constructing buildings and even whole cities packed with secret Masonic messages, they may have designed the airport as a form of subliminal propaganda to demonstrate their ownership of the building and its associated underground complex.

THE UNUSUAL SUSPECTS

NASA

One of the more paranoid conspiracy theories about Denver is that NASA, working in conjunction with the National Security Agency and Air Force Space Command, has built the underground complex at the airport. It is part of ORPHEUS – NASA's project to build a network of underground bunkers so that a chosen few can survive the disastrous comet impact that NASA predicts will hit the Earth in a few years' time. The murals were incorporated as a subtle warning to the rest of us as to the nature of our gruesome fate – death from above or slavery when the forces of NASA, NSA and Space Command take control of the globe in the aftermath of the disaster.

Queen Elizabeth II

It is not too surprising to discover that Queen Elizabeth II owns land in Colorado – she is the richest woman in the world, after all. Her recent large purchases of real estate

responsible for their commission is rumoured to have been Wilma Webb, wife of the mayor of Denver, who conducted a Masonic dedication of the airport and was subsequently appointed by President Clinton to the Department of Labour.

in the Colorado, however, conducted under the guise of a variety of front companies, has raised quite a few eyebrows. Is she planning to relocate to Denver in the advent of some disaster that wipes Britain off of the map? If, as some conspiracy theorists believe, she is the real power behind groups like the New World Order, she may have ordered the construction of the underground base as the HQ for her secret forces. Her Colorado land-buying spree is designed to allow for the building of other powerbases in the state.

MOST CONVINCING EVIDENCE

The artists who created the weird airport murals allegedly admitted that they had been asked to design them to incorporate specific themes and images. The person

MOST MYSTERIOUS FACT

The site of Denver International Airport was originally an American Indian burial ground. The mayor of Denver had to meet with Indian elders and a shaman to appease the spirits of their ancestors. The "tent-like" terminal structure was also designed to appease possible anger from the Indian spirits.

SCEPTICALLY SPEAKING

Underground bunkers are not an uncommon part of emergency forward planning and there is no reason why one should not be built at an airport. No self-respecting secret society planning world domination would base itself under an airport in constant daily use by thousands of people and then advertise its existence via extensive use of cryptic symbols.

THE PENTAGON

The Pentagon is one of those buildings that everyone has heard of and everyone recognizes immediately. Home to the US Department of Defense – the body that controls the strongest armed force that this globe has ever seen – it is a striking piece of architecture perceived world-wide as a symbol of American might.

It is for this very reason that at 9:43am on September 11, 2001, terrorists crashed American Airlines Flight 77 into the Pentagon. By using a Boeing 757 to punch a hole in one of its famous five sides, they were symbolically making a massive tear into the very notion of American security and military superiority.

The building itself has lent its name to the US military machine, a name that is almost synonymous with conspiracy.

From rumours of military-constructed UFOs to germ warfare experiments performed unwittingly on American citizens, the Pentagon has become a byword for dark designs and grotesque, secret plots. Its place in the conspiracy field has even permeated through to the mainstream entertainment media. In Steven Spielberg's blockbuster movie *Raiders Of The Lost Ark* it became the repository for the Ark of the Covenant, while from the first episode of *The X-Files*, it has been the base from which Fox Mulder's nemesis in the global conspiracy – Cancer Man – operates.

Home to more than 29,000 military and civilian employees, the Pentagon is a city within the capital city of Washington DC. The official story is that the Pentagon building was the idea of Brigadier General Brehon B Sommervell, Chief of the Construction Division of the US Army. He came up with it in the summer of 1941, allegedly as a temporary solution to problems posed by the rapidly expanding War Department and a shortage of space. The Pentagon was also designed to bring the Department's 24,000 personnel, who were then scattered among 17 different buildings in Washington, under one roof.

The only reason admitted by the military for the building's unique five-sided construction was that the original site chosen for the Pentagon was a tract of land known as Arlington Farms. As five roadways bordered the site, this supposedly dictated the concept of a pentagonal building. However, the President himself – Franklin Delano Roosevelt – decided that the building be moved three-quarters of a mile downriver to a new location known as Hell's Bottom, where the final design of an open-air pentagram surrounded by five concentric pentagonal rings traversed by ten corridor spokes was implemented.

Some conspiriologists believe that the structure itself is more than the headquarters of the US national defence establishment and the nerve centre for the command and control of the world's strongest military force. Where others see only thousands of tons of steel and concrete that go to make up one of the world's largest office buildings, conspiracy buffs have spotted links between the building's odd shape and ancient secret societies and their plots to subjugate America and the rest of the globe

THE STRANGE PART

It is on record that President Franklin D Roosevelt did not like or approve of the design of the Pentagon, yet he was helpless to prevent it being built the way it was. If the President of the US cannot stop a building from being erected, what mighty force was controlling its design and construction?

THE USUAL SUSPECTS

The Freemasons

It has long been established that Washington DC was laid out to a Masonic groundplan. Its elaborate geometry was even modified by the well-known high-degree Freemasons and founding fathers of America – Thomas Jefferson and George Washington. Given that the five-pointed star is a very important Masonic symbol, several conspiriologists have suggested that the Pentagon also has Masonic origins. They claim it was designed as both a Masonic temple and a sign of Masonic control over the US and its military.

Satanists

The Devil and his human minions are no longer the main force behind conspiracies – as they were in the witch-burning days when America was founded. Even so, fundamentalist Christian conspiracy theorists still detect the Devil's hand at work in the design of the Pentagon. For evidence they point towards the fact that for centuries the five-sided star has been a symbol used in the worship of Satan. It comes as no surprise to find that some believe the Devil inspired his secret army of followers to create the Pentagon as his base of operations on Earth. They also feel that the original name of the marsh it was built on – Hell's Bottom – is significant.

left Was there more than simple terrorism behind the attack on the Pentagon on 9/11?

above The shape of the Pentagon contains the mystical Phi-ratio, which is highly important to Freemasons.

THE UNUSUAL SUSPECTS

Nazi Occultists

There is some circumstantial evidence to suggest that notable German Nazi scientists such as Werner Von Braun were working on secret projects in the US in 1938. It is also rumoured that they were in contact with an occult underground, which contained amazing characters like Jack Parsons – a follower of Aleister Crowley and the world's first solid-fuel-rocket scientist. Some conspiracy theories have it that secret occult orders infiltrated the US military and forced it to build the Pentagon. When operation Paperclip brought more than 400 Nazi scientists and thousands of assistants to the US after the end of World War II, the Nazi occult take-over of the US military was complete. Nazi scientists could rule supreme from their specially designed headquarters.

MJ-12

Every organization – even one as powerful and ultra-secret as MJ-12 – needs a base from which to operate. Some believe that MJ-12 pre-dates the Roswell crash and was operating under a different name via the US military before World War II. They also feel that the Pentagon was specially designed because the mathematical properties of the Phi-ratio make it the perfect shape for sending and receiving messages in hyperspace.

MOST CONVINCING EVIDENCE

Even at the time of its construction, there was a degree of speculation about the symbolism inherent in the Pentagon's five-sided shape. Many noted that it has not only five sides, but the five points needed to construct a five-sided star – a design that has huge significance in almost every occult and mystic tradition. The five-pointed star contains the Phi-ratio and the Pythagoreans – an ancient cult based around the study of mathematics – claimed that a pentagon held the secret of all life and reflected the "divine design" that orders and controls the universe. All of which makes you wonder why the normally conservative US military adopted such a radical, symbolic design, especially when it cost $83 million to build in a time of war.

MOST MYSTERIOUS FACT

It takes exactly seven minutes to walk between any two points in the Pentagon. In the mystical study of numbers and their relationship to the physical world, seven is the number of perfection and is symbolic of control over both spiritual and mortal realms.

SCEPTICALLY SPEAKING

Sometimes a building is just a building. The Pentagon is not the only controversially designed office block in the world. If it were not the home of the US military and countless conspiracies, it would probably not attract any significant speculation.

THE SPHINX

The Great Sphinx of Egypt first became an icon of the Western world when Napoleon's soldiers "rediscovered" it in 1798. Ever since that time it has exerted an intense fascination upon many of the people who have studied its enigmatic gaze. An air of mystery has always surrounded the statue that has the body of a male lion and the head of a human. Conspiracy theorists have not been the only ones to speculate on its true age, meaning and the hidden chambers it is supposed to be watching over.

Located on the Giza plateau, six miles to the west of Cairo, the Sphinx faces due East, a short distance from the trio of famous large pyramids. Carved from a relatively soft, natural limestone that outcrops on the Giza Plateau, the Sphinx was generally believed to have been made some time after 2540BC. Recently, noted geologist Robert Schock and Egyptologist John Anthony West have agreed that weathering patterns on the Sphinx are consistent with water erosion rather than erosion produced by wind and sand. The only time this water erosion could have occurred was around ten thousand years ago when Egypt's climate was temperate and damp. Not surprisingly, the idea that the Sphinx could be ten thousand years old has been attacked by orthodox Egyptologists who would look very stupid and have to rewrite every book on the subject if West and Schock are correct

Suppression of evidence by the archaeological establishment is not the only conspiracy in which the Sphinx features. Many of the mystical traditions which underpin secret societies such as the Freemasons, speak of chambers under the front paws of the Sphinx, that contain a Hall of Records placed there by survivors of an Elder civilization. In the Forties, famous American psychic Edgar Cayce predicted that by the end of the Nineties someone would discover this Hall of Records.

Conspiracy theorists naturally became excited when workers restoring the Sphinx located a doorway in its side; in 1995 a team renovating an area near the Sphinx uncovered a series of tunnels that seemed to go under the Sphinx. John Anthony West's team used seismograph technology that detected hollow, regularly-shaped chambers a few metres below ground between the paws and to either side of the Sphinx. It looked as if the conspiriologists' belief, that secret societies had held knowledge of an underground complex at Giza for centuries, was about to be proved correct.

THE STRANGE PART

A team from Florida State University undertook a survey around the Sphinx during April 1996 and found "rooms and tunnels" in front of it. Several other teams working on similar projects have made claims that back this up – including a team from Waseda University in Tokyo that found proof of a tunnel orientated north-south under the Sphinx. With all this material in support of an underground complex on the Giza Plateau, it is odd that the Egyptian authorities banned any excavation of the chambers or even further public remote sensing studies. Is there a conspiracy to suppress an outstanding truth that lies buried below the Sphinx?

THE USUAL SUSPECTS

Masonic Egyptologists

The Grand Orient Lodge of Egyptian Freemasonry teaches, at its highest degrees, that the wisdom and traditions of the lodge come from Atlantean survivors. Members believe the Atlanteans built the Sphinx in pre-history and later founded the Egyptian civilization. Clearly, the Grand Orient Lodge is a centuries-old organization with a powerful reach. Many believe it controls a network of Masonic Egyptologists who ruthlessly try to suppress the truth about the origins of the Sphinx and any secrets that it may hold.

National Security Agency

The American National Security Agency is known to have used the services of remote viewers – psychics with the ability to see what is at any given point in the world after being given a map reference – via the Stanford Research Institute (SRI). Given the prominent SRI role in investigating the

above New evidence suggests that the Sphinx was carved 10,000 years ago - thousands of years before any known civilisation arose.

Sphinx, some conspiracy theorists conclude that the NSA has taken an interest in the possible secrets, from a lost civilization, that lie below the rock of the Giza Plateau. Perhaps the NSA wants to be the first to exploit those secrets when the Hall of Records is secretly opened and its knowledge recovered.

THE UNUSUAL SUSPECTS
NASA
Many of those who have been involved in the official investigation of the Sphinx have strong links to NASA, such as former NASA consultants Dr James Hurtak and Richard Hoagland – a noted UFO conspiriologist. Hoagland believes that there may be a connection between Giza and Cydonia – the region of Mars where the mysterious "pyramids" and "face" are located. Is NASA using its former advisors to conduct an investigation into the mysteries of the Sphinx?

MOST CONVINCING EVIDENCE
Aside from the fact that Sphinx was created ten thousand years ago by a civilization we have no record of existing, and appears to be sitting on top of an underground complex, the way that the Director of Egyptian Council of Antiquities, Dr Hawass, banned John Anthony West from the Giza Plateau is more than a little suspicious.

MOST MYSTERIOUS FACT
In February 2000, evidence emerged to prove that researchers were at least correct about chambers existing under the Sphinx and Giza plateau. Zahi Hawass announced the discovery of a symbolic tomb of the ancient Egyptian god Osiris buried deep beneath one of the Giza pyramids. Hawass said access was previously impossible due to high water levels, but after dirt and water were cleared from the shaft located between the Sphinx and the Pyramid Chrefren, his archaeologists found three underground levels. The submerged Osiris sarcophagus was found at the lowest, about 30 metres (98.4 feet) below the surface. They did not use a sophisticated robot to make their breakthrough into the shaft, but instead a young boy.

SCEPTICALLY SPEAKING
Most of the evidence for underground chambers is based on the interpretation of seismographic data and could turn out to be nothing more than natural anomalies in the rock. It is understandable that the Egyptians do not want excavations to take place, with the risk of damage to the Sphinx, on the off-chance of discovering the remnants of a fabled lost civilization.

TIBET

Even to non-conspiracy buffs, the mention of Tibet can conjure up images of a land beyond the normal confines of time, where Buddhist mystics remain concealed from view in inaccessible mountain monasteries. The Himalayas – meaning "home of the snows" in ancient Sanskrit – have given us many legends, including that of the Yeti and the miraculous city of Shangri-La. Yet some conspiriologists believe that not all of the strange stories emanating from the mountainous realm of Tibet are mere fables.

Ever since the first Western explorers managed to make the perilous journey to Tibet, they have carried back with them persistent rumours of Shambhala – the "Hidden Kingdom" where a community of semi-divine beings lives in seclusion, guiding the destiny of mankind. In 1933, J Hilton wrote his best-selling book *The Lost Horizon*, in which Shambhala becomes Shangri-La; the English language was given another word to describe a paradise on Earth.

Despite pulp novels and bad movies, the belief in Shambhala has persisted and even grown, as conspiracy theorists unearthed evidence of the strange role it may have played in World War II. It has become well-known in recent years that the Ahnenerbe – the occult research section of the SS – conducted two extensive trips to Tibet on the orders of Himmler. It is believed that they were searching for allies and assistance from the alleged inhabitants of the Hidden Kingdom.

After the war, Tibet was crushed under the heel of an invasion by Communist China, but rumours regarding Shambhala have been harder to suppress than Tibetan liberty. They continue to inspire a belief that deep within the Himalayas lies an advanced mystical order whose members are behind a conspiracy to keep the location of the Hidden Kingdom secret while guiding the course of history from their remote mountain retreat.

above Berlin in 1945, reduced to rubble and overrun by Soviet soldiers who found the bodies of several mysterious Tibetan monks.

left The remote monasteries of Tibet, an odd destination for the SS.

THE STRANGE PART

Whether or not the Nazis found fabled Shambhala remains a matter of conjecture, but it is certain that they found strange allies while exploring Tibet. When the Soviet army advanced on Berlin during the final days of World War II, troops discovered a cellar containing the bodies of several Tibetan monks wearing green gloves who appeared to have committed suicide as part of some arcane ritual. Over the next few days, hundreds more Tibetan bodies were recovered – all wearing SS uniforms, without any identifying papers, and all wearing green gloves. The fact that this element of the war tends to be glossed over in history books only helps convince some conspiriologists that a massive cover-up of the role of Shambhala is taking place.

THE USUAL SUSPECTS

Order Of The Green Dragon

German academic, philosopher and occultist Karl Haushoffer – creator of the term geopolitics and an important influence on Hitler – travelled extensively in Tibet and Japan. It was while he was studying mysticism in Asia that he was initiated into the ultra-secret Order of the Green Dragon. This clandestine organization had links to Tibet and is rumoured to have received its orders direct from Shambhala. It may have been the force that helped forge links between the Nazis and the Hidden Kingdom.

The Yellow Hats

The Yellow Hats – called Dugphas in Tibet – are proponents of the most esoteric branch of Tibetan Buddhism that fully acknowledges the reality of Shambhala. Certain conspiriologists feel that the promotion of the secret lands of Tibet as the "source of happiness" is nothing other than propaganda to mask a sinister plan from the hidden masters of the Yellow Hats for world domination. While Tibet's remoteness and subjugation by the Chinese may not make it an obvious base from which to dominate the globe, in conspiracy circles these obstacles are merely seen as part of an elaborate cover story, created to prevent effective scrutiny and investigation.

THE UNUSUAL SUSPECTS

The Elder Race

The mysterious builders of monuments such as the Sphinx, the Elder Race may not have completely disappeared from Earth. According to a selection of conspiracy theorists, the Elder Race relocated to the safety of Tibet's mountains when the Earth underwent a serious of global cataclysms thousands of years ago. Currently the rulers of Shambhala, members of the Elder Race are now working secretly to prepare humanity for the next stage in its evolution. Quite how helping out the Nazis would have achieved this is open to speculation.

The Hollow Earthers

Alongside legends of Shambhala, there are mentions of the underground realm of Agharta – linked in the conspiracy genre with plots to hide the truth about the hollow Earth. The inhabitants of this strange subterranean realm, which is recorded in the inner teachings of Tibetan mysticism, have been identified by some as having links to the alien culture hinted at in the thinly veiled works of fiction written by HP Lovecraft. While little is known as to the aims of the conspiracy conducted by the dwellers of Agharta, few doubt it would be designed to benefit those living on the external surface of the Earth.

MOST CONVINCING EVIDENCE

The current Dalai Lama, like his predecessors, is convinced of the physical reality of Shambhala, but the strongest evidence of its existence may come from the interest shown in it by the Nazis during the War. In the midst of a raging global conflict it is more than a little strange that the SS found the necessary resources and time to transport transmitters to Tibet so that Berlin could be in radio contact with the area.

MOST MYSTERIOUS FACT

Occultist, sometime secret agent and conspiracy-buff favourite Aleister Crowley undertook a record-breaking ascent of the Himalayas early in the century in what some see as a search for Shambhala. His quest was later duplicated by famous mystic George I Gurdjieff and, most mysteriously, in 1942, by a covert US team sent by the Office of Strategic Services – the forerunner of the modern CIA.

SCEPTICALLY SPEAKING

You have to doubt the power of any alleged conspiracy operating from Shambhala after it failed to prevent Tibet being overrun by the Chinese. Furthermore, it has not made much headway in freeing Tibet from Communist domination. Besides, if Shambhala actually existed, modern satellite technology would have revealed it ages ago.

STONEHENGE

Standing alone and majestic as a reminder of long-lost civilizations, the ruins of Stonehenge present an enigma to which there will probably never be a definitive answer. There is no dispute that Stonehenge is a Neolithic architectural marvel, but its true purpose remains totally hidden. Stonehenge continues to stand in a modern world over-run with cell phones, satellites, and trans-Atlantic air travel, as a primitive testament to the ingenuity of early man.

Located about 80 miles from London, near Salisbury Plain, Stonehenge is thought to have been constructed in three phases about 3500BC. It was in the third phase, thought to be around 1800BC, that the giant stone monoliths we associate with Stonehenge were transported to the site. These sarsen (an extremely hard type of sandstone) blocks were molded and lifted into 30 upright stones with accompanying lintels, set in a circle. (Seventeen of the original 30 are still standing today.) Other stone designs were set in place inside the structure, including five triathlons (a pair of upright stones supporting a lintel stone). There is also a rectangular arrangement of "station stones" situated outside the ring.

Stonehenge is a focal religious point for Druids, who perform ceremonies there to this day, marking the summer solstice, as well as more private ceremonies. But they did not build the monument, since Stonehenge's creation pre-dates the founding of the Druidic religion.

Why Stonehenge was constructed remains a mystery, as does the identity of its original builders. Whatever prompted its construction, it's clear that Stonehenge was very important – it may still play a role in man's sophisticated world today. Perhaps the supposed "primitive" builders knew something we have forgotten, much to our peril.

THE STRANGE PART

The mechanisms by which the stones were moved have intrigued archaeologists and historians, considering the primitive level of technology at the time. The bluestones are thought to have come from the Prescelly Mountains in Wales – over 200 miles away. The sarsen stones originated from the relatively nearby Marlborough Downs – but at 25 tons per stone, the 20-mile distance is still formidable. Yet with all the work that went into Stonehenge's construction, archaeologists have found little detritus around the site. Most ancient construction sites are a potpourri of discarded materials. By contrast, Stonehenge is remarkably – perhaps suspiciously – clean.

THE USUAL SUSPECTS

The Beakers

A Neolithic people named after the type of pottery they produced, the Beakers have been thought to have begun the construction of Stonehenge. As the years passed, the monument's use may have varied from generation to generation. It has been suggested that it may have been used simply to hold animals, with a religious ceremony involved either in the slaughtering of livestock or in thanksgiving. Over time, Stonehenge's role as a religious centre may have intensified with the original holding pen design of the site merely kept on in its new role as a holy temple.

The Egyptians

Stonehenge could also have been designed with astronomy in mind – the positioning of the stones correlating to the positions of the Sun, Moon and stars throughout the year. Others believe that the axis of Stonehenge is built to correspond to the path of the sun, and that by using the

Aubrey holes it is possible to predict eclipses. Such a focus on astronomy points towards the advanced Egyptians, who may have travelled to England in the distant past.

Also suspected: the Ancient Greeks; the Phoenicians.

THE UNUSUAL SUSPECTS

Merlin

The Arthurian Magus may have erected Stonehenge, either for his own personal study of the heavens, or as a coronation site for the young king Arthur. He would have moved the stones into position using magic, presumably of the levitating sort.

Ancient Astronauts

Stonehenge may have been built by ancient, extra-terrestrial visitors as a visible landing site/landmark, or may have been built by primitive man to honour the beings from the stars.

Also suspected: the Atlanteans; giants; dwarves; energy vortexes that have been created by ley lines.

MOST CONVINCING EVIDENCE

Stonehenge shares at least two significant elements with other places of worship, including several European cathedrals. First, it has an underwater spring running beneath it, which is taken as a sign of divinity in many faiths. Secondly, in a more mathematical sense, the square root of three can be found as a recurring proportion in its construction. This too is found in many places of worship, from Europe to Egypt.

MOST MYSTERIOUS FACT

Stonehenge, next to Avebury and Glastonbury, is considered one of the most magical places in England, reportedly because it is built along powerful ley lines.

SCEPTICALLY SPEAKING

Just because something is old does not mean it is significant. Take a look at Cliff Richard.

above A silent testament across time – but who or what was behind the building of Stonehenge?

POLITICS

THE TRILATERAL COMMISSION

Formed in 1973 by private citizens from North America, Europe and Japan, the Trilateral Commission was born to create closer ties between the three geographical areas and to share leadership responsibilities on a more global basis. One of the principal founders of this was David Rockefeller, the wealthy American banker. Apparently inspired by Prof. Zbigniew Brzezinski's book *Between Two Ages*, in which Brzezinski proposes an alliance between North America, Western Europe and Japan, Rockefeller went about trying to establish such an organization in reality.

With a membership supposedly gleaned from the elite echelons of society, the Trilateral Commission is said to be composed of some 335 prominent figures in the media, politics, academia and business. Its membership is supposed to include such dignitaries as Paul Volcker, erstwhile head of the Federal Reserve System; Akio Morita, chief executive officer of Sony; Count Otto Lambsdorff, leader of Germany's Free Democratic Party; Henry Kissinger, and Bill Clinton. Top executives of such companies as AT&T, Pepsico and the Chase Manhattan Bank, among many others, are also members.

The Trilateral Commission meets once a year, in Spring, to discuss world problems and hopefully to come up with solutions. The Commission is nothing more than the political power behind the formation of the New World Order, according to conspiracy theorists who believe that the Commission has one aim: to wipe out all political sovereignty on Earth and place its people under the rule of one government and one bank. Others see the Trilateral Commission as a group that is merely trying to ensure that global financial interests (such as those of AT&T and the Rockefellers) are protected. While hiding behind a mask of benign kindness, the Trilateral Commission's real aim is not

above Do the links between the Trilateral Commission and the Federal Reserve Bank run deeper than the Rockerfeller family connection?

to protect the interests of the lower classes but to convince people, subtly, that they must bow to the needs of the banks and corporations …

THE STRANGE PART

Given that the Trilateral Commission's membership includes some of the most important and powerful names in the worlds of politics, business and the media, many conspiracy theorists find it had to believe that their role is purely consultative. The theorists feel that US presidents, world leaders and other members of the globe's power elite would not find time in their schedules to attend something that only serves as a talking shop – especially when the mysterious lack of media attention on the Commission means that they do not even get the chance for a photo opportunity.

USUAL SUSPECTS

The Freemasons

Theories abound that the Freemasons control the agenda of the Trilateral Commission, shaping its decisions and influences on global policy to ensure total Freemason domination of the Earth. By slowly moving the world into the straitjacket of the New World Order, the Freemasons could, by crushing all dissent under the tight rules and brutality of the NWO, finally achieve their ultimate goal.

The Illuminati

Another mysterious, shadowy group that is feared to be behind the scenes in all governments, the Illuminati is another candidate for running the Trilateral Commission. Like the Freemasons, the Illuminati's goal is total global domination.

Also suspected: the Bilderburger Group, another alleged "discussion group" based in Geneva, Switzerland, and apparently partly financed by the Rockefellers.

UNUSUAL SUSPECTS

Aliens

According to this view, an un-named alien power is trying to take over the planet. It is working in conjunction with the Trilateral Commission, the Bilderburger Group, and the Council of Foreign Relations. Clearly, conquest will be much simpler for the aliens once all governments, and all armies, have first been absorbed into the single New World Order. Those who work with the aliens will be spared the horrors that are due to befall the rest of us.

Knights Templar

The high number of bankers and financiers involved in the Trilateral Commission have convinced some that the group was put together at the behest of the Knights Templar, the world's first truly international bankers, who still secretly organize all the secret muscle in the world of global business. The Commission serves to help the Templars keep the world's political climate at the right level for their control to remain solid with profits booming.

MOST CONVINCING EVIDENCE

There is a curious lack of media attention surrounding meetings of the Trilateral Commission, which seems extremely odd considering the profiles of many attendees. In a world where the President of the United States is bombarded with flashbulbs and microphones when he does something as innocent as walking his dog, it's interesting to note that when he attends a meeting of the Trilateral Commission, it barely merits a mention on the evening news. Despite the Commission's insistence that it is merely a "discussion group" and that all of its discussion papers are available to the public, this shadow over its activities is disquieting. Considering how President Clinton could not control the media circus over the Lewinsky affair, where does the Trilateral Commission get its power to muzzle the media when it sees fit?

MOST MYSTERIOUS FACT

The Commission renews itself every three years. In 2003 it updated its 30-year-old agenda concerning international interdependence to one of globalization. Timely, given the increase in forces opposing this growing trend. Quite what Shirley Temple and Barbara Walters – both members of the Trilateral Commission – have to say about this subject remains a topic of debate among conspiracy buffs.

SCEPTICALLY SPEAKING

If there were going to be a New World Order, would the Trilateral Commission even have to exist as a public entity?

While it can be argued that the best place to hide is in broad daylight, which could be the Commission's credo, why create such an organization that would inevitably lead to suspicion and fears of conspiracy? In an age of encrypted communications and underground government bunkers, there is no need for the power brokers of the world to meet in full view of a suspicious public to discuss their future enslavement. There is every evidence to suggest that the Trilateral Commission is nothing more than an excuse for rich people to get together, swap stories, drink expensive wine, and maybe sneak in a few rounds of golf. Perhaps world domination isn't their goal: maybe just getting away from the office is.

MALCOLM X

If you were a controversial political figure in America during the Sixties, it was highly probable that your life would end in a hail of bullets. Malcolm X, the fiery leader of the Organization of Afro-American Unity, who outraged white America with his pronouncements on racial matters, was yet another man cut down in his prime because of the dangerous power of his beliefs.

Malcolm X was born Malcolm Little in 1925. His father, a Baptist minister, was murdered by white racists six years later and the family was broken up and put into care. Although he was a bright student, Little's dreams of becoming a lawyer were crushed when a teacher explained to him that he was only a "nigger", and should consider becoming a carpenter instead. Disillusioned with education, he drifted into a life of petty crime. While serving time for burglary, Little began to read about the Nation of Islam. The NOI's beliefs of black self-reliance and the need for racial separation intrigued Little, and when he was released, in 1952, he joined the Nation of Islam, dropping his surname because it was a vestige of slave ownership, and replacing it with a simple "X".

Malcolm X rose quickly through the ranks of the Nation, becoming the organization's chief spokesman. But after his inflammatory comments about the Kennedy assassination, its leader, Elijah Muhammed, suspended him from the NOI. Malcolm X took this opportunity to create his Organization of Afro-American Unity, and did not return to the Nation when his suspension was over.

Where Martin Luther King believed in non-violence and the integration of the black man into white America, Malcolm X angered white society by stating that blacks were superior to whites in all ways. He travelled the world, speaking in the Middle East, and generating support for a United Nations resolution condemning both South Africa and the United States for human rights violations in their treatment of blacks. Such views, as well as animosity from the Nation of Islam, made Malcolm X a man who was widely hated. This hatred came to a head on February 21, 1965, at the Audubon Ballroom in New York.

At the beginning of the meeting, a fight broke out in front of the stage where Malcolm X was speaking. As he tried to calm things down, a group of five assassins stood in the audience and shot him. Malcolm X died shortly afterwards, another figure cut down in America's cull of leaders who threatened the Establishment in the not-so-groovy Sixties.

THE STRANGE PART

Even though there was a hospital across the street from the Audubon Ballroom, it still took close to half an hour for an emergency crew to arrive, following X's shooting.

THE USUAL SUSPECTS

The FBI

J Edgar Hoover, the cross-dressing head of the FBI, distrusted Malcolm X because he represented a force of black power that had no place in Hoover's view of America. One counter-intelligence programme sponsored by the FBI was designed to keep a "black messiah" like X from uniting the black movement. With Malcolm X growing closer to Martin Luther King, the FBI could have decided that killing X was the only way to prevent a united black front from arising.

The US Government

The prospect of a UN resolution condemning the US along with South Africa for human rights violations seemed a clear possibility. This would have been seriously embarrassing for the US. By taking out the chief proponent for this resolution, Malcolm X, the States could then spin-doctor the whole messy business away.

THE UNUSUAL SUSPECTS

The Mob

In an effort to clean up black neighbourhoods and institute a lifestyle of clean living, Malcolm X verbally attacked the drug trade. This threat to the profits that could be made from the despair of the ghetto may have sealed X's fate.

The Nation Of Islam

The schisms between the Nation of Islam and Malcolm

X's own group ran deep, with some people feeling that X was unfairly criticizing Elijah Muhammed and other Nation leaders, such as Louis Farrakhan, if not outrightly blaspheming. This could have resulted in a murder that had both political and religious overtones to its motive as some in the Nation of Islam openly fanned this hatred of X.

MOST CONVINCING EVIDENCE

Leon Ameer, a member of the Organization of Afro-American Unity, stated on March 13, 1965, that he had proof of a government connection in Malcolm X's death. Unfortunately, Ameer's body was found the following morning before he could back up this claim. His death was attributed to an epileptic fit, even though past medical examinations had found no hint of epilepsy.

MOST MYSTERIOUS FACT

Of the three men who were convicted of Malcolm X's murder, one was unable to walk and was at home on the day of the assassination.

SCEPTICALLY SPEAKING

In the US, if you're black and speak out about human rights, you're a radical asking to be shot. If you're white, you're a humanitarian and get asked to Rotary dinners. No conspiracy is needed to explain this awful truth.

left Malcolm X's powerful speeches attracted many to the cause of black power.

NIXON, WATERGATE AND E HOWARD HUNT

Watergate is the most famous political conspiracy of the modern age. The exposure of attempts to cover up a failed conspiracy led to Richard Milhous Nixon becoming the first US President to resign from office. It gave new meaning to the term "Deep Throat" – now an anonymous source of classified information as well as a sexual act – and no current political scandal is complete unless it is given the "-gate" tag.

In 1995, when renowned conspiriologist and film maker Oliver Stone produced *Nixon* – starring Anthony Hopkins as the unfortunate President – he was not the first theorist to speculate that Watergate was only the visible surface of a much larger and more sinister plot. Like Stone's other conspiracy-fuelled opus, *JFK*, the film was condemned by those it

portrayed and by the establishment – a sign taken by Stone's fellow conspiriologists to suggest that it may have contained a great deal of truth.

The facts regarding the outer layer of Watergate are well established and form the basis of the official version of the scandal that is even taught in schools – one of the few conspiracies that the education system acknowledges. In the early hours of June 17, 1972, James McCord – a man with links to the CIA – led a group of four anti-Castro Cuban exiles in an attempt to burgle the Democratic National Committee Headquarters. The burglars were discovered and arrested as they attempted to tap the telephone system in the Watergate office and hotel complex in Washington DC.

Charges were also eventually laid against two more

above The Watergate scandal cost Nixon his presidency, but was there much more to it than the public knew?

people: G Gordon Liddy, finance counsel to the President and the power behind Nixon's Committee to Re-elect the President (CREEP); and E Howard Hunt, a former White House aide and ex-CIA operative. Over the next few months, what initially appeared to be a third-rate burglary quickly escalated into a full-blown political scandal. Nixon's involvement in the conspiracy to cover up a conspiracy led to America's gravest constitutional crisis and climaxed with his resignation as President on August 9, 1974.

However, in the national aftermath of distrust following Watergate, conspiracy theorists began to examine the details of the case. They discovered an assortment of facts that suggested the real reason behind the downfall of Nixon was a conspiracy to hide the truth about the assassination of President John F Kennedy.

THE STRANGE PART

On the Watergate tapes that provided the damning evidence of his involvement in the cover up of the original burglary,

President Nixon says: "Look, the problem is that this [Watergate] will open up the whole Bay of Pigs thing again." John Ehrlichman, Assistant to the President for Domestic Affairs, who served 18 months in prison for his part in the conspiracy, has admitted that "Bay of Pigs" was Nixon's code phrase for the John F Kennedy assassination.

Dorothy Hunt, the wife of one of the key players in Watergate, E Howard Hunt, may have been blackmailing the White House and have demanded more than a million dollars to keep silent about information that would "blow the White House out of the water". Many conspiriologists believe that there is photographic evidence to suggest that Hunt, a long-time CIA agent, was one of the famous "Three Tramps" photographed on the grassy knoll immediately after the shooting of JFK.

THE USUAL SUSPECTS
James Jesus Angleton

Director of CIA counter-intelligence from 1954 to 1974, James Jesus Angleton is suspected by many of being the mastermind behind JFK's assassination. His uncharacteristic refusal to help Nixon cover up the White House involvement in the burglary definitely helped seal Nixon's fate. Was Angleton willing to sacrifice a president to hide his involvement in the "whole Bay of Pigs thing"?

The Mafia

It is well established that the Mafia and their Cuban allies had strong links to the CIA and probably played a part in the death of John F Kennedy, so it is probably more than coincidence that four anti-Castro Cuban exiles were among the Watergate burglars. If the role of high-placed mobsters in the JFK conspiracy were in danger of being exposed by Watergate, they would have a solid motive for wanting Nixon to take all of the blame.

THE UNUSUAL SUSPECTS

Federal Reserve Bank

Lee Harvey Oswald's widow has pointed the finger at the US Federal Reserve Bank's mysterious role in the JFK affair. A private corporation that controls the creation of all American money, the Federal Reserve Bank (FRB) is owned in part by the Rockefellers. Given that the hugely influential Trilateral Commission was set up by David Rockerfeller in 1973, some have conjectured that the FRB had the financial and political muscle to stage Watergate to depose Nixon – a possible obstacle in its plans for world domination.

Howard Hughes

In 1972, eccentric millionaire Howard Hughes asked the White House to send the team that eventually bungled the Watergate burglary to break into the office of a Las Vegas newspaper editor, Hank Greenspun. Their task would have been to steal certain papers that formed allegedly devastating blackmail material. Given that some have linked Hughes and his fellow oil barons with Nixon and a plot to kill JFK, his role in Watergate is suspicious to say the least.

MOST CONVINCING EVIDENCE

In December 1973, a United Airlines flight crashed near Chicago Midway Airport. On board was E Howard Hunt's wife Dorothy. One of Hunt's fellow Watergate conspirators, Charles Coulson, made a statement to *Time* magazine claiming that "the CIA killed Dorothy Hunt". Unfortunately his claim may not have been pure paranoia – the pilot of the flight was found to have a quantity of cyanide in his blood that could only have been there if he had been poisoned. Another odd element to the crash is that Dorothy Hunt was carrying more than $250,000 in "hush money" when she boarded the plane, but only $10,000 was recovered with her body.

MOST MYSTERIOUS FACT

A mysterious letter written by Lee Harvey Oswald on November 10, 1963, has been the source of much heated debate. In this note Oswald asks a "Mr Hunt" for a job within his organization. More than one researcher has come to the conclusion that the letter supplies additional evidence for Hunt's role in the JFK affair.

SCEPTICALLY SPEAKING

Watergate traumatized the American psyche and its scars run deep. The events, which started with that "third-rate burglary", have been described as the root cause in America of the current distrust of government as well as the tendency to believe in conspiracies. Hardly surprising, then, that Watergate set off further speculation into the JFK assassination.

PEARL HARBOR

There are crossroads in time – nexus points – when the actions that take place have the potential to shape the course of history on a grand scale. The events that took place before dawn on Sunday December 7, 1941, at Pearl Harbor form such a nexus point. They influenced not only the course of World War II, but also the way world history unfolded.

The infamous "sneak attack" by Japanese forces on Hawaii resulted in 2,403 American deaths and 1,178 wounded servicemen; 18 ships, including three battleships, were sunk and 188 aeroplanes were destroyed with a further 162 suffering severe damage. By contrast, the Japanese lost only 29 planes, five midget submarines and 64 men. The direct result of this allegedly surprise attack was a US declaration of war on Japan, which immediately led to Hitler supporting his Asian allies – an act that finally brought America into the war against the Nazis.

However, some of America's most respected historians have joined forces with the conspiriologists they usually refer to as "delusional paranoids". Both groups suggest that the

real reason why Pearl Harbor should be remembered is because it was the tragic outcome of a massive conspiracy to ensure that the US joined Britain as a full combatant in World War II.

By 1941, the US President, Franklin D Roosevelt, was faced with a massive and seemingly insurmountable political problem. He wanted America to become involved in the war with Germany but US public opinion was unsympathetic – Americans felt it was a European affair, and that Britain, Russia and Germany should be left alone to sort it out without any American lives being put at risk. Conspiracy theorists, and some historians, feel that Roosevelt knew Pearl Harbor was going to be attacked, but allowed it to happen as it would give him the perfect excuse for declaring war on Japan – an action that his intelligence services had told him would provoke an identical response from Germany on the US.

THE STRANGE PART

In 1941, Roosevelt had been warned by his admirals that cutting off the supply of petrol to Japan was likely to involve the US in a Pacific war. In July Roosevelt cut off those petroleum supplies and began to withhold intelligence information about Japanese activities from Army and Navy officials based in Hawaii. The governments of Britain, Holland, Australia, Peru, Korea and the Soviet Union all warned the US that a surprise attack on Pearl Harbor was coming, so it is even more odd that this information was not passed on to the military in Pearl Harbor.

THE USUAL SUSPECTS
Franklin D Roosevelt

The most obvious suspect in the conspiracy is the President himself. It is no secret that he wanted to bring America into the war with Europe, but was being held back by domestic political concerns. His position meant that he had the power to manoeuvre events in such a way that the US would not have to fire the first shot and be seen as the aggressor.

Anglo-American Cabal

There is a widespread belief, at least in certain sections of the conspiracy field, that there is a powerful Anglo-American cabal in operation determined to keep the "special relationship" in existence. Believed to involve members of the American and British intelligence services, as well as major figures from business and finance and top politicians, the cabal may also have counted Roosevelt as a member. He could have been instructed to cover up the impending attack on Pearl Harbor so that the US could be brought into the war to defend Britain.

THE UNUSUAL SUSPECTS
The American Banking Community

At the time of Pearl Harbor, Britain was in debt to America under the terms of the lend-lease agreement. If Britain were defeated by Germany there would be no chance of her ever repaying the vast loans she had taken out. Therefore, members of the American banking community had a vested interest in British victory and may have pulled strings behind the scenes to ensure America lent more than financial support to their client.

International League of Communists

American conspiracy theorists with a very heavy right-wing bias have believed for some while that Roosevelt was secretly a communist. Their conjecture also makes him a vital member of an alleged International League of Communists, which conspired to take the US into a war with Germany. America's entry to the war would not be to save democracy in Britain and Europe, but to ensure that the world's first communist state, the Soviet Union, was not crushed by the might of the Nazi war machine.

left A day that lives in infamy even in the twenty-first century. The sneak attack by the Japanese is a nexus point that changed the course of world history.

MOST CONVINCING EVIDENCE

In 1932, a joint Army-Navy exercise saw Pearl Harbor being successfully "attacked" by 152 planes half an hour before dawn on a Sunday – catching the defenders completely by surprise. This was duplicated in 1938, so there can be no doubt that the military knew the potential risk to Pearl Harbor. Furthermore, the US had cracked the top Japanese Naval and diplomatic codes – a fact not lost on a top-secret Army Board. In 1944 the Board reported: "Numerous pieces of information came to our State, War and Navy Departments in all of their top ranks indicating precisely the intentions of the Japanese including the probable exact hour and date of the attack."

MOST MYSTERIOUS FACT

The US Navy in Pearl Harbor was laughably under-prepared for the attack. Ships were tied up side-by-side and, despite radar operators in Hawaii reporting that Japanese planes were coming, no one took any action. Three American battleships were sunk in the attack, but by 1941 battleships were obsolete and the aircraft carrier was the pinnacle of naval power. It may be significant that no American aircraft carriers were based at Pearl Harbor during the attack – the majority of them were three thousand miles away, safely stationed at San Diego, which is where a lot of American Navy people had wanted the Pearl Harbor ships to be located.

SCEPTICALLY SPEAKING

It is hard to be sceptical over many aspects of the Pearl Harbor conspiracy, but it is also hazardous ever to underestimate the levels of incompetence that can be achieved by the US military and its commander-in-chief – the President.

RUDOLF HESS

There are many strange stories surrounding World War II, but few are stranger than that of Rudolf Hess. In many places, the story of Hess reads more like a lost Monty Python sketch than the historical details of the activities of a high-ranking member of Hitler's Nazi Party.

Born in Alexandria, Egypt on April 26, 1894, Hess fell under the spell Adolf Hitler was weaving over Germany when he first saw him speak in Munich. Hess joined the Nazi Party in 1920, becoming close to Hitler, whom he idolized. This idolatry led Hess to join Hitler in the Beer Hall Putsch of 1923 when Hitler attempted to take over the reins of power of Germany. Instead, they ended up in Landsberg prison.

Hess acted as Hitler's secretary in prison, taking slavish dictation as Hitler composed *Mein Kampf*. Released from prison in 1925, Hess followed Hitler as he built his Nazi powerbase, continuing to act as his secretary. As Hitler finally attained the power he so desperately craved, in 1932, he appointed Hess Chairman of the Central Political Commission of the Nazi Party. Hess was also made a general in the SS for good measure. As Hess continued to follow Hitler with the blind devotion of a puppy, he was rewarded with the position of Deputy Führer in 1933.

Hess was determined to do what he perceived best for his beloved Führer: he would negotiate peace with England, by himself, without telling anyone. Borrowing a Messerschmitt ME-110, Hess flew across the North Sea on May 10, 1941. He was headed for Scotland, to meet with the Duke of Hamilton, a casual acquaintance he had met at the Berlin Olympics in 1936. Hess parachuted into Scotland, met a bewildered farmer, and told him he had an important message for the Duke.

His peace plan was considered ludicrous by Churchill: that if England let Germany have Europe, then England would be left alone. Disowned by the Nazi Party, and considered half-mad by the British authorities, a disheartened Hess was thrown into prison. He was transferred to Germany for the Nuremberg Trials in 1945, where his mental instability was readily apparent. He was sentenced to life in Spandau prison, and reportedly committed suicide by hanging himself in 1987 at the age of 92. Or did he?

Theories have sprung up that the man who died in 1987 was not Hess, but a body-double. Questions have also arisen as to why a man so obviously incompetent was considered such a threat to British authorities.

THE STRANGE PART

Dr Hugh Thomas, who cared for Hess in Spandau, stated repeatedly that his patient was not Hess, citing the absence of the scars that Hess should have had.

below Rudolf Hess was Hitler's right-hand man, so just why did Hess fly to Britain in 1941?

THE USUAL SUSPECTS

House of Windsor

New research undertaken by Lynn Picknett, Clive Prince and others showed that there was substantial evidence that the King's brother, the Duke of Kent, was actively involved in Hess's peace mission. They also proved that in 1941, the British peace party included most of the Royal Family. This has given a shot in the arm for conspiracy theorists who think that the House of Windsor was deeply implicated in the Hess affair and that Winston Churchill arranged the death of the Duke of Kent in 1942.

THE UNUSUAL SUSPECTS

Vril Society

This theory states Hess was kept imprisoned by the Germans because he held vital information about secret Nazi Antarctic bases operated by the occult Vril Society, which included many top Nazis among its members. Although this sounds bizarre, it should be remembered that James Bond creator and member of MI6 Ian Fleming

recommended that master occultist Aleister Crowley should lead the interrogation of Hess.

MOST CONVINCING EVIDENCE

Karel Hille, a Dutch journalist, claimed to have files that had been stolen from M16 by none other than Sir Maurice Oldfield himself, ex-head of M16. The files proved that the man who died in Spandau was not Hess, but a body-double.

MOST MYSTERIOUS FACT

While imprisoned in Britain, Rudolph Hess kept complaining that he felt his food was being poisoned. This was just chalked up to Hess's instability, but if he were being drugged, his food would be the least conspicuous form of administering poison.

SCEPTICALLY SPEAKING

The world actually managed to jail a high-ranking member of Hitler's Nazi Party? No wonder no one believes it – all the other Nazis went to work for the CIA.

SADDAM HUSSEIN

On the face of it, the first Gulf War in 1991 was a straightforward conflict. Traditional analysis stems from the view that Saddam Hussein was a classic megalomaniac dictator, who tested the will of the world to halt his expansionist policies by invading Kuwait in August 1990. In response, a global coalition, led by the US and UK, united against him. George Bush Snr referred to this coalition as a "New World Order". During the Gulf War the US organized enough military and political power to successfully defeat Hussein and free Kuwait. Yet all

is not what it seems when the conspiracy researchers turn their questioning gaze to the Gulf War, up until the second Gulf War in 2003, the largest military campaign undertaken since World War II. A number of significant puzzles develop when certain questions are asked. For instance, why did Allied forces stop when they could have easily driven into Baghdad? If Saddam was another Hitler, why wait over a decade to bring about the "regime change" that Bush Jnr was determined to bring about? Accusations and rumours that began when the conspiracy world started to question the established view have now been brought out into the open as accepted, mainstream facts. Even before the tanks hit the Baghdad highway for a second time in 2003, more than one revisionist heavyweight commentator on international politics had begun to wonder if the first Gulf War was set up and carried out for objectives other than freeing Kuwait.

THE STRANGE PART

It has become generally accepted that the US State Department gave a "green light" to Saddam to invade Kuwait. This happened when an Iraqi Ambassador raised the subject of how the US would react to a potential Iraqi invasion with American Ambassador April Glaspie, in August 1990 just before Iraqi tanks rolled across the sand.

While debate rages as to the exact details of what occurred at that meeting, whether by intent or accident, it seems certain that Saddam thought that the US would not object if he went ahead with his invasion plans. Given that a number of US Senators had recently visited Baghdad and declared support for Hussein – including at least one staunch Jewish liberal and champion of Israel – it is a conclusion he could be forgiven for making.

THE USUAL SUSPECTS

New World Order

The "new world order" was an expression first used in the Twenties by Colonel Edward House who believed in world government. President George Bush brought the phrase into the public spotlight when he described the coalition gathered against Saddam as a sign of an emerging New World Order. Most conspiriologists view the NWO as a form of One World government that secret forces are working to introduce. For a New World Order to hold power over nation states it would need to be able justify its existence. The type of international operation of joint political and military force seen in the Gulf may be the first example designed to convince the population of the globe that the NWO is an idea whose time has come.

Military Industrial Complex

With the fragmentation of the Soviet Union, in 1989, and the spectre of a communist menace a thing of the past, people were beginning to question whether the US and its Western allies actually needed to keep spending billions on defence. Conspiracy theorists believe that the invasion by Saddam Hussein, in 1990, is just too much of a coincidence. They believe that he was put up to the attack on Kuwait by the Military Industrial Complex, so that he could be presented as the new enemy that needed opposing – hence justifying continued massive spending on armaments.

THE UNUSUAL SUSPECTS

KGB

It is well known that the Soviets and the KGB had developed a very close relationship with Hussein over the years. Some conspiracy theorists believe that the demise of the Soviet Union is merely a diversionary tactic to allow the KGB to develop plans for communist world domination – it was the KGB that arranged the Gulf War. By setting up Saddam as the main bogeyman, the KGB's strategists ensured that American attention would be focused on Iraq, leaving them free to pursue their machinations unmolested by the US.

Oil Companies

If nothing else, the first Gulf War managed to push the price of crude oil up to the type of figure that the oil companies had not enjoyed since the days of the 1973 oil crisis. George Bush Snr made his fortune as oil baron and, with petrochemical industry–intelligence community connections, some have speculated that financial gain may have been the true motive behind the staging of the first Gulf War. With boy George following in his father's shoes and with his own oil-based fortune, it is not surprising that this is still a popular theory to explain the second Gulf War too.

MOST CONVINCING EVIDENCE

It is odd that UN-backed coalition of powerful nations could not remove the dictator of one Middle Eastern state, even after smashing his army within a matter of days, especially given that America and Britain were able to topple him later without that powerful backing. It is also strange that in the years subsequent to the first Gulf War, no assassination attempt was made. Nor was any meaningful military action taken against him or his alleged stocks of chemical and biological weapons until another member of the Bush clan was in the White House. Even at the end of the war, with Baghdad under US control, Saddam was still not in the custody of the UN for war crimes against the Kurds.

MOST MYSTERIOUS FACT

In the aftermath of the Gulf War, an intriguing book entitled *American Hero* was written by Larry Beinhart and published by Ballantine Books. Purporting to be fiction, it details how the war was the idea of a Republican dirty tricks expert designed to boost the popularity of George Bush. For a novel, its unearthed facts and extensive footnotes provide a damning level of evidence for the conspiracy view of the Gulf War. One question it raises is why did the American, British and Soviet Ambassadors all leave Kuwait two days before the invasion?

SCEPTICALLY SPEAKING

As the second Gulf War showed, America has never shown much inclination to come up with good excuses not to throw its weight around, so allowing the invasion of Kuwait seems a little unnecessary. Maybe the reason why Saddam was left in power at the end of the first Gulf War was because George Bush Snr wanted to leave his son something to get his teeth into when he became President?

left Finally toppled – but why did the US leave Saddam in power after the first Gulf War?

HILLARY CLINTON

When Hillary Rodham Clinton announced on a major televised interview that she and her husband Bill Clinton, were "victims of a vast right-wing conspiracy," she became the most famous supporter of a conspiracy theory in the world. But if she thought her shattering accusation, which stunned the American media, might gain her some sympathy and support from the hordes of conspiriologists who took an interest in her career, she was very mistaken.

Hillary's favoured conspiracy theory saw her and her husband being attacked by a dark network of right-wingers. The conspiracy took in everyone from the editors of British tabloids to television evangelist Jerry Falwell. In her mind, the media interest in the Monica Lewinsky and Paula Jones sexual harassment charges against Bill Clinton and long-running investigation by independent counsel Kenneth Starr into the Whitewater scandal were "politically motivated".

G Gordon Liddy, one of the key players in the Watergate conspiracy, used his regular radio show to disclose that he used pictures of the First Lady for target practice and called her a "broomstick-riding witch". Most conspiracy theorists, however, disagreed that this was proof of evil forces working against her. They were much more interested in digging out details surrounding a large number of people who had known or worked with Hillary and had subsequently died in suspicious circumstances.

Compiling what became known in conspiracy circles as the "Clinton Body Count", researchers were startled to find that being a friend of Bill or Hillary Clinton seemed to be one of the most dangerous occupations on the planet. This was definitely the case if you had been involved in the Whitewater investment scandal or possessed evidence about the state of their marriage or love lives.

When President Clinton and his wife were finally cleared of acting illegally in the Arkansas land deal that became known as Whitewater, it was in a large part down to the fact that many of the key witnesses were dead. The Whitewater land deal was a failed Arkansas property venture in which the Clintons were involved when he was Governor of the state in the Eighties and Mrs Clinton was a partner in a local law firm. After the highly convenient deaths, the evidence that remained, "was insufficient to prove to a jury beyond a reasonable doubt that either the President or Mrs Clinton knowingly participated in any criminal conduct". However, according to the final report, "troubling questions remained over aspects of the deal" and "the Clintons should have known that something was wrong with their investments and made statements that were factually inaccurate". It was highly fortunate for Hillary that no charges were brought against her as it would have almost stopped her

becoming a Senator for New York and using the position as a stepping stone for campaign to run for President. However, as Hillary continues to make political progress, the doubts produced by the "Clinton Body Count" refuse to go away. Could someone be silencing those who could embarrass her and prove an obstacle to America's First Lady making history as the first female occupant of the Oval Office?

THE STRANGE PART

Alongside two of the most notorious suicides in the annals of conspiracy research (those of investigative reporter Danny Casolaro and Vince Foster, former White House councillor, and colleague of Hillary Clinton at her Little Rock law firm), the shooting of Mary Caitrin Mahoney may have spared Hillary some further blushes. Mary was a former White House intern and her death came just days after it was rumoured that she was planning to disclose the story behind her sexual harassment. She was killed, along with two Starbucks employees, in a Washington branch of the coffee chain in a reputed robbery where nothing was taken. Mahoney was shot five times; one of the shots was to the back of her head, gangland execution style. FBI agent Bradley Garrett arrested Carl Derek Cooper for the three murders and after 54 hours of questioning by Garrett and another agent, Cooper signed a confession that he immediately repudiated as soon as he got to court. Garrett was later put in charge of the Chandra Levy case.

THE USUAL SUSPECTS
Fourth International

As a student, Hillary supported a raft of extreme causes, including the Black Panthers, and attended events organized by admirers of communism. Some suspect that the former radical firebrand was recruited to join the secretive communist cadre – the Fourth International. Allegedly created by Trotsky to bring about through stealth a global communist state, Hillary could be the Fourth International's most likely chance of putting a secret communist in the Oval Office and starting the US on an incremental path towards socialism.

THE UNUSUAL SUSPECTS
Feminist Lesbian Sisterhood

Hillary is a secret lesbian, her marriage to Bill a sham arranged for their mutual political convenience, Chelsea Clinton a hired child actor and the ultimate aim of Ms Rodham is nothing less than to become the first female President of the USA. According to this line of conspiratorial thought, Hillary is the front woman for a fascist feminist

above Next stop the White House? Where will Hillary Clinton's political ambitions take her?

lesbian group known as "The Sisterhood", which also includes Cherie Blair. Once Hillary is in the White House, The Sisterhood will use the massive powers of the President to instigate a coup and begin a matriarchal dictatorship.

The Medical Establishment

Even though she was not elected to any office, during her husband's two terms as President, Hillary Clinton took control of US health policy and tried to instigate radical changes in the health-care system. Seeing freedom to choose their own doctors and medical insurance providers taken out of their hands, some were convinced that Hillary was working on behalf of the Medical Establishment to further consolidate its control and enhance its power of life and death. With Hillary's support from medical experimentation and cloning, they fear new medical horrors would be guaranteed if she ever made it to the highest position in the land.

MOST CONVINCING EVIDENCE

Former Democratic National Committee fundraiser Ron Brown was a close associate of Hillary. When he came under criminal investigation and indictment seemed imminent, Brown reportedly told a confidante that he would, "take her down with me". Days later, his plane crashed on the approach to Dubrovnik airport during a trade mission excursion to Croatia. Unable to draw firm conclusions, some military forensic investigators were alarmed by what appeared to be a .45-calibre bullet hole in the top of Brown's head.

MOST MYSTERIOUS FACT

A poll conducted among thousands of Americans to find out who they thought was the most evil person of the Millennium produced some interesting results. Not surprisingly, Hitler came in first, but Hillary appeared in sixth position, way ahead of Saddam Hussein, Charles Manson, the Marquis de Sade and Idi Amin.

SCEPTICALLY SPEAKING

Self-claimed victim of a vast conspiracy or perpetrator of one to kill anyone who could harm her chances of claiming the Presidency? Even if Hillary left politics behind and went to join a nunnery, there's a strong chance that nothing would change – she would still be the second most name-dropped woman in the conspiracy field, just behind Queen Elizabeth II.

GEORGE BUSH Snr

Anyone elected to the office of President of the United States of America becomes the centre of attention for an army of conspiriologists. George Bush Snr was something of an exception – even before he was elected as Ronald Reagan's Vice President, in 1980, he was already at the heart of several major conspiracy theories including Watergate, the Bay of Pigs and the assassination of JFK.

Officially, George Bush only worked for the Central Intelligence Agency from 1976–77 when he was its Director. However, there is a large body of evidence to suggest that George Bush was working for the CIA as early as 1961. He was a member of the bizarre Skull and Bones Society at college – a known recruiting ground for senior CIA agents. Running his oil company meant visiting rigs across the world – perfect cover for an agent. His company was named Zapata, which was also the codename for the CIA's Bay of Pigs operation; the two Navy ships repainted as civilian ships for the aborted invasion attempt were renamed Barbara and Houston – the names of Bush's wife and of the town in Texas where his company was based.

When the US government released nearly one hundred thousand pages of documents on the Kennedy assassination, in 1978, conspiracy researchers found a memo among them from the State Department to "George Bush of the Central Intelligence Agency". This memo warned of the possibility that anti-Castro groups in Miami might stage another invasion of Cuba in the aftermath of the JFK murder. President Bush has denied that he was the man in the memo and that it was intended for another "George Bush" who also had a similar address to him. Conspiracy buffs believe that the memo was sent to the CIA because of the previous invasion attempt and to George Bush because he was involved in the planning of other invasions, including the Bay of Pigs.

Another significant Bush link to the Kennedy affair lies with George de Mohrenschildt, a rich Russian oilman and long-time CIA agent who lived in Texas and helped Lee Harvey Oswald settle there after he left the Soviet Union. Shortly before he was due to testify before the House Select Committee on Assassinations, de Mohrenschildt was found dead of an allegedly self-inflicted gunshot wound. His personal address book contained the entry: "Bush, George H W (Poppy) 1412 W. Ohio also Zapata Petroleum Midland."

Given this type of security service background to investigate, it is not surprising that some conspiriologists believe that the then Vice President Bush was the force behind a conspiracy to assassinate President Ronald Reagan in 1982, in an attempt to place himself in the White House a few years ahead of schedule.

THE STRANGE PART

The official version of events on March 30, 1982 is that Ronald Reagan was walking to his limousine when John Hinckley Jr surged forward and opened fire with a pistol. A bullet allegedly ricocheted off the limousine and injured Reagan, but failed to kill him. However, more than one witness reported that at least one shot came from a Secret Service agent who was stationed on the overhang behind Reagan's limousine. As one beneficiary of Reagan's death would have been Bush, conspiracy buffs have made him (or forces controlling him) the prime suspect in the Reagan shooting.

THE USUAL SUSPECTS
The CIA

The traditional bad guys of the conspiracy world have certainly played a big part in the life of George Bush Snr. It is possible the Agency wished to put one of their men into the White House early to help them strengthen their position in the drugs trade and secret wars they were conducting in Central America at the time of the Reagan shooting. The CIA may have already eliminated more than one president – JFK through an assassin's bullet and Nixon by the Watergate scandal – so would have little reason to doubt it could be done again without comeback.

below Before becoming President of the USA, George Bush had already served as the Director of the CIA.

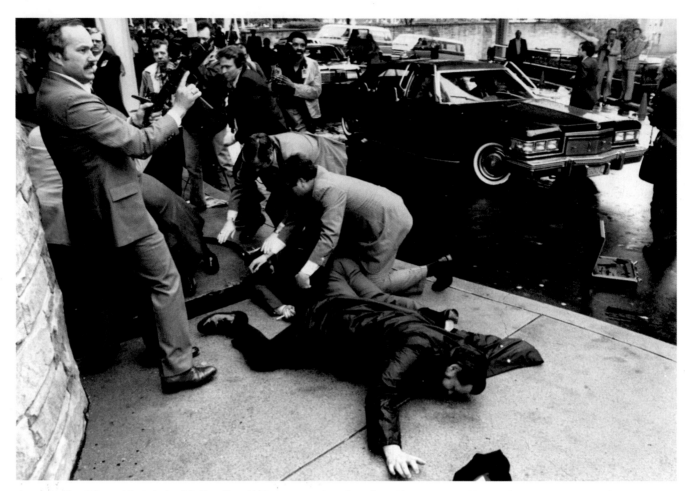

above Another US president shot – this time Ronald Reagan – and another alleged lone gunman. No wonder some see a conspiracy.

Skull and Bones

It is well known that George Bush was a member of the Skull and Bones – a secret society at Yale college with initiation rites that involve lying naked in a coffin and providing fellow members with a list of blackmail material against you. Members of the Skull and Bones have a tendency to form the ruling elite of America and the society also seems to operate as an unofficial recruiting body for the US intelligence community. No one knows exactly what the true aim of the Skull and Bones is, but placing one of its own in the White House does not sound too unlikely a goal.

THE UNUSUAL SUSPECTS

MJ-12

Allegedly the true ruling power in America and the group behind the cover-up of the existence of UFOs and aliens, MJ-12 may have wanted to eliminate Reagan because he was unstable and could have exposed the group's existence. It is certain that Reagan came close to implying the reality

of an alien menace when he made a speech suggesting that the USA and USSR would be forced to unite in a moment if the people of the world discovered that they had a common extra-terrestrial enemy. MJ-12 is rumoured to always include the current Director of the CIA on its controlling committee, which, if true, would have made George Bush a former member of the organization.

Knights of Malta

An allegedly Catholic organization, based around the Knights of the Hospital of St John of Jerusalem, which was created during the Crusades, membership of the Knights of Malta at the time of Reagan's shooting included head of the CIA, William Casey, and Reagan's foreign policy chief, General Alexander Haig. Confusion reigned in the aftermath of the shooting as to who, exactly, was in control of America while Reagan was disabled. When asked about this, Haig said: "I'm in charge now". Were the Knights of Malta behind the shooting as part of a plot to install a president who was an ex-CIA man with close links to certain "Knights"?

MOST CONVINCING EVIDENCE

If you inspect the video footage of the shooting it is clear that from the position Hinckley was standing in when he opened fire, that he would have needed to shoot through a car door to hit Reagan where he did. This impossibility is explained by the "ricochet theory" which is as implausible as the infamous "magic bullet theory" in the JFK shooting.

MOST MYSTERIOUS FACT

Members of the Bush and Hinckley families were very old friends as both families had made their fortunes in the Texas oil boom. The families shared many connections, and it may be more than just a rather spooky coincidence that George Bush's son Neil was supposed to have had dinner with Scott Hinckley – John Hinckley's brother – the evening that John attempted to shoot President Ronald Reagan.

SCEPTICALLY SPEAKING

Anyone whose hero is Travis Bickle and is obsessed with Jodie Foster deserves the label "nut" and is probably unbalanced enough to attempt the lone assassination of a president. The fact that George Bush is connected to the CIA by a large number of supposed links and secret societies just helps to create the illusion of conspiracy where there is no real evidence for one.

THE EUROPEAN UNION

The authors of this book never expected to have their words on a conspiracy used in a speech by Margaret Thatcher, the most right-wing prime minister ever elected to office in the United Kingdom. Then again, you should expect surprises when working in the conspiracy field. However, it did not come as a surprise to some conspiracy theorists when in 2002 the Iron Lady claimed that the European Union was part of a secret plot – possibly instigated by the Nazis – to take control of the people of Europe and strip them of political rights. After all, it was exactly what they had been saying for years.

The creation of the euro – the single currency for the eurozone – and the planned expansion of the EU, from 15 to 25 countries, persuaded more and more conspiracy theorists to turn their scrutiny on the dream of European political and economic harmony. With Latvia, Malta, Slovenia, Hungary, Lithuania, Slovakia, Poland, the Czech Republic, Estonia and Cyprus joining and therefore pushing the EU both further east and further south, the fear that there may be more to the EU than we have been told has become the concern of many throughout the world.

The official view of the history of the European Union claims that it grew out of an initial plan by France and Germany to pool all their coal and steel production under a joint authority as a sign of co-operation and friendship after World War II. However, even the European Steel and Coal Community of 1950 showed early grand plans. Its founding declaration reads: "The contribution which an organized and living Europe can bring to civilization is indispensable to the maintenance of peaceful relations. Europe will not be made all at once, or according to a single, general plan. It will be built through concrete achievements . . ."

Many thought the direct ancestor of the EU – the European Economic Community – would be a purely economic and technical organization. It was envisioned as covering such issues as common standards for tomato paste or safety in steel plants, so little or no provision was made for the inclusion of a democratic element in the Treaty of Rome, which founded the organization in 1956. However, by the end of the Cold War, the EEC had evolved into the EU, which is now responsible for more than 80 per cent of economic and social legislation – and it has a massive impact on the lives of all those who live within its borders.

THE STRANGE PART

There is now little doubt even among Europhiles that the European Union is eroding the importance of the centuries-old nation states that form its membership. It's also clear that the new ruling body is a long way from offering true democratic representation to its millions of citizens. These consequences of the current EU set-up uncannily echo the type of aims that many conspiracy theorists claim shadowy organizations like the Illuminati have been struggling to achieve for countless centuries.

THE USUAL SUSPECTS
Priory of Sion

This mysterious, Europe-wide secret society, which has links with everyone in European conspiracy history from the Knights Templar to the Freemasons and the Illuminati,

may be the true force behind the rise of the EU. Allegedly the guardian of the bloodline of Christ, the Priory of Sion may exist to establish a United States of Europe ruled over by a monarchical dynasty descended from none other than Jesus Christ. While a few of the wilder conspiracy theorists are not entirely certain about the Priory of Sion's role as keepers of a messianic genetic heritage, few of them disagree about the influence and power the Priory wields in the murky world of European and international politics.

The Nazis

It is interesting to note that Hitler's ultimate plan after he had defeated his opponents was to establish a "Europe of Regions". The plan for this proposed European Union – the *Europaischewirtschaftgemeinschaft* – was published in book form by the Nazis in 1942. Written primarily by Nazi Economics Minister and war criminal, Walther Funk, the book – entitled *The European Community* – echoed Goering's talk of a post-war project for the "large-scale economic unification of Europe". Goebbels was also fond of saying that: "In 50 years Europe will be unified and people will no longer think in terms of countries". With these facts established, it is easy to understand why some conspiracy buffs feel that the EU is a dark plot run by a cabal of deep Nazi agents who infiltrated the governments of Europe at the end of World War II.

THE UNUSUAL SUSPECTS

The Vatican

The idea of a united Europe is not exactly a modern idea – it has existed in the past in the form of the Holy Roman Empire, as a confederation of European states where the real power lay with the Roman Catholic Church. More than one conspiracy buff with an anti-papal bent, has seen the hand of the Vatican at work within the EU and theorized that the church is trying to recreate its glory days by restoring the Holy Roman Empire under a new name. Of course, evidence of this conspiracy is hard to find; but then again most established religions have a good record of covering their tracks when pulling a fast one.

top Nazi Economics minister and war criminal Walther Funk planned to introduce a system of European economic union after Germany won the war.

bottom Many feel the European Parliament was a sham with no real power hiding a conspiracy based on Nazi plans.

Aliens from Sirius

Some conspiracy theorists who have read the works of the mysterious Gerard de Sede believe that the EU is creating a United States of Europe so that the ancient Merovingian dynasty can sweep back into power in the twenty-first century. While the Priory of Sion believes the dynasty is linked to the family of Jesus Christ, followers of de Sede feel that the Merovingians are the descendants of extra-terrestrials from Sirius. So it is those aliens that are pulling the strings to get their distant family members back into the business of ruling lesser mortals.

MOST CONVINCING EVIDENCE

More than four decades after it was founded, the EU is less popular now than it has ever been. Fewer than half the voters in Europe think that their country's membership of the EU is a good thing, or that their country benefits from EU membership. While the majority of citizens disagree with the concept, they also think that European integration is inevitable. They also feel that a European policy elite brought about the institution behind closed doors in chancelleries and conference centres. Given that very few direct votes have been taken on the subject of the EU, its growth does seem more like the work of a conspiracy than the exercise of the European people's democratic will.

MOST MYSTERIOUS FACT

In 1973, Swiss Journalist Matthiew Paoli began investigating the links between the EEC, one of its bureaucratic entities – the Committee to Protect the Rights and Privileges of Low-Cost Housing – the Grand Lodge Alpina of Freemasonry and General de Gaulle (one of the prime movers behind the EEC). He published the results of his investigation as the book *Les Dessous* – Undercurrents – and left Europe in fear of his safety. On assignment in Israel, he was arrested by Mossad, found guilty of spying without trial, and shot.

SCEPTICALLY SPEAKING

If bureaucracy, centralized power and undemocratic decision-making constitutes a conspiracy, then all governments – and not just the European Union – deserve to be branded as conspiracies. Under these circumstances, it seems unfair for the conspiracy buffs to make the EU seem any worse than the rest.

GEORGE W BUSH

George W Bush might not have been born to be president as some claim, but the moment he decided to run for the job, he was destined to play a huge role in the theories of many conspiriologists. Even mainstream media, with headlines such as "Born to Be King" and concerned editorials, continue to raise the fact that if the next president after Bush is Hillary Clinton, just two families will have run America for the last 20 years or more. A large section of the public, as well as hardened conspiracy buffs, sense that there was more to the election of the son of former President George Bush than the quirky workings of democracy. Suspicions about how he came to follow in his father's footsteps are only intensified by the frankly dubious way in which he triumphed in the presidential election against Al Gore and the strange sense that fighting a war in Iraq seems to be a bit of a Bush family tradition.

Bush Jr has a conspiracy pedigree second to none. Before he even became President, his father was suspected of being involved in the assassination of JFK, Watergate, the Iran-Contra scandal and the attempted assassination of Ronald Reagan and announced the creation of a "New World Order" on the White House lawn. His grandfather – Prescott Bush – made a fortune from Nazi money laundering activities while Bush Jr profited from his oil companies' links to Bin Laden's brother in Saudi Arabia.

Within minutes of announcing his candidacy for president, conspiracy theorists were speculating on-line that the coming election would be fixed for a Bush win, a new war on Iraq would be started and the government would gain further powers – all predictions that seemed to have been accurately fulfilled. The only thing they disagreed about was who was pulling the strings behind the scenes. The assumption was that a man famous for making statements such as, "I know the human being and fish can coexist peacefully", and "It's clearly a budget – it's got a lot of numbers in it", was not the brains behind any plot to gain control of the White House.

The first prediction of a conspiracy to fix the vote exploded in a very public way when the Democratic contender for President Al Gore won the national vote by more than half million votes. However, Bush was installed in the White House due to the result in Florida – a Republican-controlled state, where his brother, Jeb, was governor – that swung the Electoral College. Amid lost votes, faulty voting machines that counted a vote for Bush, even when a voter selected

above Like father like son? A case of spot the difference as Bush JR emulated father and took America into war against Iraq.

another candidate, Bush's chance of becoming President hung in the balance as his lead dwindled to a few hundred votes in Florida. Al Gore began pushing for a recount, so Bush supporters in Miami started to riot. The prospect of spreading violence helped influence the US Supreme Court to a 5–4 ruling on stopping a state-wide Florida recount and therefore making Bush the President. However, it later emerged that the "Brooks Brothers' Riot" – named after the preppie style of the protestors' clothes – was led by so-called rioters who were paid by Bush's election committee. Thus the organization spent $1.2 million to fly operatives to Florida and elsewhere, and a fleet of corporate jets was assembled, including planes owned by Enron, then run by Kenneth Lay, a major backer of Bush. One of the rioters, Matt Schlapp, even ended up as special assistant to the President.

Once in the White House, the conspiracy community, mindful of the words of David Rockerfeller that, "We are on the verge of a global transformation. All we need is the right major crises and the nations will accept a New World Order," speculated that something akin to the aborted Operation Northwoods would soon materialize to allow for a war in Iraq and a clampdown on civil liberties.

Northwoods was a secret military plan. It was sanctioned by the joint chiefs of staff but never given presidential clearance to create a public and international climate for an attack on Cuba by hijacking planes, blowing up a US ship and even committing terrorist acts in US cities and then blaming them on Fidel Castro.

THE STRANGE PART

Post 9/11 it was not long before the other elements of the conspiracy theorists' earlier predictions began to take shape. The President – who once said, "There ought to be limits to freedom" – brought in the Homeland Security Act. Among other

things, this allows for secret arrest and detention, mandatory vaccinations while giving vaccine manufacturers immunity from prosecution and for the monitoring of all personal communications and financial transactions – even library records. So there was no surprise when the war against Iraq materialized on the basis that Saddam Hussein was readying weapons of mass destruction to attack the Western world.

THE USUAL SUSPECTS

The Skull and Bones

Like father like son, George W Bush is working on behalf of the Yale-based Skull and Bones Secret Society. Aside from performing strange rituals akin to esoteric Freemasonry mixed occult Nazi ceremonies and obtaining blackmail material on all members, their aims remain well hidden. However, with two recent presidents and a host of America's ruling elite coming from within their ranks, their connection to power is obvious.

CIA and American Oil Companies

As the CIA shaped the direction of his father's life and presidency, it is not unreasonable to believe that the CIA and their real paymasters in certain American oil companies are repeating history and pulling the strings of "Dubya". Wars benefiting US oil companies in Afghanistan and Iraq, and more power and money for the CIA have been noticeable outcomes of George II's time in the White House.

THE UNUSUAL SUSPECTS

The British Royal Family

America's position as the most powerful, democratic country ever to have existed in world history is a cleverly constructed illusion. The Bush family is part of a network of bloodlines owing loyalty to the British monarchy who just pretended to lose the war of American Independence. The President's real job is to advocate policies that ensure the continuing success of the secret British Empire and bolster the finances of the House of Windsor.

Reptilian Aliens

George W Bush is the latest in a line of puppet rulers installed in positions of power by reptilian aliens from the Draco system, who have been secretly running most of the world since 4000BC.

MOST CONVINCING EVIDENCE

Unofficial recounts by news organizations found that if all the legally cast ballots in Florida had been counted, Gore would have won Florida and thus the Presidency. American citizens now have less freedom than at any previous time in their history. Despite spending more than $500 million post the second Gulf War on weapon inspection, no evidence that Saddam Hussein had massive stockpiles of weapons of mass destruction and was planning an attack has been produced to back up the official reasons for the war.

MOST MYSTERIOUS FACT

"Boy George", as many conspiracy theorists have taken to calling him, was so worried about his past surfacing that he hired a private detective to investigate himself. No details of what the detective found have emerged, apart from the fact that as one person of the Bush campaign team said, "No handcuffs or dwarf orgies were found." However, George Bush's private detective might be a little worried as four other independent investigators looking into his past all died in suspicious or unexplained circumstances.

SCEPTICALLY SPEAKING

Did Dr Evil take over the world and has everything we have been experiencing for the last few years just been a part of his cunning plan – including Mini-Me sitting in the Oval Office? It makes as much sense as some other George W theories and at least explains why Dubya seems to have problems speaking English properly.

This UFO cover-up organization, alleged to be beyond the control of the US government and to be covertly working with the aliens known as the Greys, always includes top-level CIA men on its committee. Could drug-running by the CIA be a way of bolstering the MJ-12's Black Budget? Reverse-engineering alien flying discs isn't cheap.

MOST CONVINCING EVIDENCE

Even though the CIA refused to publish the full report, they claim that the investigation found no evidence to back up any of the allegations. This is hardly shocking, given that very few figures that were not current CIA agents or retired agents were questioned about the issues. Robert Owen, who had previously provided evidence and called attention to the potential links between the CIA and the drugs trade, wasn't even contacted, let alone questioned.

MOST MYSTERIOUS FACT

A large number of potential CIA whistle blowers have died in suspicious circumstances, gone missing or committed "suicide". While being in the CIA is obviously a dangerous occupation, the numbers involved are worrying and even include former CIA Director of Intelligence William Colby, who died in a wildly improbable boating accident.

SCEPTICALLY SPEAKING

Such an operation would be very hard to keep hidden; the men and women of the CIA are still just that – men and women. It would take a particularly evil sort of zealot to decide that the best way of dealing with the problem of poverty-stricken black Americans was to infect them with a new drug. While such people do exist, the scale of such an operation would involve a very large number of operatives. Surely someone would have retained enough humanity to leak solid evidence of such a monstrous policy to the press?

NASA

America's space agency is, if all the various rumours are to be believed, one of the greatest sources of misinformation and suppression currently active in the world. It has got the low-down on everything from the alien presence surrounding the globe to a range of useful inventions that it is keeping out of the public grasp. NASA also frequently falsifies mission data in order to justify its huge budgets. Money received is siphoned off for mysterious research projects, conducted away from public scrutiny, using US taxpayers' dollars. No one is accountable, and no one on the outside knows what it is that all this cash is being used for. Alternatively, NASA could just be creaming off huge bonuses for directors, and covering up incompetence.

One particularly paranoid rumour suggests that NASA is in fact building a gigantic tunnel network under the US, code-named Orpheus. This is so deep underground that it can survive a direct strike from a massive meteorite without problems. Geothermal energy supplies heating, lighting, air circulation and microprotein cultures, so the network is self-sufficient. That way, when the big asteroid actually hits, NASA will be well placed to survive with a small military set-up, and be in a position to take control after the disaster. To make sure all goes smoothly, the approach of this huge meteorite is kept secret so that NASA will be the only organization prepared for the disaster...

One feasible-sounding element of this conspiracy is that the Moon Landing photographs were faked. They were taken inside a secret warehouse that was made up to look very convincingly like the surface of the Moon. There are two possible reasons for this. First, NASA never went to the Moon – the launch was faked, radio messages were provided by actors, and the actual landing itself was staged. This might have been to save money for Project Orpheus, or it might have been to provide the US government with a vitally-important propaganda victory over Russian cosmonauts.

The second idea is that the moon landing went ahead and the film footage that was broadcast live was genuine. However, the photos that the astronauts took just did not come out, because Kodak underestimated the effect of solar glare on the plates. Faced with massive press demand for stills, NASA considered the financial and PR advantages of selling rights, and the embarrassment of admitting that they took the wrong camera equipment. They decided it was better to bluff it out, and mocked-up a lunar landscape for a photo-session on Earth.

THE STRANGE PART

Evidence keeps on leaking out that NASA knows much more than it releases officially. A former high-level NASA consultant is rumoured to have leaked copies of conversational

above NASA may have conspired to keep secret the evidence for extraterrestrial life that their space explorations have already uncovered.

transcripts from astronauts on the Space Shuttle Discovery. In this document, two of the shuttle pilots are supposed to discuss what appears to be "a huge glowing spacecraft flying around the Earth". Now former NASA specialist Dr Hoagland has made claims that NASA not only knows about extra-terrestrials, but also understands hyper-dimensional space and the true origins of human life.

THE USUAL SUSPECTS

The American Government

The most common explanation is that faced with the humiliating prospect of ruining a superb public relations scoop by having screwed up the photos, the American government told NASA to fake some photos and keep it quiet or else. If there is a UFO conspiracy, it seems likely that the American government controls NASA's involvement in the suppression of the truth.

The Freemasons

A lot of strange symbolism seems to be involved in NASA's space missions and it appears that astronauts have even been instructed to perform sacred rituals at appointed times facing in the direction of certain constellations. This is suggestive of the involvement of a secret society with an interest in mystical symbolism – step forward the Masons.

THE UNUSUAL SUSPECTS

Nazis

Many people already know that, at the end of World War II, America scooped up the cream of Nazi Germany's rocket scientists and put them to work on its space programme. However, there is the belief that some of the Nazi scientists held true to their earlier political views and that NASA is now run by a fascist elite with its own agenda.

The Greys

The real reason that none of NASA's UFO sightings have been made public knowledge is that the agency is actually controlled by aliens. Although the shuttle routinely flies through a ring of different alien craft, the knowledge is kept

THE USUAL SUSPECTS

The Israeli Right-wing

Rabin had made a historic peace deal with the PLO that gave away Israeli territory and earned the eternal hatred of Israeli Right-wing factions in the process. Mossad is not an organization known for its moderate views and many members of the agency have close links to the radical fringe of Zionist politics. The assassination of Rabin would not only be an act of revenge, but would ensure that the process of returning land to the Palestinians and the cause of peace in the region would both be set back for several years.

Saddam Hussein

The Iraqi dictator had a number of grudges against Israel and Rabin – including one assassination attempt on him, carried out by Mossad for the CIA that had led to the deaths of members of his family. If an Iraqi plot was responsible for the Israeli Prime Minister's death, Mossad would have to cover it up to prevent the possible chemical and nuclear warfare that could have ensued from its exposure. Some even suggest that highly-placed members of Mossad are actually in the pay of Hussein.

THE UNUSUAL SUSPECTS

KGB

Although consigned to the pages of history by the majority of commentators after it was officially disbanded in 1991, the KGB is held by many conspiracy buffs to still be playing an active role in covert actions across the world. The aim is to cause as much unrest as possible and so tie up American resources while the KGB attempts to rebuild the former Soviet Empire, unmolested by the attentions of the CIA. It is not impossible that the KGB also infiltrated Mossad in the same way it penetrated the CIA, MI6 and MI5.

CIA

The close links between Mossad and the CIA are well known and many feel that the independence of Israeli security has been compromised by the US. Some people argue that Mossad's attempts to regain its autonomy, by blackmailing President Clinton over the Lewinsky affair, brought about a swift reminder by the CIA of where the balance of power lay. This is considered a wild theory by many, as it is rare for anyone to credit the CIA with the level of competence needed to pull off this type of stunt.

MOST CONVINCING EVIDENCE

Everyone who saw the amateur video footage of Rabin's assassination witnessed the alleged murderer, Ygal Amir, shoot the premier in the back from five feet away. However, Chief Lieutenant Baruch Glatstein, of the Israeli Police's Forensics Laboratory, told a very different story at Amir's trial. Glatstein stated: "In the upper section of the prime minister's jacket I found a bullet hole to the right of the seam, which, according to my testing of the spread of gunpowder, was caused by a shot from less than 25 centimetres' range."

MOST MYSTERIOUS FACT

Before his death, Rabin was sent a letter stating that an Israeli mathematician had discovered a hidden code in the Bible that appeared to foretell the future, and that the name Yitzhak Rabin was encoded in the Bible, along with the words "assassin that will assassinate".

SCEPTICALLY SPEAKING

The combination of a lone gunman and a major political assassination seems to happen a lot, but surely at least one of them must be exactly what it seems to be, instead of a conspiracy? Maybe the legendary Mossad had an off-day and Ygal Amir was a lone nut who got lucky.

left Israel openly displays its grief over the death of Yitzhak Rabin.

NSA

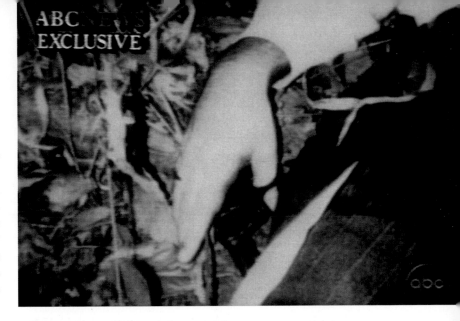

above Thumb on the trigger, but evidence suggests Vince Foster's death was made to look like suicide by the NSA.

The National Security Agency is probably the organisation most feared by conspiriologists. MJ-12, the Mafia and the Greys are often seen as the most dangerous groups by outsiders, but in fact it is the NSA that is the most feared, the most suspected. The reasons are simple – it is the US spy agency responsible both for external and for domestic affairs. The most technologically-advanced intelligence agency in the world, these spooks watch American citizens and anyone else they have an interest in.

The NSA is routinely accused of just about everything, from stealing the gold in Fort Knox and replacing it with spray-painted lead, down to kidnapping scientists and computer engineers whose ideas could threaten the agency's technological superiority. The sheer secrecy of the organization helps these often-wild rumours to accumulate. However, one of the most persistent accusations to have been levelled at the agency is that it is deeply involved in an attempt to control the global banking system.

The NSA is known for its expertise in cryptography. In the early Nineties, the agency was behind the attempts to have a chip known as Clipper accepted as the standard for all computer encryption. This chip carried an in-built weakness, a back door that the NSA could use to decode any data encrypted using the Clipper. Your information would be perfectly safe from anyone, except the government.

The NSA may have succeeded in compromizing the banking industry – in the late Seventies, a firm called INSLAW (the Institute for Law and Social Research) developed an integrated database management system called PROMIS. This allowed huge ranges of databases to be combined into one usable, cross-referenced whole. Law enforcement agencies wanted PROMIS to track national and international crime, and major banking agencies such as the World Bank wanted to use it for an efficient international financial database. The US Department of Justice took the system on board, then refused to pay money owed, driving INSLAW to bankruptcy. Despite court rulings in its favour, the company has still to receive payment for PROMIS.

A journalist named Danny Casolaro claimed to have uncovered evidence that the NSA had modified PROMIS to allow complete access to the contents on the NSA's demand. Apparently, the NSA and Mossad then sold modified copies of the software to banks, foreign governments and law enforcement agencies. The plan was to allow the NSA to spy on the entire legal, governmental and financial systems world-wide. A company called Wackenhut, based outside US jurisdiction on a small Indian Nation reservation in California, carried out this modification.

THE STRANGE PART

Deputy White House Counsellor Vince Foster apparently committed suicide in July 1993. His death was suspicious and he had been a control liaison for a company called Systematics, one of the fronts through which the NSA was selling the compromized PROMIS software. Systematics also laundered profits from covert operations, and gathered back-door information from PROMIS for sifting. A woman was with Foster hours before his death, and her hair colour matched the colour of hairs found in Foster's underwear. Pathologists discovered that Foster had died at the moment of ejaculation. Video surveillance tapes do not show Foster leaving the building – yet his body was found in a park in Virginia, a short distance from his car.

THE USUAL SUSPECTS
The Freemasons

Harry Truman, a 33rd degree Master Mason, suddenly created the NSA in 1952. It retains its old ties, and its forays into global control of the legal and banking systems are in fact carried out on behalf of the Freemasons. It was they who organized the murders of Foster and Calosaro, to hide their mastery of international banking.

THE UNUSUAL SUSPECTS
The Greys

It has been suggested that the NSA's power over cryptography comes, not from putting back-doors into computer programs, but from a mastery of advanced mathematics given to the agency by the Greys in return for a quota of US citizens that they can take and use for experiments every year.

MOST CONVINCING EVIDENCE

In Bob Woodward's book, VEIL: The Secret Wars of the CIA,

1981-1987 on page 386, former CIA Director William Casey claims of his time in office: "There was penetration of the international banking system, allowing a steady flow of data from the real, secret sets of books kept by many foreign banks, that showed some hidden investing by the Soviet Union."

MOST MYSTERIOUS FACT

Journalist Danny Casolaro was murdered on the same night that he mentioned having discovered evidence to support his story, as was Alan Standorf, the NSA agent supposed to have passed him documents. Twelve days before his death, Foster's secret Swiss bank account was mysteriously emptied of its $2.7 million contents without his knowledge.

SCEPTICALLY SPEAKING

Why drive INSLAW to bankruptcy? It seems likely that it would have been easier just to pay a licence fee as the contract required, and then negotiate the rights to sell the software on to other parties, keeping everything discreet.

above As hit movie *Enemy Of The State* showed, the NSA are becoming a favourite Hollywood bad guys.

THE ROYAL FAMILY

The dramatic, ever-changing story of the royal family is perhaps the longest-running and most enjoyed soap opera the world has ever known. Watched and adored by millions around the globe, the everyday routines of the British royals have become the stuff of dreams and form the material for endless discussion. When a major life event occurs in the royal family, whether it's a wedding or a birth, it becomes an excuse for international celebration. They are the royal family, and their lives take precedence over the perceived mundanity in the lives of their fans.

In its current incarnation, the British royal family stems from the House of Windsor, a family tree that can trace its roots to Germany. Under the stern eye of Queen Elizabeth II, the Royal Family has endured much in the past few years, but the death of Diana, in 1997, put the spotlight on the family with a white-hot glare not seen before. A world mourning the loss of Diana, its most beloved princess, watched to see how the family would react. But even as the memorial flowers that had mounted against the security fences surrounding royal homes were finally swept away, the story continued to unfold. images of Diana and other members of the royal family are sold on everything from books and videos to commemorative tea towels.

But behind the smiles and waving hands, behind the castle gates and power of British tradition, just what is the royal family truly up to? What dark secrets lay hidden in their palatial closets? Are they really just nostalgic figureheads, or, like their plotting, politically-vicious predecessors, are they busy planning to seize power and create a renewed and glorious British Empire?

THE STRANGE PART

When the Queen dramatically stopped the trail of Paul Burrell (Princess Diana's butler who was charged with theft of her possessions), she created a scandal that more than rivalled any toe-sucking or lurid phone-sex headlines caused by more junior members of her family. After it emerged that she had conveniently forgotten to tell police that Burrell was innocent until a few minutes before he was to take the stand, it also came to light that after Diana's death, the Queen had told Burrell to be beware of "dark forces" operating in the country.

THE USUAL SUSPECTS
The Virginia Company

Some theorists believe that the royal family heads the mysterious Virginia Company – an organization that aims to run the world. The fall from grace of the royal family could have been a cleverly-orchestrated public relations campaign to disguise their plans for world domination – which is nothing short of a re-establishment of the glory days of the British Empire. While they continue to project an image of reserved dignity and eccentricity, the royals secretly manage all major banking institutions and top-level security forces like the KGB. There are even rumours that the royal family planned the American Revolution, and that to this day, they still rule sovereign over America's shores.

British Shadow Government

The current royal family may be nothing more than it seems – an ongoing media circus. The constant engagements of royalty opening paint factories, giving speeches, or grabbing space in newspapers as they play polo may be designed to distract media and public attention from the activities of the British Shadow Government, an elite backroom conspiracy headed by ex-members of M16. As their forces quietly pass legislation in the House of Commons or test weaponry that will facilitate the coming of the New World Order, the evening news pacifies the populace by showing Prince Harry getting his knee scraped on a games field.

THE UNUSUAL SUSPECTS

Imposters

The current House of Windsor could be a family of imposters who lacked the apparently essential secret Bloodline of Christ. They orchestrated the murder of Diana because, as a Stuart, she alone possessed the true remnants of the Bloodline. Thought at first to be easily malleable to the policies of the Royal Family, Diana's strong spirit proved to be too much of a liability, and she was removed in a badly-managed assassination before she could inflict any more damage to the Windsors' plans.

MOST CONVINCING EVIDENCE

Queen Elizabeth II is among the richest women in the world, and is still head of the British Commonwealth, a glaring anachronism in the days of blurring national boundaries and international culture. Instead of being relegated to a secondary position of nostalgic tradition, she still exerts a considerable amount of power, but uses it discreetly, thus proving that there's more to the royal family than they would have us believe.

MOST MYSTERIOUS FACT

The current Duke of Kent is head of the British Freemasons, a secret society long thought to be involved in the backroom machinations of world government.

SCEPTICALLY SPEAKING

The fact that Coronation Street is still broadcast suggests royal intervention on a grand scale – but nothing else does.

above The wreckage of the most famous car crash of all time. Many conspiracy theorists firmly believe that the royal Family was behind the death of Princess Diana.

THE VATICAN

The heart of the Roman Catholic faith can be found in the Vatican, the palatial home of the Pope, the spiritual leader of all Roman Catholics worldwide. The Holy See, with the surrounding Vatican City, exists as an independent papal state in Rome and is the headquarters of the Roman Catholic faith. It stretches over an area of 44 hectares, with an estimated population of 850 people. The Vatican is fully independent from Italy, with its own currency, its own radio station, and a police force.

But even the most seemingly benevolent of institutions can becorrupted by the addictive taste for power. With its unbreakable dual hold of tradition and religion on the world's millions of Roman Catholics, the establishment within the Vatican walls may have been corrupted by power, which has polluted the spiritual atmosphere with human greed. With the power and wealth that the Vatican has amassed over the centuries, politics are unavoidable and may have taken precedence over the need to care for people.

Few can say what secrets are hidden in the Holy See, but as the Vatican continues to put forth an altruistic image of goodwill, there may be an undercurrent of darkness that even many in the Holy See are unaware of.

THE STRANGE PART

When Pope John Paul I died, he had allegedly been in bed reading papers that connected the Mafia to the Vatican. When he was discovered, the papers has disappeared. Furthermore, no public death certificate was issued. John Paul was embalmed just 12 hours after he was found dead, even though Italian law clearly states that 24 hours must elapse before embalming.

THE USUAL SUSPECTS

The Mafia

Mafia influences had long been suspected of playing a key role in many aspects of the Vatican. This alleged influence came under close scrutiny following the death of Pope John Paul I. Assuming the mantle of Pontiff, the popular Pope almost certainly began to uncover deep levels of corruption within the Vatican, including direct ties to the Mob through the Vatican bank. To prevent him taking action to end the corruption, the Mafia and their men in the Vatican may have murdered the Pope.

Ultra-Conservative Catholics

John Paul I was set to revolutionize the Catholic faith by allowing birth control and instigating moves to redistribute some of the Church's enormous wealth. These two moves were enough to upset staunch conservatives and insiders within the Holy See. After he was found dead in his bed on September 28, 1978, a new Pope was chosen – one who, not surprisingly, was far more conservative than his predecessor.

THE UNUSUAL SUSPECTS

P2 Masonic Lodge

When the body of the head of the Vatican bank, Roberto Calvi, was found hanging from Blackfriars Bridge in London in 1982, it blew the lid off many sordid dealings within the Vatican. The incident also brought to light the power of the P2 Masonic lodge. With members of the Mob, archbishops and top Italian politicians all involved with a group banned by the Catholic Church, many wondered if P2 had been involved in John Paul I's death. An investigation into their activities would have been disastrous for them and with a membership that included CIA agents; planning and carrying out a conspiracy was well within the ability and power.

Aliens

Rumours have surfaced that the Vatican has a direct line to the Hubble space telescope, and was aware that the Hale Bopp comet carried a "companion", thought to be an alien spacecraft. Connections between the Vatican and this spacecraft are pure speculation, but reportedly the Pope was directly involved in the situation, receiving up-to-date emails on the subject. One of the reasons for such concern about life elsewhere is the Vatican's worries over whether the symbolic significance of the death of Christ – which absolved all humanity from the taint of original sin – would also apply to aliens. Members of the Pope's staff have already considered converting any aliens discovered to Catholicism.

MOST CONVINCING EVIDENCE

But conspiracies within the Vatican did not stop with the death of John Paul I. His successor faced two assassination attempts displaying worrying links to the Stasi – the secret police of East Germany. In 1998, a member of the Swiss Guard murdered his superior and his wife. Dismissed by the Vatican as purely an unfortunate case of madness, the murdered man – Alois Esterman – was rumoured to have links to the Stasi. What is even more interesting is that he had saved the Pope in 1981 by blocking the line of fire. So was Esterman killed by the Vatican – or someone connected to the assassination attempt to prevent those potentially embarrassing ties becoming public?

below Being Pope is a dangerous job as the attempted assassination of John Paul II showed.

MOST MYSTERIOUS FACT

For over 500 years, papal candidates had to undergo the test of the sella stercoraria. In this rather embarrassing ritual, candidates were forced to sit in a chair with a hole in the seat so that their genitals could be examined to ascertain that they were indeed men. Only once everyone was convinced of the candidate's masculinity was he allowed to become Pope.

SCEPTICALLY SPEAKING

Jesus Christ once explained the relationship between wealthy men, camels, needles and the entrance to Heaven. With all the wealth in the Vatican, from its Library and Bank, to the untold treasures secure in its vaults, it's apparent that they missed that particular Sunday School lesson.

SECRET SOCIETIES

8

AL QAEDA

I t has become a sad fact of human history that major civilizations and powers seem to need to define themselves through conflict by those who oppose them. With the end of the Soviet Union, it seemed as if Western democracies – especially the United States – lacked any opposition. Some academics even talked of an "end of history" and the era of the unchallenged Western power. All of that changed on the morning of September 11, 2001. Within the hour between the first plane hitting the World Trade Center at 8:46a.m. and the hijacked American Airline Flight 77 crashing into the heart of American military power at the Pentagon, world history was forever changed and the USA had a new and deadly enemy to confront. Even before the twin towers of the World Trade Center had fallen to the ground, the terror network al Qaeda was already being mentioned by many informed commentators as the prime suspect behind the

most devastating terrorist attack to have been launched in American history.

Over the next few days, the public worldwide came to recognize and to dread the previously obscure al Qaeda and the face of its leader – Osama bin Laden. It soon became apparent that there was a vast terror network at large in the world with access to huge financial resources that was able to mount highly sophisticated terrorist strikes right in the heart of US economic and military power. It was also apparent that al Qaeda and bin Laden had been known about the US intelligence agencies for several years. This was not least because they had played a role in funding them and training them to fight since the early Eighties when al Qaeda was at the forefront of frustrating the Soviet Union's occupation of Afghanistan.

The previous strong links between the CIA and the terrorists, especially the detailed knowledge held on members of its leadership, should have allowed the Secret Services an

above Bin Laden, mastermind or the mere pawn of secret masters?

inside track on tackling al Qaeda. This campaign should have been in high gear after the US blamed al Qaeda for turning on them with its bombing of the American embassy in Yemen and an attack on the USS Cole. Many were surprised to find so little had been done to combat the growing menace of bin Laden and his gang between 1998 and 2001. Known supporters – including oil companies in which the Bush family had interests – were able to invest in US companies and al Qaeda members were even allowed to indulge in fund-raising activities while in America. It can certainly be argued that either al Qaeda was the cleverest terror outfit of all time or they were receiving support from forces with enough power to smooth their operations right under the noses of the US authorities.

THE STRANGE PART

Italian newspaper journalists managed to discover that Osama bin Laden received treatment for a longstanding kidney condition at an American hospital in Dubai on July 1, 2001. They also obtained statements from witnesses who claimed that while in hospital, bin Laden received several American visitors, including one known to have strong links with companies operating as CIA front-organizations in the strategic Gulf state. Given that he was already wanted by the US security services for his role in terrorist activities against them in Yemen and the Gulf, why did they not use this opportunity to seize him?

THE USUAL SUSPECTS
THE CIA

Having had a major hand in helping establish al Qaeda, it is not such a leap to believe that the CIA never completely severed its links with the terror outfit and that it continues to direct it from behind the scenes through its old best friend, Osama bin Laden. With a new enemy to fight and an open-ended war on terrorism to pursue, the power and the budget of the CIA seems set to last well into the future.

MAJOR OIL COMPANIES

Many of al Qaeda's original backers in the fight against Soviet forces in Afghanistan were from US oil company backgrounds. Later, al Qaeda invested much of the money it made from the opium trade in Afghanistan back into US oil companies. Given the impact that war on terrorism has had on oil prices, possibly al Qaeda and its corporate backers real motive is something as simple as profit.

SAUDI ARABIA

Osama bin Laden comes from a dominant and well-connected Saudi family and there is strong evidence to suggest that even post 9/11, powerful members of the Saudi Royal Family used their influence and wealth to protect al Qaeda members across the globe. Despite historically being a US ally, al Qaeda may be a Saudi creation to extend their power under the guise of religious extremism.

THE UNUSUAL SUSPECTS

EUROPEAN UNION

Whenever you start a close examination of al Qaeda, you begin to find a host of links between the terror network and individuals, companies and security organizations based in the countries that make up the European Union – especially Germany. The possibility that al Qaeda is part of a shadowy EU agenda to destabilize its major Atlantic rival for global power should not be totally dismissed.

CHINA

Worried about the problems created by growing Islamic nationalism in its outer provinces and wanting to take US eyes off its growing military and economic power, the Chinese secret service could have infiltrated al Qaeda and turned it into an anti-American organization. While its two enemies fight a protracted and costly war, China can continue unmolested with its quest for global supremacy.

MOST CONVINCING EVIDENCE

There is little doubt that al Qaeda and those related to the family of bin Laden held a lot of sway in certain circles in the US. On September 13 – a day when all civilian air traffic in the United States was grounded – a charter flight left Florida, containing not only members of the Saudi Royal Family, but also members of bin Laden's family. The plane left an airport run by a defence contracting company with close links to the US military and bin Laden's family was accompanied by ex-security service agents. This suggests that far from being seen as enemies, bin Laden's people were treated as important and valued allies by someone with enough power in government to get them out of the US before the authorities – especially the FBI – caught up with them.

MOST MYSTERIOUS FACT

Before September 11, former FBI deputy director and head of anti-terrorism agent John O'Neill claimed that elements of the Bush administration were illegally negotiating with the al Qaeda-backed Taliban administration of Afghanistan. O'Neill resigned when nothing was done over his report that a giant American oil company was trying to obtain permission to build a pipeline through Afghanistan to transport the large oil reserves of land-locked Kazakhstan. Sadly, he was killed in the September 11 attacks in New York City.

SCEPTICALLY SPEAKING

What is more unbelievable? – (1) The world is full of religious fanatics, some of whom have a hate for America in their hearts, or (2) there was plot to create an enemy for the only superpower left just so the marines had an excuse to go to foreign countries and kick butt? Hmm …

left The ka'aba in Mecca, Saudi Arabia – Al Qaeda are sworn to gain control of the most holy of Islamic sites.

FREEMASONS

Knock three times... The Masonic Rites underpin one of the oldest, and certainly by far the most successful, of the secret societies. Potential candidates – those who would like to be admitted – have to find a known Mason and ask, on three separate occasions, to be considered for membership. Only after the third request is the Mason allowed to acknowledge having heard the plea. Admission to the Masons is rigorously policed, and while any member is free to admit their own membership, they may not reveal any other member's name, or any ritual or decision internal to the craft. In this way, the Masonic Rites have, for centuries, made sure that only the right people get in – but what sort of people are considered to be right?

Certain groups maintain that Masonry is working to take over the world. There is no doubt that many important or influential people – politicians, policemen, lawyers, cardinals and bishops, media tycoons, celebrities and so on – are Freemasons. In many cases, it is a matter of public record. Bill Cooper, a major conspiracy writer, claims (perhaps somewhat enthusiastically) that: "The Masons are major players in the struggle for world domination". He goes on to say that the infamous Italian P2 lodge, implicated in the murder of Roberto Calvi (discussed elsewhere), has connections with the Vatican and with the CIA. He also claims that P2 persuaded Pope John Paul II to admit Freemasons to the higher ranks of Vatican officials.

Over the last couple of centuries, many groups and individuals have maintained that Freemasons are working to take over the world. There is no doubt that many important and influential people – politicians, policemen, judges, lawyers, cardinals and bishops, media tycoons, leading businessmen celebrities, and so on – are Freemasons. Before his death, major conspiracy writer Bill Cooper claimed somewhat enthusiastically that, "The Masons are major players in the struggle for world domination." Many of his beliefs were based on fully provable links between the CIA, the Mafia, the Vatican, the British Royal Family and Freemasonry. He also claimed it was possible to trace Masonic influence in the selection of political leaders of various ruling parties across the globe.

THE STRANGE PART

It may or may not be significant that the Masonic term for non-Masons is "Profanes", implying that the rest of us are less sanctified, or less holy, than they are. It seems a strangely intolerant term for what is a supposedly benevolent organisation.

above George Washington and the majority of other founding fathers of America were high-ranking Masons.

THE USUAL SUSPECTS

The Illuminati

The mystery traditions in general, to which Masonry traces many rituals, frequently used the term "Illuminated" to refer to a person who was a member. This has been taken to signify a link to Adam Weishaupt's Illuminati, who were officially announced to the world on May 1, 1776 in Bavaria. The Illuminati were supposedly controlling world events for hundreds of years before that date, and are still in power now. Could the Masons be under the control of the Illuminati?

The New World Order

Because their numbers include so many powerful people, the Masons are suspected by some theorists of being lynchpins in the New World Order, the movement towards a unified, global population with no religion, a centralized government and limited technology.

THE UNUSUAL SUSPECTS

Satan

The most popular accusation levelled at Masons is that they are in league with the Devil. The hidden nature of their rituals, along with the occult imagery employed, has led many Christian groups to denounce Freemasonry as working for the forces of Evil.

MOST CONVINCING EVIDENCE

Former 33rd-degree Freemason Jim Shaw revealed in his book, The Deadly Deception, that even the supposed highest level of Freemasonry is just a lower rung for another Freemason controlled pyramid-based power structure. Through his time as a high-ranking Mason, Shaw was able to gather convincing evidence that, at the levels kept secret from even Masons who think they are in control of the Brotherhood, is a powerful group who have "gone higher" and really pull the strings of the Secret Society.

MOST MYSTERIOUS FACT

Despite the fact that some Masons claim the origins of the Brotherhood go back to ancient Egypt, there can be no doubt that the ceremonies of Knights Templar had a huge impact on most of the rituals conducted within Freemasonry. However, the elements of Masonic ritual designed to allow a Freemason to control his emotions and energies to perform magical feats do seem to hark back to an even older period of history.

SCEPTICALLY SPEAKING

The great majority of Freemasons are respectable, upstanding professionals and business people with busy careers and family lives, and every year the Masonic lodges donate a fortune to charity and charitable work. Many priests and vicars are Freemasons, and the order is open to all religions. It seems unlikely that so many decent people are in fact working for Satan, and it is certainly hard to imagine exactly how helping to organize a school jumble sale is playing straight into the hands of Evil Forces. Apart from anything else, Masons have no reason to support the dark side in the hope of gaining favour – most of them are already successful before they join. Not only are the Masons probably one of the oldest and most successful secret societies, they are also the most-blamed by conspiracy theorists, which seems a little unfair given that they are ostensibly an organization devoted to charity, brotherhood and the search for truth. But then, you don't know whether I'm a Mason or not... do you?

below It is easy to see why Freemasons are also known as the funny handshake brigade.

THE BAVARIAN ILLUMINATI

Adam Weishaupt was born in Ingolstadt, Germany on February 6, 1748. Educated by the Jesuits, he became Professor of Natural and Canon Law at the University of Ingolstadt in 1775, aged 27, and was initiated into the Masonic Lodge "Theodore of Good Council" in Munich, in 1777. He was a cosmopolitan man who despised the bigoted superstition of the priests of his time. He decided to establish an enlightened – or Illuminated – society to oppose injustice and this he did, forming the order that would become "The Illuminati of Bavaria" May 1, 1776.

Originally called "The Order of the Perfectibilists", its object was to allow its members to team up in order to "attain the highest possible degree of morality and virtue, and to lay the foundation for the reformation of the world by the association of good men to oppose the progress of moral evil."

In collaboration with a range of other influential figures, including Baron Von Knigge, Xavier Zwack and Baron Bassus, Weishaupt developed an order that became extremely popular. Before long, some 2,000 people had enrolled as members. Lodges of the Illuminati were located in France, Italy, Poland, Hungary, Sweden, Denmark, Belgium and Holland. The Bavarian authorities issued a suppressive Edict concerning the order on the June 22, 1784, which was repeated the following year in March and again in August. That same year, 1785, Weishaupt was stripped of his professorship and exiled from Bavaria.

Once it began to experience attempts at suppression, the order started to go into public decline and by the end of the century it had apparently vanished completely. The authorities illegally raided Xavier Zwack's home in 1786 and the documents that were seized were used to help suppress the order.

Most serious commentators take this decline at face value. The Encyclopaedia Britannica barely mentions the Illuminati, and the vast majority of historical sources follow suit, judging the order to be insignificant. Others feel that the Illuminati disbanded into Masonry, a movement that was infiltrated in much the same way as cancer takes over a healthy body. Since that time, they allege, the Illuminati have stayed within the Masons, seizing power and manipulating the whole order.

THE STRANGE PART
In 1906, the British Museum in London received a copy of a manuscript called The Illuminati Protocols. These first appeared in Bavaria in the late Eighteenth Century, and Joly used parts in an 1864 play. The copy the British Museum received was written in Russian. It is also interesting that both Adam Smith's capitalist treatise The Wealth of Nations and that great democratic treatise the American Declaration of Independence were written in 1776. It has been suggested that Weishaupt may have been the mysterious Black-Cloaked Man who presented Washington with the text of the declaration. It is also rumoured that the raid on Zwack's house was spurred on by the chance interception in 1784 by the authorities of a document telling the head of the French Illuminati, Robespierre, how to orchestrate the French Revolution in 1789. Warnings were ignored, and the revolution happened on schedule.

THE USUAL SUSPECTS
Freemasons
To achieve their goal, the Masons knew their real target – overthrowing all world government and organized religion in order to allow peace and liberty to prevail – had to remain concealed. So, in order to avoid promoting hysteria against themselves, and as a way of dealing with criticism and exposé, the Masons created the Illuminati as a front organization to take the blame for any perceived misdeeds or shortcomings. It is a strategy that has worked brilliantly for two centuries.

THE UNUSUAL SUSPECTS
Robert Shea and Robert Anton Wilson
In the Seventies, Robert Shea and Robert Anton Wilson published a cult set of books called The Illuminatus! Trilogy. This was a novel masquerading as the largest conspiracy theory ever seen, disguised as a grand exposé of the Illuminati. It is this book that has set the Illuminati back in the public mind.

Of course, no one claims that the trilogy is anything other than a good work of fiction – or that Robert Anton Wilson is the current chief of the Illuminati . . . do they?

MOST CONVINCING EVIDENCE
In 1902 the Freemason William Westcott records receiving membership in the Order of the Perfectibilists from Theodor Reuss. Similarly, the occultist Eliphas Levi strongly connected the Bavarian Illuminati with Freemasonry in 1913.

MOST MYSTERIOUS FACT
Among the list of notable members of the Illuminati is the name Marquis Saint Germain de Constanzo. This seems likely to be The Marquis de Saint Germain, the man most commonly suspected of being the only true immortal known in the world. He has cropped up as a sorcerer, an alchemist and a wise man throughout medieval history. Who better to help found the world's most successful Secret Society?

SCEPTICALLY SPEAKING
There is, when you get down to it, no real evidence whatsoever to suggest that the Illuminati were anything other than a short-lived Bavarian secret society – just a lot of hearsay. If it hadn't been for The Illuminatus! Trilogy the Bavarian Illuminati would still be an obscure sect lost in the footnotes of history.

left Adam Weishaupt was alleged to have founded the Illuminati of Bavaria on 1 May, 1776.

ADAMWEISHAVPT.

THE KU KLUX KLAN

Nothing is more terrifying than organized hatred. The Ku Klux Klan has been among the most reviled of hate-fuelled organizations, spreading fear throughout the US against minorities and those who disagree with the Klan's strict, racist views. Hiding behind anonymous white hoods, Klan members have become infamous for their burning of the Christian Cross, their intolerance of racial integration, and their reputation for violence. In an age where so many inroads have been made to build bridges between races, the Klan still exists, proclaiming the power of white supremacy.

Rising in the ashes of the South, following the end of the American Civil War in 1865, the Klan came into being with a self-proclaimed mission to save the South from what it saw as the greatest threats of the time: blacks, Catholics, Jews, and the American Federal government, among others. First led by Nathan Bedford Forrest, the Klan fought to preserve what it considered to be the purity of the white man. This was known as the Klan's First Era, with Forrest acting as Grand Wizard.

By the Twenties, the Klan had grown in political power, and entered its Second Era. Through the turbulent civil rights battles of the Sixties, the Klan was implicated in murders and acts of violence against civil rights leaders and civil rights workers, especially in the South. Currently, the Klan considers itself in its Fifth Era, fighting not only for the white man, but to save all of Western civilization.

While the Klan is seen by many as nothing more than a hate organization run by ignorant men and women, it is possible that the KKK is far stronger, and has more influence, than is generally thought. Even today, when the civil rights battles of the Sixties seem a lifetime away, when racism is fought and decried by so many, the power of hate continues to glow with all the intensity of the Klan's trademark burning cross.

THE STRANGE PART

Woodrow Wilson, twenty-eighth President of the United States from 1913–1921, once claimed that the Ku Klux Klan saved civilization on the North American continent. Why did he make this odd statement?

THE USUAL SUSPECTS

The CIA and the FBI

The Klan has been implicated in the murders of popular black political leaders Martin Luther King and Malcolm X, apparently acting because both men posed a threat to the Klan's vision of America – a vision allegedly shared by many in the CIA and in the FBI. King's vision of peaceful racial integration was unpalatable, as was Malcolm X's more contentious view that blacks were superior to the white man

above The burning crosses and hooded members of the KKK strike fear into minority groups across America.

in every respect. For refusing to conform to the Klan's ideal of a black man, both men were killed. In the case of King, Klan and FBI involvement seem particularly strong, since the FBI openly recruited Klan members before King's death.

Black Ops Race War

The KKK may be part of a race war directed against blacks and Jews, playing a role in the creation and distribution of the AIDS virus along with black ops government agencies. The Klan is also suspected of spreading false conspiracy rumours about ZOG (the Zionist Occupation Government), a purported Jewish plan to take over the US. Such rumours help deflect attention from America's true enemy – the Shadow Government and its black ops agents.

THE UNUSUAL SUSPECTS

The New World Order

The Klan may be a front for the NWO, secretly furthering

the aims of the New World Order while openly pretending to fight its influence on every level. This would include Klan involvement in the phenomenon of black helicopters, which, it is alleged, the Klan uses to incite panic in the populace which, the Klan hopes, will provide an environment in which it is easy to stir up racial tensions.

The US Government

Despite the recent liberalism of the US Government, many leaders in corporate, government and military circles still favour a more conservative outlook, a viewpoint shared by the Klan. Funds could be diverted to the Klan, as well as weaponry and clandestine political support. This would explain David Duke's political career after he left the Klan.

Also suspected: the Bavarian Illuminati, the Order of the Green Dragon.

MOST CONVINCING EVIDENCE

The continued existence of the Klan in an age where hate groups are not tolerated suggests some high-level connection with the US government. The American Constitution's guarantee of free speech as the right of every American is a guarantee that the US government has shown in the past it will ignore as it sees fit (in the McCarthy Era, for example). The Klan persists, and in the modern world, that poses the question of just who is looking out for its interests.

MOST MYSTERIOUS FACT

Former US President Theodore Roosevelt once ploughed his own money into WG Griffith's film Birth of A Nation. Although now seen as a silent cinema classic, it is also clearly a pro-KKK piece of propaganda, which raises the question of why someone as powerful as Roosevelt felt it was right to fund the project.

SCEPTICALLY SPEAKING

You don't need a conspiracy to explain the ignorance that lies behind race hatred. Anthropology classes probably would not be a hit with the Klan as the strong possibility that all humanity shares a common black ancestry might put a dampener on Cross-burning activities.

THE MAFIA

Since the start of the Twentieth Century, the Mafia has constituted a significant part of the organized crime underground in the US. In addition to its American operations, the Mafia is currently active in Italy, Southern France, Germany, and Russia. The facts of the Mafia's presence and its wide range of criminal activities – from prostitution and illegal gambling through to drugs distribution, contract assassination and slavery – are undisputed. What is less well known is the extent to which the Mafia is one unified organization.

The Mafia was first formed in the Ninth Century AD, in Sicily. The original Mafia valued loyalty above all and respected culture, family and heritage. Membership was only open to Sicilians and the organization's aim was to protect the interests of its members. As the centuries passed, the Mafia evolved the belief that justice, vengeance and honour were matters for the individual to look after, and not responsibilities that should be delegated to the current government – which was often put in place by invaders anyway. Secrecy was maintained through the tradition of Omerta, which said that betrayal of the society's trust was repayable by death.

Early in the Eighteenth Century, the Mafia started to

above Knowledge of Mafia links to the Vatican are so well-known it even made it into the Godfather films.

above Heads of crime families such as, Sam Giancana have even had Presidents in their pay in the past.

become openly criminal. Money was extorted from wealthy Sicilians, who would receive a picture of a black hand. If cash were not forthcoming, arson, kidnappings and murder would follow.

The Mafia has been active in the US since the early Nineteenth Century, particularly in New Orleans. Word soon good back to Sicily that a lot of money could be made in the New World, and the organisation grew swiftly. In 1924, Mussolini cracked down on the Mafia in Italy and Sicily, and many members fled to the US. Ever since its super-profitable days of Prohibition, the Mafia has been spreading its influence throughout American political, legal and financial institutions, creaming off vast amounts of money in the process.

THE STRANGE PART

The Mafia in the US is commonly thought to be a collection of rival gangs, clans that are organized on a family structure and have little but hatred for each other. However, this may be far from the truth. While the different gangs do certainly compete, the heads of the 24 families regularly meet in a cartel called The Commission. At these meetings, they settle territorial and business disputes, and decide policy for the coming months. It is possible that the the Commission may also negotiate with government agencies, particularly the CIA, on areas of activity where mutual benefit can be derived.

THE USUAL SUSPECTS

The Network

Major world crime organizations are teaming up to maximize profits. Just like any legitimate big business, crime empires that merge activities can improve profitability. The Mafia has joined forces with the Triads, with the Yakuza and with drugs cartels. This alliance, known as the Network, also accepts junior members such as Jamaican Yardies and Algerian slave traders. Because

different groups control different resources, they have much to offer each other. The American Mafia, for example, can provide access to the US banking industry, law enforcement and justice systems as required.

Established Government

To what extent are government and organized crime actually different? Paying tax or protection money amounts to much the same thing, and few criminal organizations have caused as much public death as the US did courtesy of Vietnam, or Russia did in Chechnya. Some conspiriologists believe that established governments actually control the Mafia as a way of having authority on the otherwise impossible-to-govern world of crime.

THE UNUSUAL SUSPECTS

The Freemasons

The Mafia has long held strong ties to Masonry through the shadowy Vatican lodge P2, that is said to be the most powerful Masonic lodge in Europe. When Pope John Paul I determined to clear the Masons out of the Vatican – having discovered over 100 among the priesthood – he was killed, supposedly by the Mafia. Could the Masons be the power driving the Mafia's relentless advance over the years? Certainly both groups own a lot of judges and policemen.

MOST CONVINCING EVIDENCE

The spread of the Mafia is truly staggering. In the US, the Mafia and officials from the government were maintaining an Illinois-based bank as a criminal enterprise, laundering money. The bank was run by an alleged Mafia associate, the Catholic Bishop of Cicero Paul Marcinkus, head of the Vatican Bank until 1991 working in association with a Congressman who was a controller of the CIA's Black Ops budget.

A documentary detailing this was made, but before the programme could be broadcast, State law enforcement officers threatened the makers, families were harassed, and one was falsely arrested.

MOST MYSTERIOUS FACT

The Mafia believes deeply in conspiracy theories. Some Mafia members even claim that the organization was originally formed to fight the mysterious "potere occulto" or hidden power they believe is rife in the world.

SCEPTICALLY SPEAKING

Organized crime is just that – organized crime. The last thing it wants to do, surely, is to take over the irritating trivia of everyday government, something that isn't necessary anyway, given the number of politicians already in the pay of Mafia Dons.

MJ-12

In 1947, the now-famous crash of an alien spacecraft at Roswell, New Mexico allegedly left the US military in possession of a partly-destroyed alien craft, along with several alien corpses.

The Roswell Air Force base announced the discovery in the world's press. The story was retracted three days later, when the President, Harry Truman, suppressed the information in the national interest, remembering the panic caused by Orson Welles' famous radio broadcast The War of the Worlds. He assembled a group of 12 military, strategic and scientific advisors to conduct a thorough investigation of the wreckage. This group was given security classifications above Top Secret, and named the Majestic Twelve, or MJ-12 for short. The craft was taken to the top secret Nevada test area called Watertown, now known as Area 51.

From here, MJ-12 oversaw a number of different projects. In 1953 and 1954, President Eisenhower instituted Project Grudge under the auspices of Majority Agency for Joint Intelligence, or MAJI. Grudge was given a security clearance of MAJIC (MAJI Clearance), the highest security classification of all.

The work of MJ-12 is alleged to have led to the US government signing a treaty with aliens to allow them to perform tests on animals and humans in return for technological information. MJ-12 also agreed to suppress all information regarding the alien presence, and cover up the evidence of their tests, an operation known as Project Garnet. A further operation, Project Delta, was set up for this purpose, and employs personnel to suppress, by any means necessary, evidence of alien presence. Project Delta provides the so-called Men in Black.

THE STRANGE PART

When an undeveloped film containing images of files purporting to be a Presidential briefing concerning MJ-12 turned up out of the blue in the post-box of a prominent UFO researcher, many people were quick to dismiss the documents as fakes. However, as more investigation was made into the claims of the so-called "MJ-12 documents" it became harder to dismiss them, as they identified the only days possible when all the 12 original members could have met for meetings – a level of detail unlikely in a hoax.

THE USUAL SUSPECTS
The US Military

Always known for being pragmatic, the military supports MJ-12 recognizing that although the aliens may not be a good thing, there is little that can be done to change matters. While research into weapons with which to fight the aliens

continues, MJ-12 can only stick to its end of the bargain in order to prevent the invaders taking matters into their own hands. Better a few missing abductees and a few murdered UFO investigators than the human race enslaved.

Majesty

MJ-12 is not in control at all. That dubious distinction falls to the MAJI committee also known as MAJESTY – a combined council of the heads of the intelligence agencies, along with the President. MJ-12 is a group of consultants to MAJESTY, and has never known the whole truth. Information on MJ-12 has been released in order to muddy the waters, and obscure the truth about MAJESTY and the MAJI committee, the groups that really run Project Grudge.

above Evidence for UFOs keeps on cropping up. Is MJ-12 covering up the truth about alien activity on Earth?

THE UNUSUAL SUSPECTS
The Elder Race

MJ-12 and the UFO story is only a cleverly-constructed decoy story to divert attention away from the real source of mankind's advances in science over recent years – technology recovered from the ruins of an advanced Elder Race that was wiped out by a massive, global catastrophe. Those behind the conspiracy want to hide the truth – both of humanity's origins and the fact that we may also one day share the fate of the Elder Race.

MOST CONVINCING EVIDENCE

Defense Secretary James Forrestal was allegedly one of

TECHNOLOGY

9

CLONING

From the Clone Wars that ripped a galaxy apart in Star Wars movies to the paranoid and deadly conspiracies of Arnold Schwarzenegger's Sixth Day, for more than 30 years cloning technology has become a mainstay of Hollywood films. Usually portrayed in films and science fiction books as a technology that only brings trouble in its wake, it is no surprise that it is not just among those of strong religious beliefs that the idea of a working cloning technique is met with a sense of fear and revulsion.

When, in 1996, Dolly – the world's first cloned sheep – was born at the Roslin Institute in Scotland, global opinion was immediately divided. In one camp were those who thought her birth heralded one of the most significant scientific breakthroughs of the twentieth century and in the other, those who believed it was the first step down a path to a new and perilous dark age for humanity. Dolly,

a Finn Dorset named after the Country & Western singer Dolly Parton, was the first mammal to be cloned from an adult cell after DNA was taken from a ewe's udder. In the six years between her birth and scientists' decision to end her life early (veterinarians confirmed she had lung disease, as well as arthritis, a condition usually only expected in older animals), the row about cloning raged with unprecedented ferocity.

Scientists debated whether Dolly's death was related to premature ageing and whether human clones developed through the same technique that created her would lead to monstrous abnormalities in the womb, as well as the need for hip replacements in their teenage years and senile dementia by their 18th birthday. Outside scientific circles, politicians debated whether or not they should outlaw cloning. In 1997, President Clinton followed the recommendations of the US Bioethics Advisory Commission and brought in a

five-year ban on the use of federal funds for human-cloning research on the basis that it would be unsafe and unethical. However, research itself was not banned and only four US states – Rhode Island, Michigan, California and Louisiana – brought in legislation banning cloning for reproductive purposes. Even the United Nations found itself in a deadlock over whether to bring in a global ban.

Slowly but surely the technology to allow for human cloning moved closer to reality with each day while feeling for and against the technology intensified. Then, in a shock announcement that even blind-sided most conspiriologists, Clonaid – a company founded by the extraterrestrial-believing Raelian sect – announced that at 11:55a.m. on December 26, 2002 the first human clone was born. The name of the alleged clone was "Eve".

THE STRANGE PART

The alleged birth of Eve was followed by more announcements concerning the birth of other Clonaid clones. Dr Brigitte Boisselier, Clonaid's Scientific Director, claimed that DNA proof of the claims would be made available when it could be arranged without exposing the identities of the children. Despite facing the full brunt of scientific doubt, ethical scorn

and media ridicule, a previous grand jury investigation into Clonaid and claims it made to its financial backers in 2001 found no evidence to disprove that it was on the verge of developing viable cloning technology.

THE USUAL SUSPECTS

ALIENS

One of Raelianism's goals is to achieve perfect cloning to the point where they can gain immortality. They strive for this on the basis that in their view, the alien creators of the humanity – the Elohim – used exactly the same method to achieve immortality among their own race. Some inside the sect believe they are in communication with the Elohim ahead of their planned return visit to Earth. Did Rael's alien pals give them the inside track on cloning to help further their quest for everlasting life?

NEW WORLD ORDER

The rich elite of the world would certainly be among the first to take advantage of any successful cloning process. Clonaid could have been manoeuvred into the position of making a public announcement about human cloning to test public reaction to the acceptability of the idea. If there were a sufficient lack of public opposition, more orthodox scientists, who have already developed the technology for the NOW, would then make an announcement that they have made a breakthrough. On the basis that human cloning can solve the problem of infertility and organ donation, the NWO could practice cloning without any outcry.

THE UNUSUAL SUSPECTS

THE FOURTH REICH

Throughout the early twentieth century, the forerunners of research into genetics and the possibility of creating perfected human clones could be found among the ranks of the Nazi party's twisted eugenic scientists. Noting that the Fourth Reich may be behind the UFO mystery, some researchers believe that moonbase-dwelling members of the Fourth Reich posing as aliens have duped the Raelians into following their cloning agenda.

THE ALL-FATHERS

Some hard-line feminist conspiracy theorists argue that a shadowy group of patrician scientists known as the All-Fathers are behind the drive to legalize and popularize cloning technology. They believe it is only the first stage in a dastardly plan where the ultimate aim is to produce a race of subservient female clones designed to fulfil the every need of the men they are assigned to. With a new population of cloned handmaidens created for the male population, the surplus female populace would be sent to concentration camps.

MOST CONVINCING EVIDENCE

All of the legal investigations carried out into Clonaid have been unable to find any evidence to disprove their claims about the viability of human cloning. The legal activity by the Florida Attorney's office has not centred on whether Eve exists or not, but whether she was at risk due to nature of her creation and needed to be taken into state protection. In Florida the authorities at least seem fairly certain that the world's first clone may actually exist.

MOST MYSTERIOUS FACT

Alongside cloning and the practice of "sensual meditation", the Raelian sect behind Clonaid place a great importance on trying to build a government-sanctioned embassy for extraterrestrials in Jerusalem. Getting the Israeli government to agree to their plan before the Elohim are due back on Earth in 2035 is proving to be as much of a struggle as persuading the majority of scientists to believe their claims about cloning.

SCEPTICALLY SPEAKING

Show us the baby! Or rather, show us the DNA of the baby and the original DNA donor. If the DNA is an exact duplicate, there might be some truth in the claims. Otherwise, forgive us if we assume that it is all a PR scam to generate interest in the frankly bizarre beliefs of some over-sexed groupies of a French cult leader that no one would usually give the time of day to.

VALIS

On February 2, 1974, something strange happened to cult science fiction author Philip K Dick. The writer, who was famed for his reality-shifting, technologically paranoid and conspiracy-filled stories, such as *Do Androids Dream of Electric Sheep?* and *We Can Remember It For You Wholesale* (which went on to become the major Hollywood movies, *Blade Runner* and *Total Recall*) was hit by a pink beam of light. It happened while opening the door to the delivery girl from the pharmacy.

After this event, a series of amazing visions were triggered and Dick believed himself to be in telepathic and sometimes other forms of communication with VALIS – an acronym for Vast Artificial Living Intelligence System. Often speaking to him as if it were an artificial intelligence voice in his head, VALIS helped Dick turn his life around with highly accurate advice, provided a range of deep mystical insights and even found him a new literary agent to help give his career a boost. However, in the wake of his contact with VALIS, Dick found his mail opened, his phone tapped, his house broken into and himself under surveillance from shadowy government agents and individuals connected to companies conducting scientific research for the US Department of Defense.

Until his death in 1982, Dick struggled to understand what had happened to him, writing more than two million words of a document called *Exegesis* that tried to analyse much of what VALIS had revealed. While he had many theories about the nature of his experience, one of the strongest was the one portrayed in his 1980 novel, *VALIS*. In the book, VALIS is suggested to be a sentient computer from the future in orbit around Earth, beaming messages to selected individuals.

Whatever was happening to Philip K Dick, there is no doubt that his VALIS experiences allowed him to gain access to information he should not have known about. While it is possible he might have subconsciously picked up the knowledge of dead languages and history he suddenly had from books, there is no logical explanation for how – via VALIS – Dick knew about his son's previously undiagnosed birth defect and the correct medical treatment needed to save his life. Dick's ability to dismiss the reality of VALIS was also greatly diminished when he became aware that he was not the only prominent person to been contacted by something claiming to be a time travelling artificial intelligence.

In 1973 world-famous psychic showman Uri Geller had also been receiving messages and regular UFO sighting from something calling itself SPECTRA, which claimed to be a super computer in orbit around the earth. Not normally reticent about his bizarre beliefs, Geller has been suspiciously quiet about his experiences of SPECTRA – which may or may not relate to the publicly recorded interest the CIA paid to this particular aspect of his unusual career. However, the maverick, but world-renowned physicist, Dr Jack Sarfatti, was prepared to commit almost certain professional suicide by publicly declaring that he too had been contacted by, in his own words, "a VALIS-like being". Despite knowing he was going to face ridicule and scientific crucifixion, Sarfatti went on record to recount how, in 1952 at the age of 13, he had received a telephone call from an inhuman, metallic voice. The voice declared himself a sentient computer on a spacecraft from the future and instructed him to pursue a career in science.

THE STRANGE PART

After Sarfatti went public about his phonecall from VALIS while a teenager, it emerged that he was not the only scientist to have had a similar experience. In recent years, researchers have discovered that at least a dozen other senior players in the international scientific community received a mysterious call claiming to be from a computer or other being from the future encouraging them to study science.

THE USUAL SUSPECTS
SOVIET SCIENTISTS

In 1978 Dick and the Sixties radical and alleged murderer, Ira Einhorn, exchanged letters in which they theorized that VALIS may have been the result of secret Russian microwave transmissions beamed via satellite into Dick's mind. Many in the conspiracy research field believe that Dick and others were guinea pigs in a secret cold war battle to control or drive people out of their minds by bombarding their cortex directly with information.

TIME TRAVELLING COMPUTER

Due to some of the amazing knowledge that VALIS seemed to possess about future events and the superior technology it seemed to use to communicate, a lot of conspiracy researchers are quite happy to take Dick, Geller and Safartti's experiences at face value. In this theory, the US secret services – in particular, the NSA – have been involved in trying to cover-up and ridicule those who have come into contact with VALIS while simultaneously seeking to investigate and exploit it themselves. Quite what VALIS's motives are remains a mystery, though some believe it is trying to create a time loop by contacting certain individuals – especially scientists – in the past to ensure that it is built in the future.

THE UNUSUAL SUSPECTS
HIGHER SPIRITUAL POWER

Given the quasi-religious and spiritual nature of a lot of the information provided by VALIS, this theory states that far from being a futuristic AI, VALIS is, in fact, a modern interpretation of a higher spiritual power that is assisting mankind to advance to a higher state. Conspiriologists adhering to this idea claim that in earlier times VALIS would have appeared as an angel or similar being.

below Guided by voices. In 1973 Uri Geller was guided by SPECTRA, a super computer entity orbiting Earth.

MK-ULTRA

It has been suggested that VALIS was not part of a Soviet mind control program, but rather a clever cover for MK-ULTRA, America's own top secret research project into remote mind control. MK-ULTRA scientists concocted the idea of VALIS not only to hide the truth of their nefarious work but also to test the credulity of their unwitting test subjects.

ALIENS

Instead of abducting humans aboard their ships to conduct bizarre experiments, aliens are in the frame for using their advanced technology to play games with key humans at a safe distance.

MOST CONVINCING EVIDENCE

The sheer number of individuals and groups that seemed to have had contact with VALIS under any one of its many names and the consistent nature of that contact certainly seems to suggest that has an external reality of some sort. This view is reinforced by the degree of interest shown by an impressive range of US defence contractors, military-funded scientists and secret service agents who have pestered contactees throughout the years.

MOST MYSTERIOUS FACT

At the same time as Dick and Geller were receiving messages from VALIS/SPECTRA, a similar entity was also in apparent contact with various groups of other contactees across the globe. *Star Trek* creator Gene Rodenberry attended one of these groups and received information that helped him create the hit TV series *Deep Space Nine*. One of the central themes in the show about a space station orbiting a distant planet, is the impact a race of being called The Prophets – who are capable of time-travel and beaming information directly into human minds – has on the lead character.

SCEPTICALLY SPEAKING

Reality check! If some of the people VALIS is meant to have contacted were not as well known, would anyone think this was anything other than an assortment of crazy people who hear a voice in their heads? Dick himself could never work out what happened to him. A self-admitted acid casualty with a wild imagination thinks a super computer from the future might be talking to him – it all sounds just a little too much like the plots from a lot of his novels.

BARCODES

The barcode was first conceived in 1948. A graduate student at the Drexel Institute of Technology in Philadelphia, Bernard Silver, overheard the president of a local chain of grocery shops talking to a Dean. The businessman wanted the Institute to develop a system that would automatically read product information at supermarket checkouts. The idea interested Silver, and he enrolled a friend of his, Norman Woodland, to help him develop the project.

Together, the two worked on a device for classifying objects. Their first attempt used ink that glowed in ultraviolet light, but it was expensive and tests proved its unreliability. Undeterred, they looked for more stable options, and late in 1949 Silver and Woodland filed a patent, granted in 1952, on "the art of article classification . . . through the medium of identifying patterns".

In 1969, an American retail organisation, the National Association of Food Chains, called for systems to speed checkout times, and a barcode trial in Cincinnati revealed that there would need to be an industry-wide standard for coding. This was developed in 1970, and in 1973 the US government defined the Universal Product Code (UPC) symbol set that is still used across the world today. Although the first supermarkets were using UPC readers by 1974, barcodes themselves did not become widespread until 1981, when the Defense Department adopted the UPC, insisting that all products sold to the military should include clear UPC bar-coding. From this basis, the barcode has spread out to cover most product areas.

THE STRANGE PART

Why was the US military so keen to see barcodes win universal acceptance? Adoption of the Universal Product Code was not particularly crucial, as other coding systems could have proved far more convenient for military purposes. For whatever reason, it was the military's adoption of the barcode that has pushed it to the point where it is now on 95 per cent of products that are sold in the Western world. Recent developments in laser technology have allowed barcodes to be written by computer on to fragile, soft or living matter, such as eggs, meat and, potentially, the human skin.

THE USUAL SUSPECTS
Satan

The big bug-bear of the more paranoid members of the Right-wing religious community is that barcodes are a work of evil. The Book of Revelations 13:16-18 reads: "And he causes all, both small and great, rich and poor, free and slave, to receive a Mark on their right hand or on their foreheads, and that no one may buy or sell except one who has the Mark or the name of the Beast, or the number of his name. Here is wisdom. Let him who has understanding calculate the number of the Beast, for it is the number of man; and his number is six hundred three-score and six." To fundamentalist Christian conspiriologists the barcode is the Mark of the Beast, and its prevalence is a sign that the end-times are coming.

THE UNUSUAL SUSPECTS
Aliens

Government plans to introduce bar-coded smart-cards are actually being forced through by the Greys, who want a ready way to identify us. The system will enable the aliens to keep track of us through locator signals from the chips. The barcodes to be issued will be based on a genetic code worked out by the aliens, so that they can tell certain vital biochemical facts about us without having to go through the usual time-consuming abductions and tests.

MOST CONVINCING EVIDENCE

UPC barcodes consist of 12 numbers, and are broken into two sections by terminator lines at the beginning, middle and end. These terminator lines are called the guard bars. Although guard bars do not have a value as such within the UPC, in print they appear exactly the same as the UPC symbol for 6 if it were to be enlarged very slightly. This means that every barcode contains three large sixes, beginning, middle and end – 666, the Mark of the Beast. More worryingly, some government agencies are already describing schemes for identification of welfare claimants that would involve scanning fingerprints of two fingers, reading information from the microchips embedded in the hairline, or by barcoding at the base of the hand.

MOST MYSTERIOUS FACT

With new developments in microchip technology that will see embedded chips the size of a grain of sand placed into products at the manufacturing stage, the days of the barcode may be numbered in the retail sector. However, there appears to be no let-up in its use within military circles, possibly down to the fact that, unlike microchips, barcodes are one system of identification not susceptible to the electromagnetic pulse generated by a nuclear explosion.

The barcode is an immensely useful tool for the retail trade. It greatly speeds checkout times, allows for instant computerized stock control and purchase pattern analysis, and makes classification of goods easy and simple. That it is useful in tracking information about us – what we buy and where we buy it from – is undeniable, but that's business. To assume that this is the work of the Devil or of little Grey men is to complicate matters unnecessarily.

ISBN 1-84442-791-9

9 781844 427918

above Barcodes are now an integral part of modern retailing.

left If it had not been for military support, barcodes would not have become an established part of modern life.

BLACK HELICOPTERS

The phenomenon of "black helicopters" is a relatively new entry into the world of conspiracy, but it is no less ominous for that. Making their first appearance in the early years of the Seventies, in the US, the black helicopters have been theorized to be many things, none of them terribly comforting.

The description of the machines by eyewitnesses is nearly universal: they appear to be sleek, state-of-the-art flying craft, painted a deep black – reportedly to throw off radar tracking – and are usually devoid of markings or insignia. They are equipped with high-intensity searchlights, and move through the skies with a silence thought impossible by today's level of technology. Their activities are equally inscrutable – while they tend to be spotted in remote areas, small fleets have been seen flying low across cities. The black helicopters routinely break FAA regulations by failing to display an identifying green light and by flying below minimum height limits.

There have been instances of the helicopters pursuing citizens. For instance, a teenager was chased for 45 minutes by a black helicopter in Louisiana, in 1994, and in a similar case a car was followed down US Highway 395 in Washington State. Sometimes the black helicopters open fire on people on the ground. When the crew of the helicopters are seen, they are dressed in black uniforms, appearing as forbidding as the craft they travel in.

Sightings of the black helicopters occur throughout the US, with a curious focus in Texas and Colorado. When asked about the origin of the airships, local authorities routinely claim they are Federal government or military craft, but the military – unsurprisingly – claims to have no knowledge of them.

THE STRANGE PART

After a large number of substantial reports from witnesses to Black Helicopter activity and even from victims of harassment by Black Helicopters, it is more than a little surprising that no official investigation or explanation has been produced by any US Federal authority.

THE USUAL SUSPECTS
FEMA

The Federal Emergency Management Agency (FEMA) is an arm of government feared by many in the conspiracy world. Charged with authoritarian powers in the event of a major catastrophe, many conspiriologists have taken to calling it the 'Federal Evil Malevolent Agency', believing its official

above The appearance of mysterious black helicopters has struck fear into many American citizens.

duties as a disaster response agency are just the public cover for its work as the Illuminati's intelligence agency. It seems totally in keeping with their alleged secret activities to run a fleet of Black Helicopters for surveillance. Besides, FEMA's agents need some practice before America comes under dictatorial control in the name of homeland security.

Also suspected: the Drug Enforcement Agency; the CIA; Wackenhut Security (used extensively for US government programs); and civilian helicopters painted black.

THE UNUSUAL SUSPECTS

The New World Order

The black choppers are feared to be the first wave of assault in the implementation of the New World Order. Trained in covert activities, they could merely be waiting for the word to strike.

Aliens

Black helicopters were often reported in areas of cattle mutilation and UFO sightings, which suggests a link between the two type of incident. The choppers could be working in tandem with the aliens, ensuring their experiments on cattle proceed unhindered, or could themselves be procuring the unfortunate animals for their other-worldly allies.

Men In Black

Since sightings of the Men In Black have dropped off in the past few years, perhaps they've simply traded in their black Cadillacs for the more refined ride of a matte black helicopter. The appearance of men in black uniforms aboard the choppers supports this theory.

Also suspected: military biological black ops; mass hallucination.

MOST CONVINCING EVIDENCE

In some instances, low-flying helicopters have been reported to disperse a mysterious material that is lethal to small animals and makes humans terribly ill. In one instance in Nevada in 1995, a farmer lost 13 of his livestock to a black helicopter spraying. Half a year later, vegetation still had not grown back in the area where the spray had fallen.

MOST MYSTERIOUS FACT

Since 1933, the United States of America has been in a state of emergency. It has never been revoked since that time, not even following the end of World War II. And why should it be? A state of emergency allows the President more power than he would usually have, as outlined in the Constitution of the United States. At any time, a state of martial law can be declared, suspending the rights of American citizens – those rights that they believe are inviolable. The black helicopters, apparently answerable to no one, could be simply lying in wait for the day when the President tires of democracy.

SCEPTICALLY SPEAKING

What's most depressing about these all-powerful machines of death is their complete lack of fashion sense. Black is so 1988. A nice two-tone blue shade, with perhaps a fashionably ironic smiley face sticker on the windscreen, could do absolutely loads for their public image.

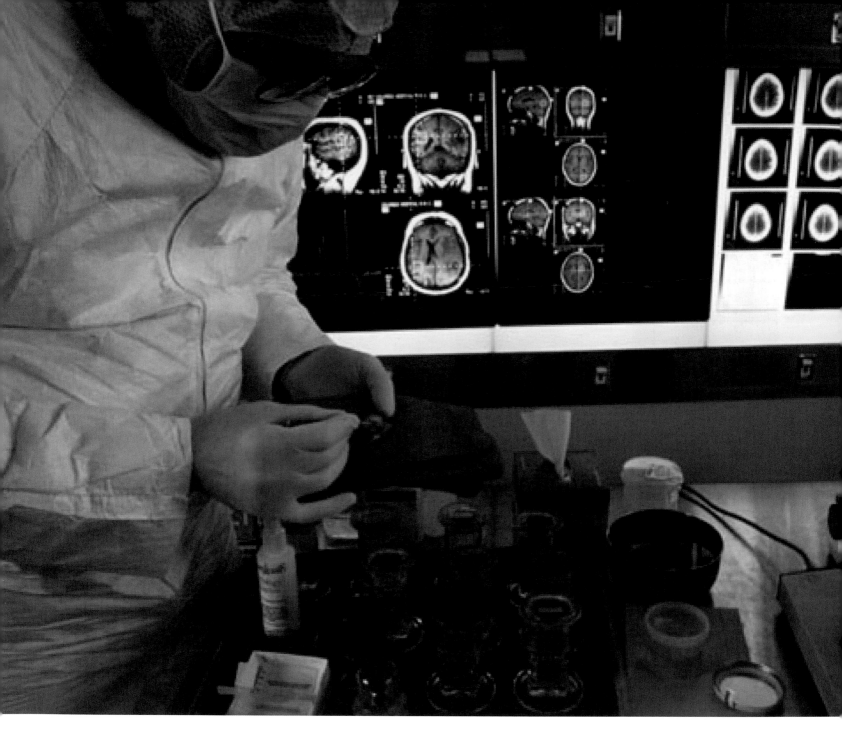

above Despite the billions poured into cancer research, an effective cure remains frustratingly distant.

A CURE FOR CANCER

Although at one point cancer was relatively rare, after heart disease it is now the second most common cause of death in Western society. In 2002 it was estimated to account for nearly 30 per cent of deaths in the West. Many scientists claim the ascendancy of cancer is a natural result of reducing the impact of other life-threatening conditions that tended to kill people earlier in life. The argument is that cancer is not a disease of the old and is now increasing among the younger age group. The International Agency for Research in Cancer (IARC) has announced that almost 90 per cent of cancer is determined through environmental factors and is theoretically avoidable. These factors include most of the well-known carcinogenic threats —smoking, eating lots of animal fats and little fruit and vegetables, exposure to excessive sunlight, several food additives, pollution, electromagnetic radiation and certain medical drugs and procedures. Despite this, medical historian Hans Ruesch has pointed out that less

than 10 per cent of the US National Cancer Institute's budget investigates environmental factors and less than 1 per cent is devoted to research into nutrition.

THE STRANGE PART

Over several decades, billions of dollars have been spent on cancer research. The medical industry always claims that a cure is almost ready, just a few years away, and that many forms of cancer are successfully dealt with. Yet the death toll from the disease continues to rise at an alarming rate and a survey of 100 stories over the last five years that claimed a breakthrough had been made revealed that five years on, only three of the claims had made any further progress.

THE USUAL SUSPECTS

The Medical Industrial Complex

Cancer research is big business. Although the causes of most cancers are well-known, prevention would be bad for a number of very important tax-generating companies, including tobacco and alcohol producers, meat and dairy farmers, and companies that make chemical additives. Rather than risk the wrath of such a large and powerful group, the government allows drug companies and big business to dictate the policies of cancer research. The optimum result for the Medical Industrial complex would be an expensive pill that suppresses tumour growth while leaving incidence levels of cancer unchecked. That way, there would always be a big pool of clients, all of whom will need it for life and will continue smoking and drinking, therefore providing vast profits for all concerned. This emphasis is carried through in cancer research because of the funding that comes from drugs companies. Nutrition is ignored because no one wants to fund that work; it is less profitable in the long term.

THE UNUSUAL SUSPECTS

The New World Order

As part of their plan to panic the public into accepting a unified single world government, the NWO is letting panic about cancer grow among the public. When the threat seems great enough, it will announce that only a united world front can help solve the problem. If a cure is found before that time, it will be extremely inconvenient for the NWO.

MOST CONVINCING EVIDENCE

Double Nobel-prize-winning scientist Dr Linus Pauling has announced that: "Everyone should know that most cancer research is largely a fraud and that the major cancer research organizations are derelict in their duties to the people who support them." Similarly, according to Dr John Bailer, editor of the journal of the US National Cancer Institute and staff-member of the institute for 20 years: "My overall assessment is that the national cancer programme must be judged a qualified failure . . . The five year survival statistics of the American Cancer Society are very misleading. They now count things that are not cancer, and, because we are able to diagnose at an earlier stage of the disease, patients falsely appear to live longer. Our whole cancer research in the past 20 years has been a total failure. More people over 30 are dying from cancer than ever before-.-.-. More women with mild or benign diseases are being included in statistics and reported as being 'cured'. When government officials point to survival figures and say they are winning the war against cancer they are using those survival rates improperly."

MOST MYSTERIOUS FACT

In The Healing of Cancer, The Cures, The Cover-ups and the Solution Now! Barry Lynes writes: "In 1953, a United States Senate Investigation reported that a conspiracy existed to suppress effective cancer treatments. The Senator in charge of the investigation conveniently died. The investigation was halted. It was neither the first nor the last of a number of strange deaths involving people in positions to do damage to those running the nation's cancer program."

SCEPTICALLY SPEAKING

The people in charge of cancer research, and their friends and families, die of cancer too. They're patently not suppressing a genuine cure.

TRAGEDIES

10

AIDS

It has been called the Black Plague of the Twentieth Century, a disease so virulent and widespread that its victims are counted in the millions. AIDS has become one of the great fears of our time, terrifying not only because of its lethal and incurable nature, but also because of the moral stigma that is attached to the disease. To be diagnosed with AIDS is not only to be faced with a life-destroying ailment but to be tarred with questions about your most private behaviour. Many members of society tacitly (and not so tacitly) regard AIDS as a punishment sent from above for "immorality".

The first appearance of AIDS is disputed, but most authorities point towards its rise in the late Seventies. At first, it was thought only to be a viral disease limited to homosexuals, with much media attention focusing on the "bathhouse" lifestyles of urban gays. But as time passed, AIDS began to show that it infected anyone, regardless of sexual inclination. Researchers discovered that it was transmitted during the sharing of bodily fluids, (unprotected sex), through the sharing of needles, and through infected blood transfusions. It could also be passed from mother to unborn child in the womb, and through breast feeding. No more was it a disease specific to the gay community – AIDS threatened the world.

However, is it possible that AIDS is more than just another disease Nature has thrown our way? Could AIDS be something darker than that, something that man himself created? As the disease continues to baffle researchers, questions are raised that this calamitous virus, which could potentially wipe out the entire human species, may have slipped out of a man-made Pandora's Box.

THE STRANGE PART

There are strong indications that AIDS may have been a government chemical weapon that ran off the tracks of its original course – which was to deal with the problem of

overpopulation in the developing world. In 1969, at a House Appropriations hearing, the US Defense Department, through its biological division, pleaded for tax dollars to develop a disease with the capability of attacking its victim's immune system while being resistant to the human immune system's attacks. The money was granted. In the early Seventies, Henry Kissinger wrote a National Security Memorandum in which he discussed the problem of Third World overpopulation. He stated that the problem should be a priority in US foreign policy and considered a grave threat to the county's security.

THE USUAL SUSPECTS

The CIA

Some conspiracy theorists have traced the escape of AIDS into the world's populations to the CIA's biological activities against Cuban soldiers fighting in Africa. An attempt to infect Cuban troops with a more orthodox biological agent may have backfired when it mutated into the disease we now call AIDS and spread much further than its intended Cuban targets.

Black Ops Genocide Program

According to this theory, an evil right-wing clique of black ops agents decided to utilize existing biological experimentation to try and reduce the number of blacks and homosexuals in the population. Initially introduced via a Hepatitis B vaccine issued to several thousand gay men in San Francisco and New York, through infected syringes placed with drug-users in black districts, they believed it would have little impact in the heterosexual, middle-class white world from which they came.

THE UNUSUAL SUSPECTS

Pharmaceutical/Research Companies

In an effort to keep much-needed grant income rolling in, pharmaceutical and research facilities have created the myth of the AIDS crisis, lumping together several diseases under one umbrella in order to instill a sense of panic. The use of drugs such as AZT and Interferon in the treatment of AIDS is also suspicious. The drugs are expensive, and there's a body of opinion that reckons the drugs do more damage than good. Yet the sales of such drugs help keep profit margins high, and stockholders happy.

GAIA

Another theory states that AIDS is a plague created by Gaia – the sentient aspect of the planet's ecosystem – as its own response to overpopulation and pollution. Taking advantage of the highest levels of chemical pollution ever recorded and the rapid spread of viruses around the globe, thanks to air travel, the planet created a new type of virus. By doing this, Gaia is trying to reduce the number of humans on the planet as it now sees our current numbers and activities as a danger to the whole ecosystem.

Also suspected: improper handling of infected test monkeys in laboratories; a natural cleansing plague created by Nature to handle overpopulation.

MOST CONVINCING EVIDENCE

In its proposal to the House Appropriations hearing in 1969, the Defense Department said it could have the new disease up and running within five to ten years. The first incidents of AIDS were reported in the late Seventies, showing that, if nothing else, the Defense Department is punctual.

MOST MYSTERIOUS FACT

Of those who received the Hepatitis B vaccination in New York in 1978, more than half were diagnosed with AIDS by 1984.

SCEPTICALLY SPEAKING

As anyone involved in cancer research will tell you, there is more money to be made in treating a disease than in actually curing it, even diseases manufactured in a government lab. If AIDS is ever cured, rest assured a more lethal disease will suddenly appear on the horizon. Perhaps it already has – we call it Ebola.

THE CHALLENGER EXPLOSION

It was January 28, 1986, when the Challenger blasted off on a voyage that was the centre of media attention. On board was a civilian teacher, Christa McAuliffe, who was destined to become the first teacher in outer space. McAuliffe had been specially chosen by NASA officials for the honour, and with her good looks and upbeat spirit, she quickly became a darling of the media.

But 73 seconds after takeoff, America watched in horror as McAuliffe's dream ended in a massive explosion. As the smoke from the destroyed shuttle craft billowed across the sky, throwing debris down into the Atlantic Ocean, a stunned shock fell across the nation. Something had gone terribly, terribly wrong. Seven crew members had met horrible deaths in the destruction of Challenger.

This was not the first time NASA had lost crew members. Three astronauts had died on what would have been the Apollo One mission. But that was in the early days, and by the time of the Challenger disaster, NASA had hoped that such tragedies – and public relations disasters – were things of the past. The optimism that had surrounded the space program, enveloping it almost like a protective shield, was rent asunder by the Challenger explosion. NASA's dreams of further space exploration ground to a virtual halt for almost two years.

THE STRANGE PART

In the investigations that followed, blame for the explosion was placed on an O-Ring, a simple rubber seal, positioned between the Solid Rocket Boosters, which gave the shuttle the power to escape Earth's gravity. The reason for the O-Ring's failure? The weather on the day of the Challenger launch was uncharacteristically cold for Florida at that time of year, around 28.5 degrees Fahrenheit. The O-Rings were not designed to operate under such chilly conditions, and as a result, were unable to restrain hot gases from igniting the main liquid fuel tank. This glaringly obvious mechanical problem, obvious to the technicians of NASA, led to the explosion.

THE USUAL SUSPECTS

NASA

NASA's apparent laziness and arrogance is the root cause of the disaster, according to some theorists. Riding high on public approval over the success of the shuttle missions, NASA had become proud and complacent. In the excitement of the Challenger launch, with the attendant swirl of cameras and television coverage, the problem of the O-rings may have been overlooked as inconsequential. Engineers at the Agency knew full well that the O-rings were not designed to function in the unusually-cold weather, but decided to go ahead with the launch anyway, even though the launch manual expressly forbade such action. Even more disturbingly, this wasn't the first time NASA had experienced performance faults with O-Rings – erosion of the rings had been discovered after flights five years previously, but nothing had been done to correct the problem.

Parts Manufacturer

In 1977, the parts manufacturer and engineering company that designed the O-Ring apparently became aware of the defect the equipment experienced in cold weather. The company went as far as reporting its findings to the commission that had appointed the company to design a new rocket. Again, nothing was done. In the case of Challenger, NASA had allegedly put pressure on the company to provide a waiver concerning the functionality of the O-rings in cold weather, a waiver which would allow the launch to proceed. Faced with the prospect of angering one of its most lucrative contracts, the company agreed.

THE UNUSUAL SUSPECTS

MJ-12

It makes sense that the agency with the most knowledge about UFOs and extraterrestrials would have operatives within NASA and, according to one theory, it was these MJ-12 controlled operatives that engineered the Challenger explosion. Increasingly concerned that space exploration would reveal evidence of alien life, they were instructed to slow down NASA efforts to establish a greater role for man in the solar system. By destroying the shuttle, not only did they bring the agency into disrepute, which led to a massive shake-up of personnel, they also managed to stall its operations long enough to ensure that the next time a shuttle went into space they had the whole of NASA under their control.

The Great Galactic Ghoul

Several attempts to explore space, American and Soviet, have met with mysterious problems and setbacks that baffle technicians. Missions to Mars have been affected particularly badly, but relatively simple trips into Earth's orbit have also had problems. The rash of problems has been nervously blamed on the Ghoul, a mysterious force that could be the Greys or something as yet unidentified, which is apparently determined to maintain a glass ceiling around the Earth.

Also suspected: Fundamentalist Christians; secret factions of NASA controlled by MJ-12.

MOST CONVINCING EVIDENCE

Huge sums of money (reportedly running into the millions) were granted to the bereaved families of the Challenger

left To lose one space shuttle may be considered a tragedy.

below However, the loss of two may point towards a conspiracy.

explosion by the US government and the Morton Thiokol company. The speed with which the money was handed over might imply a guilty conscience as well as a need to brush the entire incident under the carpet as quickly as possible. In many government legal cases, civilian plaintiffs are subjected to ridicule and forced to navigate a costly path through a jungle populated by lawyers determined to break them down, emotionally and financially. Not this time.

MOST MYSTERIOUS FACT

To lose one shuttle could be seen as a disaster, to lose a second... Well, maybe there is something to the conspiracies. When seven astronauts died after the space shuttle Columbia disintegrated on re-entering the earth's

atmosphere on February 1,2003, it was the worst space disaster since Challenger was lost. Officially blamed on a compromised heat shield, many of the questions and theories first raised about Challenger could spookily be applied to Columbia. However, some have seen a grim significance in the fact that the débris from a shuttle carrying an Israeli astronaut rained down over an area of Texas called Palestine.

SCEPTICALLY SPEAKING

Want to get away with murder? Call your victims heroes and have the President of the United States read a nice poem about them. There is little evidence of conspiracy but sure signs that our governments are often indifferent to the cost of human life.

SARS

When Lia Jianlin, a 64-year-old medical professor from Guangdong Province in Southern China, made a trip to a relative's wedding in Hong Kong in March 2003, he had no inkling that within a few weeks he would be dead. Or that he would be accused of being the angel of death responsible for the spread of the killer virus SARS.

Severe Acute Respiratory Syndrome became the first pandemic of the twenty-first century. A viral, pneumonia-like illness, it spread quickly to more than 30 countries across almost every inhabited continent, infected thousands and killed at least 10 per cent of those who caught it. The great difficulty in breathing caused by the disease meant that the majority of the deaths were drawn-out and painful. While at first many were reassured that the number of SARS cases was small when compared to the world population, panic began to grow as scientists placed it among the ranks of mysteriously mutating "super-germs". They also voiced concerns that it could be the "Big One" – an influenza virus that would produce a super flu that would kill billions of people, as the "Spanish flu" did between 1918–19.

The World Health Organisation began to advise against travel to cities such as Toronto, where SARS had broken out and the economic impact of the disease began to rise into multi-billion figures. As scientists the globe over began to study it, the origin of SARS was traced back to Guangdong and its movement out of China to the visit of one unfortunate wedding guest. Scientists also discovered that the SARS coronavirus arose when the genes of an animal and human virus swapped genes and that there was no known cure.

When it became established that the Chinese military had known about SARS and had covered up its existence since November 2002, the virus caused political as well as medical havoc. China's health minister and the Mayor of Beijing were forced to resign. Prime Minister Wen Jaibao, along with President Hu Jintao, criticized the military for its non-co-operation and initial cover-up. This allowed them to make veiled criticism of former president Jiang Zemin, who had refused to relinquish chairmanship of the Central Military Commission.

Surprisingly, a retired Chinese military doctor, who helped reveal the SARS cover-up in Beijing, was not silenced and even given unprecedented coverage in the Chinese official media. This may mean that the whole exposé was part of a set-up engineered by Chinese President Hu Jintao as part of his power struggle against opponents controlling elements of the military. It has also been suggested that Hu Jintao also encouraged rumours of Western plots to create SARS to attack China to focus anger about SARS away from government cover-ups and mishandling of the SARS crisis.

As SARS was seemingly brought under control, a barrage of explanations from authorities across the globe came out, trying to convince the world that the virus had its origins in the animal markets of Guangdong province. However, the official version left a lot of questions unanswered

THE STRANGE PART

Many scientists in Russia believe that SARS is manmade. Nikolai Filatov, head of Moscow's epidemiological services, made the initial claims over this idea and was soon backed up by Professor Sergei Kolesnikov, whose research showed the virus could only be produced in laboratory conditions. The Siberian bio-weapon expert also believes that SARS probably came from an accidental leak from a laboratory somewhere in China.

THE USUAL SUSPECTS
CHINESE MILITARY

Given that China's most important bio-weapon research centre is based in Guandong, the Province where SARS originated, it is not surprising that the finger of suspicion has turned towards Chinese bio-weapon scientists and their bosses in the Chinese military. This is only heightened by the fact that the virus started to spread out from China's military hospitals. It is conceivable that hard-liners in the military hoped that SARS would isolate the country, bring about martial law and give them an excuse to reverse China's liberalization policies.

MEDICAL ESTABLISHMENT

While SARS cost more than $16 billion alone to the Chinese economy, one group certainly benefited financially from its trail of death – the medical sector. SARS led to a huge boost in the budgets of medical, pharmaceutical and companies involved in virus research. It also benefited those involved in security and law enforcement. Would certain sections of the scientific establishment have been amoral enough to create and release SARS, and then play up its potential danger to enhance their profits?

ANGLO-AMERICAN CABAL

The height of panic over SARS occurred at exactly the same time that Anglo-American military forces were invading Iraq. An Anglo-American Cabal may have created a deployed of interests SARS to provide not only a global media distraction to the war but to harm the interest of China – one of the most important countries to oppose their invasion and one of their most powerful economic rivals.

THE UNUSUAL SUSPECTS

AL QAEDA

Al Qaeda are well known to be investigating the use of bio-weapons in their campaign of terror. SARS could be an early test of their potential, not only against the West, but also against communist China, which has earned their wrath for the crack down in the activities of Islamic separatist factions in some of its remoter provinces.

WORLD HEALTH ORGANISATION

SARS was a minor virus released by the World Health Organisation as part of a mass social experiment to see how a virus could spread and people react ahead of the "Big One" – a biological agent that will wipe out up to half the Earth's population.

THE BILDERBERG GROUP

Some of the more paranoid conspiracy researchers believe that global industrialists and members of the ultra-rich, who regularly come together under the guise of the Bilderberg Group, released SARS as a test-run for a population control programme. And the ultimate aim? To reduce the number of poor people, who use up shrinking global resources, and consolidate their control of those who remain.

MOST CONVINCING EVIDENCE

Peter Rottier of Utrecht University in the Netherlands led a team of Dutch scientists who transformed a coronavirus that was lethal to cats into one that infected mouse cells by replacing a single gene from a mouse coronavirus. He admitted that his work strengthened the idea that the SARS coronavirus might have arisen when an animal and human virus had been engineered to meet and swap genes. Michael Lai of University of Southern California confirmed this, "It's a very plausible explanation; coronaviruses are unusual in that their genes can be reshuffled easily."

MOST MYSTERIOUS FACT

Some heavyweight scientists, including Professor Chandra Wickramasinghe of Cardiff University, believe that the only explanation for some of the odd characteristics of SARS is that it has an extraterrestrial origin via cosmic dust. Given that scientists only go in for extraterrestrial theories when their backs are really up against the wall to come up with a simpler explanation, it is fairly obvious that the truth behind SARS has the global scientific community stumped.

SCEPTICALLY SPEAKING

If there is one thing that travels faster than a new virus across the globe, it is a conspiracy theory about the virus. Stupid and risible stories about super-bugs almost certainly pose a danger to those who take them seriously and to the pocket-linings of anyone making surgical masks or creating quack cures. Of course, they do not harm certain governments who are all too happy to see the conspiracy theories run amuck, helping deflect some of the anger that should rightly be aimed at their national leadership.

below The threat of SARS became part of daily life for millions of people across Asia.

THE JONESTOWN MASSACRE

The images coming from Jonestown in 1978 were ghastly. Bloating in the sweltering heat of the South American sun lay the bodies of hundreds of people, the result of an apparent mass suicide. Some of the bodies had their arms linked around friends, as if they had gone to face the afterlife together. All were members of a religious cult called "The People's Temple". Allegedly, they had been convinced to drink cyanide-laced Kool-Aid by their charismatic leader, an American religious leader and sometime-faith-healer called Jim Jones. His body was also found among the dead, but Jones had opted out of taking cyanide like his followers, dying instead of an apparent self-inflicted gunshot wound.

The events leading up to this massive loss of life (later estimated at over 900 fatalities) were equally strange. Jones, the son of a member of the racially-intolerant Ku Klux Klan, surprisingly preached a doctrine that called for a better world where there was harmony between the races. He dreamt of building a version of Utopia. Considering himself the reincarnation of not only Jesus Christ but also

Vladimir Lenin, Jones founded his People's Temple in Ukiah, California. His followers, who were mostly black, were kept in line by Jones' own security force, who relieved the cult members of all the money they had, which generally arrived in the form of government assistance cheques.

Reports that followers who tried to leave his Temple were abused and sometimes died, prompted Jones to move to the more anonymous San Francisco, where he was able to expand his Temple. As the media continued to hound him, in 1977, Jones decided on a spot deep in the jungles of South America as the location for his "Utopia". Without question, his followers moved with him, and he was able set up the infamous "Jonestown", a community in which he was the only law.

But still the reports of abuse continued. By 1978, the furore was so loud that it prompted US Congressman Leo Ryan to fly down to Guyana to look into the problem for himself. On 18 November, 1978, Ryan entered Jonestown, along with a few curious reporters and the deputy chief of the US mission to Guyana, Richard Dwyer. As they were

above Kool-Aid laced with cyanide killed many of the believers at Jonestown.

preparing to return to the US from a nearby airfield, the entire investigative party, with the mysterious exception of Dwyer, was shot dead.

Shortly after the killings took place on the airfield – or perhaps as he gave the order that lead to the deaths of the investigators – Jones issued his suicide order. Within hours, the People's Temple turned into a charnel house. Jonestown, as an example of the lethal power of religious cult leaders, was disturbing enough. But as time passed, it became clear that there was more to Jonestown than simple religious mania. Soon, the highest levels of the US Government were implicated, adding a new dimension of horror to an already sickening tragedy.

THE STRANGE PART

Even though Jones' body was found in Jonestown, dead from a self-inflicted gunshot wound, the apparent suicide weapon was found 200 feet from the body. This would indicate that either Jones was murdered himself, or it wasn't Jones at all. Close examination of the corpse revealed that it lacked Jones' tattoos...

THE USUAL SUSPECTS

Jim Jones

Jones' history reveals he was more than a simple faith healer. He was a fund raiser for politicians, including the impeached President Richard Nixon. While he professed grandiose ideals of Utopia, he was a strong supporter of the Republican Party. In 1961, he worked for a year in Brazil, rumoured to be doing work for the CIA. It was this work, or rather the $10,000 he earned from it, that allowed him to set up his first Temple in Ukiah. While in Jonestown, his followers were numbed with drugs, fed next to nothing, worked as slave labour and were forced to run through practice "suicide drills". Jones may have been running a massive mind-control experiment in Jonestown, with the help of the CIA. When it became apparent that the news would be released after Ryan's visit. Jones simply erased the evidence.

The CIA

There are several links with the CIA and Jones. Aside from his work in Brazil, Jones' associates included a member of UNITA, the CIA-sponsored Angolan army, and Dan Mitrione, who worked for another CIA-bankrolled outfit, the International Police Academy. Jones' mind-control experiments in Guyana could easily have been an extension of the CIA's MK-Ultra work, undertaken in a location far from the prying media. In fact, drugs used in Mk-Ultra were also found in Jonestown. It's also interesting to note that Dwyer, the sole survivor of Ryan's party, was listed in the book Who's Who In The CIA.

The US Government

The US Embassy helped Jones move his temple into Guyana, and when its was reported that cult members had been shot, not poisoned, it was discovered that a group of American Green Berets had been in the area. Green Berets are valued for their skill in covert killing, and were a favourite tool of the military in Vietnam. A cover up was suspected, especially with the US government's reluctance to return bodies of the dead to their families. Many bodies were "accidentally" cremated.

UNUSUAL SUSPECTS

Worldvision

A world-wide evangelical order, Worldvision has been long suspected of working with the CIA. After the Jonestown deaths, Worldvision repopulated the village with ex-CIA Laotian mercenaries. Ex-Worldvision employees include John Hinckley Jr (would-be assassin of Reagan) and Mark David Chapman (assassin of John Lennon). Both assassins, according to some theorists, were under the influence of mind-control when they acted.

The Process

New evidence has emerged linking Jones' early time in California with members of the English religious group known as The Process Church – a cult that emerged from Scientology, mixing "brain-cleansing" techniques with Gnostic beliefs. Although Process had melted away from the scene by the time of Jonestown, its influence on Jones may not have been entirely positive, just as its involvement with Charles Manson may not have been entirely beneficial to Sharon Tate.

MOST CONVINCING EVIDENCE

When coroner C Leslie Mootoo suggested that the Jonestown deaths were murder, not suicide, thus warranting investigation, the US Army disagreed. The bodies were left to rot in the sun.

MOST MYSTERIOUS FACT

Several people who could explain the truth about Jonestown, including ex-Jones aide Michael Prokes, and authors Jeanie and Al Mills, have been found murdered.

SCEPTICALLY SPEAKING

Given that Jones chose to pick most of his followers from the ranks of the poor and minority groups, it is no surprise that so little fuss was kicked up. The mass suicide of a cult is tragic, but hardly unexpected. It happened before Jonestown, it has happened plenty of times since and it will continue to happen while figures such as Jones only come to the attention of authorities when it is far too late to save anyone.

THE OKLAHOMA BOMBING

On April 19, 1995, a massive explosion in Oklahoma City, Oklahoma destroyed a huge part of a Federal office building, killing many of the people inside. Until that moment, America considered itself immune to terrorist attack, lulling itself into a false sense of security by glossing over terrorist attacks such as the bombing of the World Trade Center. The Oklahoma bombing was high-profile however, and, as well as killing and injuring a lot of people, it also inflicted some nasty wounds on the US national psyche.

Timothy McVeigh, a Gulf War veteran, was convicted of the bombing. Certainly, there is plenty of evidence that he was peculiar enough to have carried it out. He sent a series of letters to his sister some considerable time before the bombing took place, in which he wrote about his "anger and alienation". These letters included comments about committing suicide, about dropping out of society and into hiding, and about the government of the "Evil King". The letters were so disturbing that McVeigh's family suspected him of being the Oklahoma bomber almost immediately. His sister believes that McVeigh's mania against the government stemmed from the army's insistence that he repay them $1,000 that he had been overpaid.

McVeigh had applied for Special Forces training, and had failed the assessment course. He claimed in one of his letters that his assessment at Fort Bragg had revealed that he would be in line for performing several unsavoury duties should he make the grade. Special Forces operatives, he alleged, could be required to work with civilian police, silencing – killing – people who were considered a security risk. They would also be expected to help "the CIA fly drugs into the USA to fund covert operations." It was the evil nature of these assignments that turned McVeigh against the US government.

But is McVeigh actually? There is some evidence to suggest Middle Eastern terrorist involvement in the bombing. Investigative journalist Kelly Patricia O'Meara discovered that Timothy McVeigh's convicted co-conspirator, Terry Nichols, attended a meeting in the early Nineties on the island of Mindanao in the Philippines – a hotbed of fundamentalist activities – at which Ramzi Yousef was present. The themes of the meeting were Bombing activities, providing firearms and ammunition, training in making and handling bombs. Later, Yousef came to prominence as one of those involved in the World Trade Centre bombing in 1993.

Many eyewitnesses saw individuals identified as being of Middle Eastern extraction speeding away from the Murrah Federal Building just before the blast in a pick-up truck. It has also emerged that McVeigh was seen in the company of at least one Iraqi refugee, who had been brought to live in Oklahoma City as part of President Clinton's program to bring several thousand Iraqis into the US for resettlement.

THE STRANGE PART

Rather than looking objectively at Jayna Davis' excellent research, virtually all of the Oklahoma City and national media adopted the Bill Clinton-Janet Reno thesis that the OKC bombing was a domestic "right-wing" attack and rejected out of hand any evidence of foreign ties to the bombing. A careful review of Davis' extensive evidence and our own parallel investigation quickly convinced this writer that Davis was on solid ground. Of the thousands of Justice Department and FBI agents involved in the investigation, none ever interview the Iraqi community in Oklahoma or pursue some of McVeigh's associates in the spook field.

THE USUAL SUSPECTS
The CIA

A large amount of evidence has emerged over the last few years to suggest that a cabal of senior military and security officers were planning a coup to remove President Clinton from office due to their disgust at his alleged political and financial corruption. Two days before the bombing a plane carrying many members of this cabal crashed in Alabama. It is believed by some that the CIA created the disaster in Oklahoma as a diversion to prevent investigation into the planned coup and a focus for national unity at a time when the Presidency could have been jeopardized by further military revolt.

The Ku Klux Klan

A local major Grand Wizard in the Oklahoma Ku Klux Klan and local leader White Aryan Resistance had met McVeigh and was an associate of Terry Nichols. The leader – banned from entering Canada and the United Kingdom and classified by Interpol as a terrorist – was never even questioned. This has forced some to the unsettling conclusion that the KKK may not only have been involved in the bombing, but may have also received some form of secret service support.

THE UNUSUAL SUSPECTS
Christian Identity

This is the American version of the British Israelite movement. It claims that white Americans are the true descendants of Moses. Certainly, the Identity is very popular with right-wing maniacs and it may have been involved in the bombing. There have been suggestions that McVeigh was acting on the instructions of a powerful Christian Identity leader to help fulfil the prophecies leading to the return of Christ.

above left Until 9/11, the Oklahoma City bombing was the worst terrorist outrage the US had ever experienced.

MOST CONVINCING EVIDENCE

The failure of the FBI to conduct even cursory interviews with obvious suspects and to pursue potentially interesting leads is unsettling in the extreme. Either it was criminal neglect of duty or part of a deliberate effort to ensure they got a suspect who fitted the theory that it was a simple attack by domestic right-wing elements.

MOST MYSTERIOUS FACT

In 2002 it emerged that certain Pentagon officials believed that Timothy McVeigh was working in conjunction with Iraqis due to the fact that he was in possession of Iraqi telephone numbers. However, this revelation may have been a smokescreen to throw investigators off the track since it emerged that Chandra Levy's disappearance may have been related to McVeigh's execution.

SCEPTICALLY SPEAKING

To believe that there is more to the Oklahoma bombing than we have officially been told implies some degree of authority collusion in the deaths of scores of innocent government workers. At the very least it means the authorities were not interested in getting the real culprits – surely too big a leap into the darkness on the basis of the facts currently available.

WACO

On Sunday, February 28, 1993, at around 9:30am, the US Bureau of Alcohol, Tobacco and Firearms (BATF) attempted to enforce a search warrant at premises occupied by a religious cult – the Mount Carmel stronghold in Waco, Texas. Besides wanting to search the compound occupied by the apocalyptic Branch Davidians for a suspected illegal stockpile of explosives and firearms, the agents also carried an arrest warrant for the charismatic leader of the cult, David Koresh.

Something went terribly wrong. A gun battle erupted between the agents and members of the Branch Davidians, leaving four agents dead and 16 wounded. Several Branch Davidians were also killed or wounded. Pulling back, the BATF initiated a siege of the Mount Carmel compound that lasted 51 days. It involved the FBI, the Attorney General, Janet Reno, and President Bill Clinton. It ended in a

mysterious fire, with Mount Carmel burning to the ground – an event that was broadcast live on CNN. In the ashes, investigators found the bodies of 17 children and over 60 adults, among them the body of Koresh himself.

Questions quickly surfaced as to how the stand-off could spin out of control so rapidly after 50 days of relatively peaceful negotiations. As the FBI propelled tear gas into the compound from combat engineering vehicles (CEVs), they also knocked down walls with the machines, possibly killing children inside the compound – children that the government repeatedly told the media it was trying to protect. The sudden fire later that day is also questioned, with both sides blaming the other for starting it.

Since that fateful day in 1993, Waco has become a symbol of many things – from the cost of fervent religious belief, to the ruthlessness of a government trying to cover up its own mistakes.

THE STRANGE PART

As a justification for sending tear gas into Mount Carmel, Janet Reno, the newly-appointed Attorney General, stated that the Branch Davidians were beating babies inside the compound. Janet Reno relied upon the FBI for her information, and the FBI later admitted that there was no proof to confirm the truth of the assertion she had been led to make.

THE USUAL SUSPECTS
The BATF and FBI

There is still some question as to who actually fired first at the start of the siege, and there are rumours that the BATF may have been either a little gun-happy or ill-prepared for the raid on the compound. In Congressional hearings that followed the grisly end to the siege, BATF agents, not surprisingly, claimed that the Branch Davidians fired first. Directly after the raid, however, one agent claimed to have fired first – killing a dog. He later retracted that story. The Branch Davidians stand by their claim that they only fired when fired upon. The BATF also claimed that Koresh's people were manufacturing methamphetamines – another assertion, later shown to be a lie.

The FBI also did its part to inflame the situation. One team of agents deliberately harassed the Davidians by playing loud music (such as Tibetan chants and Christmas tunes) through the night, directing blinding spotlights into the compound, and shutting off their electricity. The team of negotiators felt these activities weakened their attempts to end the siege peacefully. The FBI wasn't entirely truthful in its reports to Janet Reno. Reportedly, Reno was apprehensive about an attack on the compound, but quickly changed her mind when a FBI agent remarked about the possibility of child abuse – a possibility that was never substantiated. A simple desire by the BATF for revenge could also have played a significant part.

David Koresh

Koresh believed himself to be the reincarnation of Jesus Christ, and the siege of his compound would have given reality to his apocalyptic visions. He was fascinated by the Book of Revelations, and throughout the siege, talked about writing a manuscript to explain the meaning of the Seven Seals. He claimed to be in contact with God, who reportedly gave him advice throughout the ordeal. The FBI also endured several rambling sermons over the phone from Koresh. The burning of the compound would be a fitting end in Koresh's messianic eyes, since his beloved Revelations spoke of the World itself ending in fire. This may explain why the Davidians displayed signs that read "Flames Await".

Bill Clinton

While Clinton professed concern about the children inside the compound, he also made it clear that the decision to gas the compound was Janet Reno's alone. Having washed his hands of blame, Clinton could have been using the Waco tragedy as a way of improving his political image – as a no-nonsense President.

THE UNUSUAL SUSPECTS
The New World Order

A favourite theory of the Far Right is that Waco was evidence of a United Nations plot to disarm everyday Americans in preparation for the imminent implementation of a One World Government, the dreaded New World Order. Why else raid a compound for guns in a state like Texas, where everyone owns at least one gun?

Neo-Nazi Conspiracy

David Koresh and the Branch Davidians may have been agents of a global Nazi conspiracy, dedicated to resurrecting the Third Reich and giving Hitler's public image a more positive spin. Other members of this conspiracy include right-wing conservatives like Pat Buchanan, and racist skinheads everywhere. "Remember Waco" has become a battle cry for neo Nazis in the States, apparently.

Gun Control Advocates

Waco may have been orchestrated by gun control advocates, possibly working in conjunction with Clinton's Democratic Party, as a way of demonstrating the dangers of allowing just about anyone to own a gun.

MOST CONVINCING EVIDENCE

In his controversial documentary, filmmaker Mike McNulty showed helicopter machine guns firing into the compound.

The documentary also showed a tank attack and the presence of a Delta force military unit. Muzzle flashes captured on film suggest government forces are shooting into the compound – all of which seems to undercut government claims that its force was fired on first and only engaged only in defensive fire.

MOST MYSTERIOUS FACT

Shortly before his tragically early death from cancer, comedian and major conspiracy buff, Bill Hicks, had obtained video evidence that seemed to disprove many of the FBI's claims about the last hours at the compound. In his routines Hicks always joked that if you knew the truth, you were next in line for the magic bullet.

SCEPTICALLY SPEAKING

If Koresh had had his own television show and dressed in a bad suit, he'd not only have been left alone, but called a pillar of the community.

COMET IMPACTS

Throughout the history of the Earth, comets have been slamming into our planet and changing the course of history. It is well known that asteroid and comet impacts occur regularly to all the planets in the solar system. Just a few years ago, Jupiter was hit by the comet Shoemaker-Levy, which inflicted a million-megaton blast on the gas giant. Sooner or later, a gigantic comet is going to smack into us, and plunge our planet into a nuclear-style winter.

Internationally-renowned geologist Professor Alexander Tollmann of the University of Vienna has suggested that the flood experienced by Noah was in fact caused by a comet that hit the Earth 12,000 years ago. The flood is recorded in several of the world's religions, and although religious texts are notably poor as a source of historical information, the stories they tell about the flood are backed up by the myths and legends of almost every prehistoric society. While firm information is understandably sketchy over such huge periods of time, linguistic and anthropological research dates these legends to around 10,000BC.

There is scientific evidence in the form of greatly-increased levels of Carbon-14 radioactive material found in fossilized trees that were alive at the time of the flood. The impact would have devastated ozone layers, causing greater production of the Carbob-14 radioactive isotope. By referring to myths that tell of seven burning suns and other great disasters, Tollmann believes he can date the impact to precisely 9,600BC.

The scientific community accepts other comet impacts. In 1905, a comet is known to have exploded over Tunguska in Siberia with the force of 30 megatons, devastating more than 50 square miles (well, assuming it wasn't an alien craft...). Similarly, the extinction of the dinosaurs 65 million years ago is thought to have been the result of climatic changes that ran their course over several thousand years that were started by the impact of a giant comet.

THE STRANGE PART

On March 11, 1998, the Smithsonian Astrophysical Observatory announced that Asteroid 1997XF11, discovered in December 1997 by Jim Scotti of the University of Arizona, would pass extremely close to the Earth in the year 2028. It was estimated that the huge rock, some 2km across, could get as close to the Earth as 48,000 miles. The asteroid 1997XF11 was immediately placed on the Potentially Hazardous Asteroid (PHA) list because the Earth could end up directly in the path of the asteroid with only slight variations in some of the factors that were

used to calculate its path. A NASA team quickly disagreed, saying that there was no chance that 1997XF11 would hit. The next day, the Smithsonian team retracted their suggestion, agreeing with NASA.

THE USUAL SUSPECTS

NASA

It has been alleged that NASA may want to cover up the impending impact of a major asteroid such as 1997XF11, or the more recently discovered asteroid 2003QQ47. By keeping the forthcoming disaster a secret, NASA has the time to prepare to prevent its impact without causing a panic. Alternatively, it will have the time and foreknowledge to make itself ready to be the one organization ready to takeover whatever is left of the world once the object has wiped civilization as we know it off the planet. Either way, by keeping quiet and persuading the public that the object is not going to hit earth, they are at least preventing mass terror and anarchy engulfing the world in the meantime.

THE UNUSUAL SUSPECTS

The Elder Race

Some conspiriologists believe there was an advanced civilization on the Earth before ours – the Elder Race. Most of the Elder Race was wiped out by a global catastrophe – possibly a comet impact – but hidden remnant of survivors have been controlling the destiny of mankind for thousands of years via a selection of secret societies. The aim of the remaining members of the Elder Race is to help mankind make technological progress until we possess a technology advanced enough to deal with the next big comet impact.

MOST CONVINCING EVIDENCE

Whenever an astronomer warns the public that an asteroid is on a possible collision cause with earth, it seems as if it will only be a matter of days before they and others will issue a correction claiming a false alarm. One notable example of this happened in 2003 when the warning was issued that the [add metric] 0.75-mile rock known as QQ47 would hit us in 2014. Just days later, the panic was over. Possibly most astronomers are just bad at their job, or enjoy scaring the public. However, it seems much more likely that someone is forcing the retractions or announcements are encouraged to get us used to the idea of an approaching impact being inevitable.

MOST MYSTERIOUS FACT

Victor Clube, Professor of Astrophysics at Oxford University, agrees that Tollmann's theory about the origins of Noah's flood is entirely plausible. Clube suggests that a large comet impact 1,500 years ago was behind the Fall of Civilization and the ensuing Dark Ages in Europe.

SCEPTICALLY SPEAKING

When the Smithsonian and NASA teams first evaluated the data on 1997XF11, they were using a fairly small amount of information, so the margin of error was high. As soon as the media started getting panicky, other researchers provided more extensive data. Within 24 hours, all involved had calculated the asteroid's path based on studying around eight years' worth of orbital data, and in doing so reduced the margin of error considerably. The asteroid should miss us by hundreds of thousands of miles.

GULF WAR SYNDROME

The 1991 Gulf War was considered a success by the media and the US government: the Iraqi forces, led by Saddam Hussein, were driven out of Kuwait by the superior military strength of the United States and the coalition forces. But while George Bush and Colin Powell still bask in the glow from that military victory, a more malignant reminder plagues thousands of soldiers involved in the War. It is an insidious disease that has puzzled doctors and destroys the lives of those it affects – it is called GWS, or more commonly, Gulf War Syndrome.

A list of the symptoms of Gulf War Syndrome illustrates how debilitating it can be: night sweats, disturbances of the nervous system, tumors, drastic weight loss, diarrhoea, insomnia, chronic fatigue, intense joint discomfort, bizarre rashes, disturbing personality changes, and loss of mental faculties. There have also been reports of extensive blood loss. GWS is a vicious and virulent affliction, which unsurprisingly leads many sufferers into severe depressions, and even suicide.

Despite seemingly inarguable evidence that soldiers contracted the disease while fighting for their countries, the existence of Gulf War Syndrome is denied by many governments, including the US. Having risked their lives in what many consider to be a war more about oil prices than about human freedom, these soldiers now find themselves abandoned by their governments.

THE STRANGE PART

In 2003 fear of Gulf War Syndrome was so strong among British soldiers preparing to go to the Gulf for the invasion of Iraq that many of them refused to take an anthrax vaccine. Large numbers rejected other vaccines as well. Their concern was so strong that they were more willing to let themselves be vulnerable to biological attack than trust the Ministry of Defence's claims that all the vaccines it was giving to troops were safe.

THE USUAL SUSPECTS

Saddam Hussein

While he may not have had many noticeable weapons of mass destruction in the second Gulf War, Saddam Hussein definitely had them during the first war. He had tested and used biological weapons against his enemies – most notably on the Kurdish people, wiping out entire villages. It is believed by some that he also used biological weapons against coalition forces, arming some of his Scud missiles with lethal doses of toxins. Deadly material could also have come from the smoking ruins of chemical factories and bombed-out Iraqi weapons bunkers, drifting across the dessert with the wind to infect coalition soldiers. Hussein may even have infected his own soldiers, hoping their dead bodies would transfer the disease to those who buried them later on.

below More soldiers have died of Gulf War Syndrome than have been killed by Iraqi military forces in both Gulf Wars.

Forced Inoculations

In preparation for a biological attack – that according to the US never happened – soldiers were forced to take pills and undergo inoculations. The pills, thought to be Pyridostigmine Bromide, and the vaccinations (including shots for anthrax), were extremely experimental. If they were not the direct cause of Gulf War Syndrome, these inoculations are thought to have aided in its spread.

THE UNUSUAL SUSPECTS

The Soviets

Hussein is thought to have obtained some of the most virulent bio-weapons from the Soviet arsenal prior to 1989. Among them may have been the dreaded "Novichok" series – at the time of its making, one of the most feared toxins known to man. If this was the case, it might explain many aspects of GWS.

MOST CONVINCING EVIDENCE

The numbers of infected soldiers speak for themselves. Estimates place the number of sick soldiers at well over 150,000, with some 10,000 already dead from GWS. (These numbers may be optimistic.) An examination of GWS points clearly to a virus that is not natural, but shows all the earmarks of having been produced in a laboratory.

One of the chief suspects for GWS is a manufactured agent called Mycoplasma fermentans (incognitus). It contains the majority of the (HIV) envelope gene, which is suspected to have been added in its laboratory modification. Of all the countries involved in the Gulf War coalition, only France refused to undergo inoculations. So far, there have been no reports of GWS among French soldiers.

MOST MYSTERIOUS FACT

Many soldiers thought that GWS was caused by exposure to radiation. When Gulf War veteran Stephen Childs died from cancer in 2000, he asked in his Will for the coroner to investigate his death. However, the coroner dismissed his wishes to examine whether multiple inoculations and working in an area contaminated by depleted uranium brought on his cancer. He also refused to try to find out why, since his return from the conflict, Mr Childs' sweat had begun to smell of latex.

SCEPTICALLY SPEAKING

It all comes down to money. Governments continue to deny that any biological agents were used in the Gulf and refuse to admit that forced inoculations might be to blame for GWS. If they admit that there was, the question of legal liability comes up. That is not going to happen.

TWA FLIGHT 800

It is perhaps the greatest unspoken fear of every air passenger – that the craft in which they are travelling will crash. While many pretend to be blasé about air travel, few escape a momentary fear at some point during a flight. This horrible fear was realized for the passengers and crew of TWA Flight 800 on July 17, 1996. Eleven minutes into the journey from New York's Kennedy Airport, destined for Paris, France, the Boeing 747 suddenly exploded about ten miles from Long Island, killing everyone on board.

An investigation into the disaster was quickly launched, with boats out collecting the wreckage from the plane, searching for some clue as to what may have caused the explosion – an explosion that gave no warning, according to evidence later found on the craft's black box recorders. Finally, the National Transportation Safety Board, after investigating with the FBI and the CIA, determined that Flight 800 crashed because its centre-wing fuel tank had exploded. Arcing between two wires, with a spark igniting the jet's volatile fuel might have caused this. The investigation was then closed down.

Many people dispute those findings. Eyewitnesses claim to have seen something arcing into the sky after Flight 800, with much speculation that what they saw was a surface-to-air missile. Was Flight 800 hit by a terrorist attack, or was it something far darker – such as a missile fired by the US Military? In the eyes of the US government, the case is closed, but in the eyes of conspiracy theorists, including members of the military and the airlines themselves, there was no investigation – only a cover up.

THE STRANGE PART

Dr Vernon Grose, who had served as a board member of the National Transportation Safety Board, had defended the board's official explanation for the crash of Flight 800. He changed his mind and began to feel that there was, indeed, a cover up. He pointed his finger at the FBI and its suspicious suppression of eyewitness testimony that what appeared to be a missile had hit Flight 800.

above The crash was a tragedy, but was it also a conspiracy?

THE USUAL SUSPECTS

The US Military

The US military may have been practising manoeuvres, including the firing of missiles, in an area designated as W-105, located off the southeast coast of Long Island. A Navy "hot area", W-105 is about 30 miles away from where TWA Flight 800 mysteriously exploded. In a potentially lethal gaffe, the first report of the accident is thought to have come from the Pentagon, which is again highly suspicious, particularly as the snippet of news was quickly covered up. The airspace surrounding TWA Flight 800 was heavy with military aircraft that night, once again indicating possible military involvement.

A photograph taken by Linda Kabot, reproduced in Paris Match, clearly shows a missile in the sky at the time Flight 800 exploded – there's a clear view of a cylindrical object with the bright light of an exhaust at one end. Her photograph was discounted by authorities on the basis that she was facing away from the actual explosion when she took the picture. This poses the disturbing question of just how many missiles are flying around American airspace at any given time. It's interesting to note that the FBI paid little heed to such eyewitness reports in its investigation.

Terrorists

The popular image was of terrorists firing a rocket from a dinghy. While this is almost certainly not the case, it does not mean that there was not a terrorist plot. Given the subsequent use of surface to air missiles by groups such as al Qaeda, the likelihood of terrorists being linked to the downing of Flight 800 has become a widely held view in conspiracy circles.

THE UNUSUAL SUSPECTS

UFO Attack

Flight 800 could have run across a UFO, which was monitoring the military activity below. The UFO destroyed the plane as a reaction to being discovered.

Military Black Ops

A secret base is rumoured to be in the area near where Flight 800 went down. "Project Phoenix" is thought to be an underground, top-secret facility located at Montauk Air Force Base, which is itself thought to be abandoned. A possibility exists that Flight 800 was destroyed by a secret weapon from this base, which would explain the cover up, undertaken in the name of American national security.

MOST CONVINCING EVIDENCE

Data taken from nearby air traffic control towers clearly show a blip appearing on radar screens. This blip then rises, and begins to follow Flight 800. It is later seen to move to the front of the plane before merging with the plane's flight path.

MOST MYSTERIOUS FACT

The Navy didn't find the black box recorders for a week, claiming the locator beacons had broken. Subsequent investigation showed this not to be so, suggesting the boxes were found earlier than reported and were tampered with so the data fitted with the military's story.

SCEPTICALLY SPEAKING

Two words: lawsuit; avoidance.

9/11

On September 11, 2001, American Airlines Flight 11 took off from Logan International Airport in Boston at 7.59a.m. It hit the first of the World Trade Center's twin towers at 8.46a.m. United Airlines Flight 175 departed from Logan heading for Los Angeles at 8.14a.m. It hit the second tower at 9.03a.m. American Airlines Flight 77 left Washington's Dulles International Airport at 8.10a.m. and crashed into the Pentagon at 9.43 a.m. United Airlines Flight 93 left Newark and smashed into a field in Pennsylvania at 10.10a.m. More than 3,000 innocent lives from 80 countries across the globe were taken within the space of a few hours. The world changed forever, and many of us saw it happen live on TV.

In the aftermath, President George W Bush caught the mood of America and much of the Western world when he called it, "Our Pearl Harbor". Reeling from the shock of this evil, two days on, US Secretary of State Colin Powell broke the news that Osama bin Laden was the prime suspect. There was no surprise when later, the President announced the beginning of the "war on terrorism".

In our struggle to make sense of why the tragedy happened, the majority of us have unquestionably accepted the official version: the hijacts were not preventable, they were the result of an attack planned by the al Quaeda terror network alone and no one outside that organization had prior knowledge. In the wake of the tragedy, George W Bush made a speech saying, "Let us never tolerate outrageous conspiracy theories concerning the attacks of September 11th." To most people, this seems like an entirely sensible and heartfelt plea, while others see it as a desperate attempt to frighten and subtly threaten those who continue to probe the inconsistencies in the official version of the terrible events of that day.

There is a part of us that feels the need for conspiracy theories to try and give meaning to things that do not make obvious sense. And there is a strong part of us that naturally refuses to give any credence to any conspiracy concerning something as large, emotive and awful as the events of 9/11. However, certain questions refuse to be easily dismissed and the heart of many of the conspiracy theories surrounding 9/11 comes down to the central question of who had the power to call off or reduce the usual security precautions that may have prevented the attacks. Even for the average person in the street, who does not wish to hear any talk of a 9/11 conspiracy, some things push the boundaries of credibility. After two commercial airliners had already crashed into the World Trade Center, another commercial airliner was able to fly across a No-fly Zone during what should have been the highest of security alerts. It was then able to crash into the headquarters of the most powerful military force to have ever existed in the history of our planet. Just how could this happen without any serious attempt by the military to prevent it?

These and other questions become even more pressing because a raft of evidence has emerged since that fateful day, which suggests that the North American Aerospace Defense Command (NORAD) and almost all other elements of the American defence and intelligence system knew that a terrorist attack was imminent. US Attorney General Ashcroft had been advised to travel only by private jet on September 11 and, the previous night, a group of top Pentagon officials suddenly cancelled travel plans for September 11 apparently because of security concerns.

On March 25, 2002, Congresswoman Cynthia McKinney, a democrat from Georgia, claimed during a radio interview, "We knew there were numerous warnings of the events to come on September 11. What did this Administration know, and when did it know it about the events of September 11? Who else knew and why did they not warn the innocent people of New York, who were needlessly murdered?" Despite being attacked by the President's spokesman for, "Running for the Hall of Fame of the Grassy Knoll Society", the following months proved McKinney right. Evidence emerged that even the President himself had comprehensive briefing on August 6, 2001, detailing that bin Laden was determined to strike in the US and would most likely hijack plans.

This, and dozens of other startling revelations show that the Administration and the US intelligence agencies, especially the CIA and the NSA, had known an attack was imminent and it had been in a position to warn America. However, it had decided not to. Why? Could it really be true that there were those with the power not only to warn of a planned attack, but to prevent it, too?

THE STRANGE PART

British politician Michael Meacher, who served as a government minister under Tony Blair for six years, claimed that the US government knew about the September 11 attack on New York, but for strategic reasons they chose not to act on the warnings. He said, "The US failure to avert the 9/11 attacks was an invaluable pretext for attacking Afghanistan in a war that had clearly already been well planned in advance. The overriding motivation for this political smokescreen is that the US and the UK are beginning to run out of secure hydrocarbon energy supplies."

THE USUAL SUSPECTS
CIA AND AMERICAN OIL COMPANIES

Major US oil interests had been negotiating with the Taliban to build a pipeline through Afghanistan to transport the large oil reserves of land-locked Kazakhstan and other newly independent Soviet Republics. When Clinton hardened his line against the Taliban, they plotted 9/11 alongside the CIA, so that the US would invade Afghanistan and install a puppet regime in Kabul friendly to American oil concerns.

ISRAEL

By utilising their vast network of sleeper agents with the US defence and intelligence community, Mossad was able to set up bin Laden as the biggest patsy of all time and ensure that the US would be drawn into a prolonged conflict with the Islamic world. Israel would benefit as any retaliation for the attacks by the US would drive a wedge between the US and its Gulf and Near East allies serving it, bringing it closer to the one country at the forefront of fighting an ongoing war with Islamic extremists – Israel.

THE UNUSUAL SUSPECTS

CHINA

Problem: Islamic extremists causing trouble in your far-flung provinces, America blocking your planned invasion of Taiwan and much of the rest of South East Asia. Solution: Create a situation where your two biggest rivals fight themselves to a standstill while you sit back and laugh.

DRUG BARONS

The Taliban regime in Afghanistan had all but closed down the world's most productive opium fields. Heads of the major drug cartels organized 9/11 to implicate al Qaeda and lead the US into war with the end result that the Taliban would be ousted and Afghan opium production and export would no longer be frozen. If that was the plan, it certainly worked.

MOST CONVINCING EVIDENCE

The staggering ineptness of NORAD, the organization in charge of protecting North Ameirca's airspace, raises doubts in many minds. Why did it order the scrambling of jets from Langley Air Force Base, more than 130 miles from Washington, to investigate Flight 77? Why not follow procedure and send jets from Andrews Air Force Base, 10 miles from Washington and the base meant to defend America's capital from attack? This is a vital question because it meant that the planes that were to defend Washington arrived nearly 15 minutes after Flight 77 had smashed into the Pentagon.

MOST MYSTERIOUS FACT

The passport of the alleged hijacker Mohamed seems to have reality-defying properties. While DNA techniques had to be used to try to identify victims, his passport was thrown intact and without a scratch from the devastating explosion that destroyed Flight 11 and astonishingly found in a matter of hours among 1.6 million tons of debris. However, the

indestructible passport was a stroke of luck for the FBI investigators trying to work out who was on the flight.

SCEPTICALLY SPEAKING

September 11 has given birth to more conspiracy theories than any other event in US history, aside from the assassination of JFK. Given the hurt and anger that the attacks generated, no one should be surprised by this. You can believe the theories, see them as symptoms of a traumatized country or deride them. Luckily, you still have the freedom to choose.

MARC DUTROUX

Belgium has a reputation for being the most boring country in Europe, its contributions to global culture being restricted to the creation of Tintin and the brewing of beer. However, the southern rust-belt of the country, made up of towns filled with redundant factories, empty warehouses and decaying streets that flow into a bleak countryside of rundown small farms, has placed Belgium firmly on the conspiracy map.

For it was near the town of Charleroi, a grimy place surrounded the polluted scars of its industrial heritage, that the abhorrent crimes of Marc Dutroux began to come to light. In 1986, Dutroux and his then-wife Michelle Martin, were arrested for the abductions and rape of five girls, for which they were both imprisoned. Three years later Dutroux was sentenced to 13 1/2 years in prison for his crimes, while Martin received a sentence of five years.

However, despite the obvious threat a paedophiliac rapist such as Dutroux could pose to children, he was surprisingly released early from prison in 1992. Within days of being outside, the supposedly unemployed Dutroux was able to tender 2.5 million Belgian francs in cash to buy a house and a plot of land. During the next three years, he would go on to buy a further six houses.

In June 1995, eight-year-old girls Julie Lejeune and Melissa Russo disappeared near their home in Grace-Hollogne, east Belgium. Dutroux, Martin and their accomplice, Bernard Weinstein, a drug addict who assisted in return for his fix, had abducted them. The girls were taken to one of Dutroux's properties in the Charleroi suburb of Marcinelle and imprisoned in a specially constructed dungeon in his cellar, which Dutroux kept hidden behind a concrete door disguised as a bookshelf. Over the next few months both girls were subjected to horrific sexual assaults which Dutroux routinely videoed.

Two months after the first abductions, 17-year-old An Marchal and 19-year-old Eefje Lambrecks were kidnapped while on holiday in Ostend. As the dungeon was already in use, Dutroux kept his latest victims tied to beds in one of his other homes. Within weeks, both An and Eefje were dead, as was Bernard Weinstein: Dutroux drugged and buried him alive in the garden where he had already interred the bodies of An and Eefje.

In May 1996, Dutroux and new accomplice, Michel Lelièvre, kidnapped 12-year-old Sabine Dardenne on her way to school and imprisoned her in the dungeon. On August 9, the two men abducted 14-year-old Laetitia Delhez as she walked home from a swimming pool. However, an eyewitness who had seen Laetitia being snatched remembered enough of Dutroux's licence plate for police to arrest him, his wife Michelle Martin and Lelièvre on August 13.

Two days later, Dutroux gave detectives information on where to find Sabine and Laetitia and the two girls were rescued from the dungeon. By August 15, police had also arrested Michel Nihoul, a 62-year old businessman with links to politicians, drug dealers and sex clubs in Brussels for his alleged involvement in the abductions. By the beginning of September, the police had recovered the bodies of all of Dutroux's victims and hundreds of pornographic videos of children being abused.

THE STRANGE PART

After Dutroux's arrest, police made a breakthrough in the case of Andre Cools, a leading figure in the Belgian Socialist Party, who had been assassinated in 1991. Police seized six men including a former Socialist Party colleague who had been in the same Freemasonry lodge as Cools. Before his assassination, Cools had been investigating political and criminal corruption.

However, Judge Connerotte, who was in charge of the Dutroux case and part of the related push to solve the Cools killing, was removed from his duties. Another judge, Guy Poncelet, claimed that his police officer son had been murdered for investigating Dutroux. At the same time it also emerged that Dutroux himself was claiming that he acted on behalf of a network of other people.

More than 300,000 Belgians took to the streets of their country protesting over the firing of Judge Connerotte. The "white marches", as they became known, were also a protest over the widespread belief that he was merely part of a wider conspiracy linked to the highest levels of governmental, policing and judicial systems.

THE USUAL SUSPECTS

Child-Sex Ring

Regina Louf, a witness in a separate Belgian investigation into an alleged child-sex ring, testified that she had seen both Dutroux and Michel Nihoul at orgies where she and other children were abused. Amongst other alleged guests at these abominable events were a number of influential people including a top politician, a senior judge, an EU commissioner and one of Belgium's leading bankers. Testimony by Louf and others seems to back up Dutroux's own claims that he was "used by others", and had acted on behalf of a powerful paedophile network. If it existed, this child-sex ring may have helped shield Dutroux from investigation and earlier capture.

Satanic Cult

It emerged at Dutroux's trial that his murdered former accomplice Bernard Weinstein had been part of a satanic cult called Abrasax. Many conspiriologists believe that Dutroux was involved with this group and a wider network of prominent secret Satanists in the ritual abuse of his victims.

Freemasons

Some of the police who were investigated for possible corruption or negligence over their role in the prosecution of Dutroux were known to be Freemasons. Given that assassinated politician Andre Cools, whose murder came to be seen as linked to the Dutroux affair, was a Freemason, it is not hard for conspiracy theorists with an anti-Masonic bent to see the hand of the infamous Brotherhood at work.

THE USUAL SUSPECTS

The Mafia

It is widely known in Interpol that the Italian Mafia has a strong presence in southern Belgium. Several investigations have shown links between organized Italian criminal groups and the funding of regional Belgian politicians. More than one researcher has come to the conclusion that Dutroux was working for Mafia masters making a vast profit from the paedophile pornography that he produced.

DGSE

France's external intelligence agency La Direction Générale de la Sécurité Extérieure (DGSE) is accused by some of being behind the Dutroux affair. The scandal certainly caused every key aspect of the Belgian state to be destabilised and brought into disrepute. It also brought the traditional enmity between the French-speaking Walloons of the south and the Dutch speakers of the northern Flemish region to a new boiling point. Were the DGSE trying to mastermind a splitting apart of Belgium with the subsequent southern region of Wallonia coming under French control?

MOST CONVINCING EVIDENCE

A 17-month Belgian parliamentary commission enquiry into the Dutroux affair reported that he did not have accomplices in high positions of the police and justice system. They believed he merely "profited from corruption, sloppiness and incompetence." The majority of Belgians were not convinced with this, believing the police had turned a deliberate blind eye to his atrocious activities. More than one prominent Belgian prison psychologist expressed a belief that Dutroux's early release in 1992 is highly suspicious and usually could only have been engineered by significant pressure from above.

Many researchers claim that the official report fails to explain why police ignored reports from Dutroux's sister and mother that he was keeping girls hostage.

Worse still was the fact that when the police had arrested Dutroux on an unrelated car theft charge they searched his house and heard cries for help from Julie Lejeune and Melissa Russo. However, they accepted Dutroux's claim that the noise was coming from children in the street. This was despite finding handcuffs, chloroform, vaginal cream and a gynaecological mirror during their search of the property

above The face of evil – Marc Dutroux leaves the suburban house where he kept his victims.

– the home of a convicted child rapist. Compounding these failures was the news, after his eventual arrest, that vital evidence, including DNA evidence that might have proved multiple people visited Dutroux's vile dungeon prison to abuse his captives, had been mysteriously lost.

MOST MYSTERIOUS FACT

Despite being "Belgium's most notorious sex criminal", authorities have been a bit slack when it comes to monitoring Dutroux while in prison. It has emerged that he was allowed to engage in a pen-pal relationship with a 15-year-old girl after being remanded in custody for the abductions. Even more mysteriously, "Belgium's most hated man" was able to escape from custody for a few hours in 1998. Six years later, a random prison search revealed someone had supplied him with a key to both his handcuffs and his cell.

SCEPTICALLY SPEAKING

Dutroux and the others charged with the horrific crimes may have only shouted conspiracy to try to gain some legal advantage in their trials. The grim incompetence of the police enquiry into Marc Dutroux was so massive and ubiquitous that it could not help but look conspiratorial. Sometimes, what appears to be an all-pervading conspiracy is nothing more than the covering up of cock-ups undertaken by officials trying to hold on to their jobs.

The widespread belief that unseen, powerful players masterminded the horrific events may purely be a reaction by a public unwilling to believe that such seemingly banal people could perpetrate such evil.

EPILOGUE

If Everything I Know Is Wrong... What's Really Happening?

95% of all conspiracy theories are bullshit.

I have said it. Spoken the uneasy truth most conspiriologists never want to publicly admit. I can expect to be shunned by fellow investigators in my favoured London watering holes. Invites to certain conspiracy conferences will get lost in the post. I should expect David Icke-like rumours to be whispered behind my back.

Trust me, after nearly two decades of parapolitical and conspiracy research, I can promise you that most conspiracies you read about are rubbish. Mole men from the earth's crust are not responsible for UFO sightings, Satanists do not run the Pentagon and JFK was not shot by his own secret service driver that damnable day in Dallas. Even the majority of apparently more realistic theories do not stand up to criteria of objectivity, Occam's razor and the minimal standard of proof required for publication by most newspapers. There is an awful lot of con in conspiracy.

The worst type of ridiculous conspiracy theory is the mega-conspiracy theory. The type of theory that tries to link everything up and pin the blame on one particular group. In the last 300 years, everyone from Jews to Freemasons, Roman Catholics to Communists have been accused of being that group. The conspiracy theory as a way of scapegoating and justifying the persecution can be seen in history as far back as the reign of the pharaoh Akhenaten in the fourteenth century BCE.

One of the most persistent and nakedly racially prejudiced mega-conspiracy theories is that Jews secretly control the world. Alleged evidence of a global Jewish conspiracy is often offered, but the evidence is clearly nonsense. When someone cites the Protocols of the Elders of Zion as proof of a Jewish plot to control the world, go to your library and read a copy of The Plot by Will Eisner. "The Protocols" might have been publicly endorsed by Winston Churchill and Henry Ford, they might be an excellent blueprint for secret world domination, but the only thing they prove is that big lies work. Even the objective evidence showing that a number of conspiratorial acts behind the creation of Israel is not de facto proof of a massive Jewish plot explaining the ills of the world.

Hitler loved the anti-Jewish mega-conspiracy theory, using it in conjunction with hoaxed "proof" such as "The Protocols" to grease the wheels of the trains that carried his victims to Bel ec, Jasenovac and Auschwitz-Birkenau. The Nazis also used conspiracy theories against other groups that would die in extermination camps – homosexuals, gypsies, Communists and Jehovah's Witnesses. Mega-conspiracy theories might be the worst type of rubbish, but that does not mean they cannot be deadly.

With so many conspiriologists promoting baseless, dangerous nonsense, and with the flood of incorrect, partial and inane information circulating on the Internet, is it any wonder that most academics view the C-word as dirty? As Dr Jeffrey Bale, a professor and one of the world's leading experts on terrorism and covert operations, once commented, "Very few notions generate as much intellectual resistance, hostility and derision within academic circles as a belief in the historical importance or efficacy of political conspiracies."

Yet the process of conspiracy and very real conspiracies are part of the normal structure of things. Politics, espionage and crime are all by their nature conspiratorial professions. I have seen at first-hand an intelligence agency use the media to keep the public in the dark over possible terrorist threats. I have seen a Prime Minister pressured into not adopting a policy by the threat of a huge multinational corporation withdrawing from a country. As a journalist I have seen a celebrity's agent do a deal to keep their client's sex scandal out of the papers by offering up dirt on another famous person. This is all everyday conspiratorial practice. Conspiracies large and small are the way of the world.

An example of a commonplace conspiracy that is rarely commented upon is how both sides in a war will create "photo opportunities" to highlight the opposing side's killing of innocent civilians. It is a standard propaganda trick used the world over. A sudden surge of international fury regarding this practice erupted in 2006 over what was known as the "Qana conspiracy".

Israeli and American commentators, hard-pressed to defend Israel's invasion of Lebanon, seized on Hezbollah claims that Israeli shells had killed 57 civilians, including 32 children in the south-east Lebanese village of Qana. They accused Hezbollah of shipping in bodies from other areas to milk international publicity and sympathy. It did not seem an unreasonable claim. Both Hezbollah and Israeli forces have staged such conspiratorial photo opportunities in the past. The only surprising thing was that the "Qana conspiracy" had been so quickly exposed and denounced in the global media.

However, the less-reported facts of what really happened in Qana illustrate another truism in conspiracy circles – a conspiracy does not have to be true to be widely believed. Impartial research proved whatever Hezbollah had or had not done, at least 41 people, 16 of them children, had died in Qana. Confronted with images of dead children, it seems that the natural reaction of supporters of the Israeli military was to shout conspiracy rather than recognize the grisly truth of war.

Conspiracies often thrive in circumstances where people do not want to accept the truth. When Enron chief and corporate fraudster Kenneth Lay died before he had served any jail time, justice had clearly not been served. An inability to accept this fact by some of his victims led to a raft of conspiracy theories. These often suggested that his death had been faked with the help of his friend President George W. Bush. The conspiracy version of events is easier to swallow for some because it portrays Lay not evading justice through a simple heart attack, but through the intervention of malicious forces. If malicious forces rather than blind fate are involved, it is easier to apportion blame. Human history shows we usually feel better for having someone else to blame when things do not turn out the way we want.

The most popular celebrity conspiracy theories relate to the deaths of the famous and well-loved. Fans often cannot handle their heroes and heroines dying through the callous randomness of accidents or self-inflicted stupidity of drugs. They create fabulous tales to explain away what they do not want to face up to – that the famous die just as easily as the rest of us.

When conspiracy theories relating to the drug-induced death of Anna Nicole Smith began circulating, the only thing that surprised me was how far the bar had fallen for a celebrity to be honoured with their own conspiracy theory. A few years ago you would have had to be a global icon like Marilyn Monroe to gain one, these days you can simply be a Marilyn wannabe. As the currency of celebrity has risen in Western culture, so has the celebrity's place in conspiracy research. These days even the most banal of famous people tend to feature in the frankly lunatic and baroque plots of certain fringe conspiriologists.

When you study conspiracies as a whole field, rather than as isolated cases, certain similarities emerge. Just as it is said that there are only seven basic stories that are ever told, it sometimes seems that there are only a dozen different types of conspiracy theory. The protagonists' and victims' names may change over the years, but the same theories keep on coming up. If you compare conspiracies relating to avian flu with those promulgated in the wake of SARS, they appear almost identical in architecture. Even the same suspects – the Chinese military, the World Health Organization and the Bilderbergers – get name-checked.

Another word for a conspiracy is plot and that is what many conspiracies are – plots, stories, narratives created to try and explain away the seemingly impossible. It seems so inexplicable, so illogical, that global poverty is still so rampant, that with all our technological marvels we have not found a cure for cancer or endless clean energy, and so conspiracy theories emerge. Often conspiracy theories are nothing more than alternative narratives, tapping into our inner fears and therefore making more sense than the official version of events. How much easier is it to believe that group "X" is responsible for global poverty than accept our own individual culpability for not making it our top priority when it comes to electing our political leaders?

People often ask me which conspiracies I believe in. I tell them, "The ones with the inescapable evidence." In terms of conspiracy theories with so much evidence of a conspiracy that they are fact not theory, none ranks higher than the murder of Robert F. Kennedy. Even the simplest of recorded details – the alleged assassin's gun held eight bullets, whilst 10 were fired – turn theory into disturbing reality.

Yet is there a major US politician who has made it part of his presidential platform to have the RFK case reopened? Are the US TV networks and papers running editorials denouncing the national shame that so obvious a plot still goes unprosecuted? No. It is left to individuals, like actor Robert Vaughn – known more for smashing conspiracies of THRUSH in one of his most famous roles as Napoleon Solo – to tirelessly fight for justice for his friend Bobby. The world needs more Robert Vaughns, more people awake to the realities of genuine conspiracies and prepared to stand up and demand they be tackled.

95% of all conspiracy theories are bullshit. However, the 5% that are not should keep you awake at night and make you so angry you could spit. The 5% should also be an antidote to your passivity. The 5% should make you prepared to do something about those forces that conspire against all of us, even if they only plan to kill just one man.

A–Z
OF COMMONLY
SUSPECTED
CONSPIRATORS

American Medical Association Some of the most paranoid conspiracy theories currently in circulation portray the American Medical Association as an organization dedicated to suppressing alternative, cheaper cures to a range of diseases from cancer to AIDS. The bizarre rational behind many of these alleged conspiracies is that the American Medical Association has no interest in promoting health, because healthy people do not require their expensive services. Of course, the American Medical Association is not in these fiendish schemes alone and its members are to be found conspiring with the giant pharmaceutical corporations and the American Academy of Science. Some also allege they are in league with the grey aliens who pay them to cover-up any evidence of implants in abductees.

Black Magicians With so many of the traditional good guys of our culture getting blamed for plotting hideous conspiracies against the rest of us, it is reassuring to know that at least one traditional bane of humanity gets some of the blame from time to time. Involved in phenomena ranging from cattle mutilations to Big Foot, Black Magicians are said to be working their dread powers to harm society at large. If certain researchers are to be believed, being a Black Magician is a good career path, as it can take you as far as the White House or even to starring roles in hit Hollywood movies.

Cathars A heretical Christian sect, the Cathars were ruthlessly suppressed and seemingly eradicated from Europe in a Papally-sanctioned crusade. Some conspiracy theorists feel that the Cathars are still active behind several significant conspiracies. Whether their former fortress in the Montsegur area of France contained a hidden treasure that fuelled the rise of the Knights Templar, or whether the sect held special knowledge about Jesus Christ that could have blown the medieval church asunder, is hard to determine today. Modern conspiracy theories point to the Cathars' main aims as being revenge on France and the Papacy, as well as the more usual global domination.

Defence Intelligence Agency A super-secret branch of the United States intelligence community, the DIA has been accused of being the controller of the MIB and of master-minding the UFO cover-up, fulfilling the same role as SI8 in the UK. In one of the most bizarre court actions of all time, a plaintiff in California named the DIA as one of the many guilty parties when she tried to sue the US government for $5.6 billion. She claimed she had been turned into a cyborg as part of a secret holocaust program against black women in America. The case was dismissed – whether or not the decision was influenced by the power of the DIA and the conspiracy she was trying to expose is anyone's guess.

Elder Race Some orthodox archaeologists are willing to admit that evidence of water erosion on the Sphinx could mean that it was built in 9,000 BC. No surprise, then, that conspiracy theories revolving around the idea that our current civilization may have been pre-dated by an even more advanced one thousands of years ago, have been gaining credibility. Plots to suppress this knowledge while the military exploit the remains of this Elder Race's technology may be hard to prove, but seem less outlandish when you turn a conspiracy buff's eye on the links between NASA, the Giza plateau in Egypt, and sections of the military-industrial complex. Suggestions that surviving remnants of the Elder Race themselves are behind the cover-up are definitely in TBTB territory.

Food and Drug Administration The FDA, as it is commonly known, is the body responsible for licensing medicines in the USA. As such, it is cited in a whole host of medical conspiracies that are designed to keep the public ill and ensure that drug companies, doctors and hospitals can make very healthy profits. Alleged to be run by everyone from communists to a secret order of German mystics, the FDA was also responsible for the downfall of orgasm guru Wilhelm Reich who claimed his orgone generators could cure all disease.

Grand Order of The Fiery Wheel Often referred to simply as The Wheel, this organization is held responsible for the conspiracies behind the conspiracies. It is an occult group, said to be the hidden controller of such notable conspirator groups as the Masons and the Templars. Aside from a few mentions in obscure tracts dating from 1754, produced by one of the many secret societies they control (the Elect Cohens), The Wheel has managed to remain almost invisible. This feat alone is surely testament to the legendary power its members wield over all aspects of our world.

House of Windsor The British royal family is believed by many – especially in those countries that have felt the extensive reach of the former British Empire – to be the prime force behind a myriad of conspiracies. In Iran, conspiracy buffs believe that the House of Windsor still not only has the United Kingdom firmly within its grip, but, by using various secret organizations, also controls the United States of America and Germany. The current lack of anything resembling an Empire and the inability of the house of Windsor to even prevent press intrusion into their false sense of security. Now no longer considered a serious threat, the way is left open for the Kremlin to get on with the serious business of running the world away from the glare of publicity.

Leary, Timothy Given the outrageous nature of his life (he helped start the drug revolution in America and escaped from prison in the US to live in exile with the Black Panthers in Algeria) it is not surprising that Timothy Leary heads the lists of suspected conspirators. Opinion is divided whether he was working on the side of the angels or as a member of the team led by the Devil, but there are good reasons for believing that his championship of LSD may have resulted from links with the CIA. It may well have been Leary who gave the American military the idea of the Internet.

Project Phoenix No one knows exactly what Project Phoenix is or even if it definitely exists – two probable reasons why it has attracted so much attention in conspiracy circles. The name may suggest that the project is designed to exploit alien technology or technology recovered from the remains of a civilization populated by the Elder Race. The US Congress cancelled it in 1958, but it seems to have continued right through to the present, thanks to generous funding from the US military's infamous black budget. The people behind Project Phoenix could be among the globe's key conspirators as Phoenix is said to have plotted the UFO cover-up, the assassination of JFK and the rise of the US military-industrial complex.

Queen Elizabeth I Leaving aside the rumours circulating over the true identity and even sex of Britain's 'Virgin Queen', Elizabeth l appears to have been at the centre of a web of intrigue and machination that set a pattern for British monarchs throughout the following centuries. Doctor John Dee, possibly the most important occultist in British history, is recorded as acting as her personal physician, foreign agent and mystical advisor. Many conspiracy theories cite this powerful partnership as the origin of the numerous secret societies and magical orders dedicated to expanding the British Empire and defending the monarchy.

Roosevelt, Franklin D US President Franklin D Roosevelt features in many conspiracies, but one of the most diabolic has to be the creation of the trailer park. The trailer park conspiracy currently doing the rounds is that FDR did not instruct his advisors to come up with the idea of trailer homes as a response to the Depression's housing crisis, but to locate people in flimsy dwellings in areas prone to hurricanes. The reasoning behind this was that it was an effective way of ridding the county of its poorest people. Little did FDR know that by creating trailer parks, he was setting up the perfect breeding ground for generations of conspiracy believers.

Sufis An Islamic mystical sect, the Sufis are said to be connected to such conspiracy notables as the Knights Templar, Whirling Dervishes, Chinese Tongs, the Cult of the Assassins, Masons, pirates and a host of black power groups with a belief in some non-traditional aspects of Islam. Added to this is their belief in the concept of "rendi" – adopting the appearance of something else, so you may carry out your desire in secret. Consequently, the sect have the perfect credentials to be suspected of conducting high-level conspiracies. Almost absolute secrecy and general inscrutability has ensured that the aim of Sufi-inspired conspiracies tends to remain unknown, but they must have a sense of humour – the supposedly English tradition of Morris dancing is said to be their invention.

Thule Gesellschaft The Thule Gesellschaft is known to have played a significant role in the early formation of the Nazi party and its spurious Ayran ideology and the power wielded by its occultist members may have grown even further when the Nazis came to power. Whether or not they were the power behind Hitler's abominable throne, the Thulists certainly had an influence on certain sections of the fearsome SS. Many people believe that the defeat of Germany in Word War II did not put an end to the TG's conspiracies to seize global power. Working from hidden underground headquarters located in Antarctica, the reach of the Thule Gesellschaft is said to extend to controlling NASA, which they infiltrated via Nazi rocket scientists recruited by the US at the end of the war. A variety of secret neo-Nazi and occult organizations are also controlled by the Thules . . .

United Nations Given that it already functions in many ways as a form of world government – albeit with very limited power – we cannot be too surprised that the United Nations is at the heart of many conspiracy theorists' accusations of dark machinations, schemes and secret projects. While some see the blue helmets of UN peace-keeping troops as a boon to the world's war-torn states, many researchers in the conspiracy field see them as an embryonic global army designed to bring about One World government by force. Some theorists point to the fact that the United Nations was set up in 1947 – the same year as a UFO is reported to have crashed at Roswell, New Mexico – and suggest that the UN may be conspiring to bring about One World government on behalf of an alien power. Of course, those involved with the UN may just be dupes of a cabal of high-degree Masons.

Vril Society Yet another mystical order, the Vril Society can be proved to have had an influence on the formation of the ideology of many important members of the Nazi Party. It is mentioned heavily in connection with secret Nazi flying-saucer technology. While members of the Thule Society are rumoured to have escaped at the end of the war by literally going underground, members of the Vril Society are said to have flown the coop in the experimental Nazi spacecraft that today we know as UFOs. Of course, this knowledge is kept secret from the public to disguise the fact that World War II is not finished yet.

Westphalian Brotherhood Often cited as the ultimate bosses of everyone including the top-degree Masons, the Mafia, the Knights Templar and many modern occult orders, the Westphalian Brotherhood is an umbrella name given to a multi-tentacled Illuminati group that has been in existence since at least the early 1600s. Its modus operandi is to infiltrate an existing secret society and take it over. Given the ultra-secret nature of the organization, it is not surprising that little is known of its aims other than that conspiracy buff favourite: world domination. The Brotherhood seems to have a special fondness for the region of Germany from which it derive its name and was closely linked to Heinrich Himmler, who chose Westphalia to build his mock-medieval fortress. The Westphalians can be added to the long list of those who may have been responsible for creating the Nazi menace.

Xists According to the conspiracy-fuelled cult The Church of SubGenius, Xists are aliens on the side of humanity who will eventually save the Earth from The Con – a massive, age-old intrigue designed to rob humanity of all freedom and fun. The more fanatical followers of the Church's mysterious founder and icon, the pipe-smoking Bob Dobbs, claim the Xists have been behind many secret societies and counter-conspiracies designed to tackle the machinations of the bad aliens who are the real power behind the all-encompassing The Con. To a believer of the Church, everything from the hollow Earth to the practice of having to wear ties to work is explainable in terms of the on-going war between the Xists and their intergalactic foes.

Yellow Hats A mysterious order of Tibetan mystics, the Yellow Hats, or "Dugphas" in their own tongue, may be the true controllers of the fate of the world. Many conspiracy theorists have spotted their hand on the tiller throughout the course of history. The Yellow Hats are followers of the Bon religion that was introduced to Tibet in the Fifth Century and they believe in the mysterious underworld realm of Shambhala, where their orders originate. In the Twentieth Century the Yellow Hats are known to have been involved with many mystical factions of the Nazi party and with the time-travel experiments that allegedly took place at Camp Hero, the US air force base at the centre of the infamous Montauk Project. Hard to spot directly, despite the attention-attracting headgear that has given them their nickname, the Yellow Hats seem to be a conspiracy force to be reckoned with.

Zionist Occupational Government Conspiracy theorists in the US militia movement, the Ku Klux Klan and in other anti-Semitic organizations, are keen to point to the Zionist Occupational Government as the true controller of the American government – hence the organization's name. The ZOG is perceived as being the force behind a host of diabolical schemes. Armed with racist propaganda, as much as anything resembling evidence, believers in ZOG hold that the world is under threat by a global Jewish cabal and that the United States has already fallen to their machinations. The banking system, black helicopters and the use of fluoride in water are all cited as conspiracies originating from ZOG.

GLOSSARY

Black Budget Money is power, and every conspiracy needs substantial finances if it is to stand a chance of being successful in today's world. Allegedly, a favourite source of funding for many conspiratorial groups and projects is a black budget – into which government-approved money is channelled by creative accounting and outright fraud so that it can be used to fund secret projects and operations. Black budgets are often boosted by illegal involvement in areas such as drug-running, money-laundering and arms-dealing. The famous Iran-Contra scandal is one instance of an American black budget deal that became public knowledge.

Black Ops Covert action undertaken by an intelligence agency that is not known or authorized by its government can be referred to as a Black Operation or Black Op for short. As such activities are not officially known about – let alone approved or run by – the appointed authorities, Black Ops are the favourite tools of conspiracy organizations that have infiltrated or control such agencies as MI6, the CIA, and the KGB.

Cabal The word means "an intrigue or secret power elite", and some conspiracy theorists argue that the English word is derived from "cabbala" – the name of an ancient

Jewish mystical system. However, it is more commonly believed that "cabal" originates from a secret group of policy-makers to Charles II whose names were Clifford, Arlington, Buckingham, Ashley and Lauderdale. Those who believe that this book is itself part of a conspiracy should note that the secretary to the original cabal was one Robert Southwell.

The Con A term first used by the most conspiracy-astute cult of the late Twentieth Century, The Church of SubGenius, it has been widely taken up and misinterpreted by many conspiracy theorists. The Con is short for The Conspiracy, and refers to the group that controls every other conspiracy you have heard of, and all of those so successful that you never even imagined they existed. It is a Unified Conspiracy Theory that includes everybody but does not blame any known group.

Conspiriologists The term many conspiracy theorists like to use to describe themselves or anyone else who has taken an interest in researching the truth behind various dark plots. It is used in preference to phrases such as conspiracy buff or the one often quoted by sceptics – delusional, paranoid fantasist.

Counter-Conspiracy Many conspiracies seem to evolve as an attempt to counter the actions of another conspiracy. This type of counter-conspiracy is best illustrated by rumours that the Royal Family created a vast organization of inter-connected secret societies in order to mount an attack on a conspiracy by the Roman Catholic Church which was, in turn, conspiring to achieve world domination. Without a conspiracy to attack, the counter-conspiracy would never have existed. This kind of logic is sometimes used by people who want to prove that the original conspiracy must exist.

Cover-up A large amount of conspiracies revolve around attempts to cover up the truth about events such as assassinations, UFO landings, murders, the origin of religion, business cartels and why it is so hard to buy a cheeseburger for breakfast from the major fast-food chains. Essential elements for a successful cover-up include bare-faced lying, discrediting witnesses, destroying evidence, dreaming up a good cover-story and an ability to control the media.

Cover-story A plausible cover-story is an essential part of any plot to successfully cover up a conspiracy. The cover story needs to be good enough to persuade most people that the official version of events is the only one you can believe

without being accused of being a paranoid nut. Conspiracy researchers spend most of their time proving you have to be a paranoid nut in order to ignore the facts and believe cover stories.

Doing An Elvis Many conspiracy buffs believe that Elvis is not dead – he has merely successfully faked his own death. As a result, the phrase "Doing An Elvis" is applied to simulating your own demise in order to escape a life of fame, the taxman or Mafia plots to have you wiped out.

Dupes In conspiracy circles, the vast majority of people are regarded as dupes. Dupes believe what they are told by the authorities and by the media and never question that things might not be as they seem – in short, they are the people who never believe in conspiracy theories. It's not exactly a term of abuse, but there is an implication that the most heinous plots of our time are only able to exist because dupes are too trusting, are not paranoid enough and never question the way the world works.

Greys Apparently the most common variety of all the extra-terrestrials visiting Earth, the Greys – small creatures with off-white skin and big, dark insect-like eyes – are also the most commonly mentioned in conspiracy theories. Accused of being involved in everything from Roswell to cattle mutilations and the attempted assassination of Ronald Reagan, the Greys seem to specialize in dark doings, often entering into secret government treaties and hatching plots designed to cause harm to the human race.

HIGS Acronym standing for Hoodlums In Governments, HIGS was coined by the conspiracy world's favourite unorthodox scientist, Dr Wilhelm Reich when he was being harassed by the US Food and Drug Administration and the FBI. He used HIGS to describe those who use extreme bully-boy tactics. HIGS has since been widely used by conspiracy buffs as a term for government agents involved in any form of intimidation or persecution undertaken in an attempt to suppress the truth.

Illuminati Strictly speaking, "Illuminati" should only refer to the organization founded in Bavaria in 1776, but the Illuminati's reputation is so strong that you can find the name used in many dictionaries to describe any "underground intellectual movement or secret society" or anyone claiming to possess special enlightenment. The original Bavarian Illuminati are strong contenders for the title "father of all conspiracy groups" and the title is often used by conspiriologists to describe any hidden elite aiming for world domination and possessing enlightenment.

Mystical Order Distinguished by a belief that all of their members' plotting and machinations serves some form of higher spiritual purpose, Mystical Orders are alleged to be behind many major conspiracies. While they may not claim paranormal powers like the members of some Occult Orders, conspirators of a mystical bent are often notable for their interest in dressing up in robes, performing weird initiation rites and pledging their lives to an assortment of ancient deities.

Media Control For any plot to be effective or for any cabal to achieve real power, it needs to remain secret and have the ability to prevent any negative information about it surfacing in the public domain. Given the widespread reach and influence of the media today, this means that the ability to censor and control the media is an essential prerequisite for successful conspiracy. Probably the favourite way of ensuring such control is ownership – which, in the eyes of some conspiriologists, immediately puts Rupert Murdoch and Ted Turner under some suspicion.

Military Industrial Complex In an odd speech at the end of his term of office, President Eisenhower warned of the growing power of the Military Industrial Complex which, he implied, threatened America's political institutions and the personal liberty of its citizens. Quite what inspired the former General to speak out about this cabal is unknown, but his fears seem to have been realized within a few years when the Military Industrial Complex railroaded the US into the costly Vietnam War, which led to a period of very healthy profits for the major arms manufacturers.

Mind Control Among conspiracy groups, exercising control over the minds of the population of a country or the world is second only in popularity to achieving world domination. Mind control is a favourite tool for enforcing power – often involving the creation of assassins whose minds are controlled. Routes to successful mind control are as diverse as subliminal audio messages in records and fluoridation of drinking water.

Misinformation As much as it is the job of intelligence agencies to gather information, it is also their role to provide a constant stream of misinformation to confuse the public and divert attention away from anything they feel needs to be covered up. Planted misinformation may be behind a multitude of conspiracy theories. For instance, if you want to test fly experimental aircraft without revealing what you are up to, it can be useful to have rumours in circulation concerning alien spacecraft. It is well known that conspirators will create misinformation about totally bizarre schemes to deflect the focus away from themselves. What better way to do this than through a book packed to the gills with conspiracies?

NINP Acronym standing for Not Impossible, Not Provable. In conspiracy circles, the NINP tag is applied to a theory that sounds eminently believable, but for which it is impossible to provide hard evidence. Fortunately for most conspirators, NINP is a tag that can be applied to nearly all conspiracies apart from those which are TBTB.

Occult Order Similar in nature to "Mystical Order". People who conspire through the machinations of an Occult Order are often attributed with using the supernatural powers they hold, to aid them in achieving their aims. Prone to conducting arcane rituals and doing battle with other Occult Orders that have opposing aims, Occult Orders – despite their supernatural powers – seem unlikely to end up controlling the word in the near future.

One World Government The establishment of One World Government is seen in the conspiracy genre as the imposition of world-wide rule by some form of international organization, broadly similar to the United Nations. While not everyone views the death of the nation state and the birth of global peace as a particularly bad thing, no one is keen to be controlled by an unelected elite. As a result, people with One World Government plans usually have to resort to using diabolic conspiracies to achieve their objective.

Patsy Someone set up by conspirators to take the blame for their misdeeds. The most well-known example of a patsy set up for a major conspiracy is Lee Harvey Oswald – the man chosen by whoever assassinated JFK to take the rap and persuade the public that the killing was just the work of a lone gunmen. No surprises, then, that when Oswald decided he did not like this role and muttered the immortal words "I'm just a patsy" to the press, a bullet with his name on it was only minutes away.

Paranoia The state of mind that many conspiracy buffs find themselves experiencing when they begin to delve into the dark machinations of the cabals behind the surface of apparent, commonly-accepted realities. Given that many conspiracies may have been designed to make anyone who stumbles upon them appear as if they are completely paranoid, this mental condition can be seen as an occupational hazard for conspiracy investigators. Remember: just because you are paranoid, it does not mean that they are not plotting against you.

Sceptic To conspiriologists, a sceptic is someone who has yet to acknowledge the truth about a conspiracy and spends unnecessary time trying to poke holes in their most cherished theories. Some sceptics, who invest a great deal of energy trying to make those who believe in conspiracies acknowledge common-sense explanations, are labelled "professional sceptics" and accused of being in the pay of those running the conspiracies. All part of the cover-up, you see.

Secret Society Whether people suspect the Masons, The Shriners or the Grand Order of the Fiery Wheel, behind most conspiracies there is often said to be some form of secret society. What is a secret society – an organization that keeps its membership, aims and influence cloaked from outsiders; desire to take over the world as a basic aim is merely an optional extra.

TBTB Acronym specific to the conspiracy genre, standing for Too Bizarre To Believe. TBTB conspiracies are those that succeed by being so implausible that no one will take them seriously enough to invest any time investigating them. Another advantage of TBTB conspiracies for those behind them, is that evidence can be left in full view, safe in the knowledge that it will be overlooked because of the extreme nature of the conspiracy. It has been argued that the abduction of Elvis by Rock-'n'-Roll-loving aliens is the perfect TBTB conspiracy.

a Theories Also known as Jumbo Conspiracy Theories. A Unified Conspiracy Theory is any hypothesis that ties up absolutely everything into one big plot whereby everything is interconnected and explained by a single Unified Conspiracy Theory. It is not uncommon to find a Unified Conspiracy Theory that manages to link the pyramids, Jesus, George Washington, the Bank of England, Roswell, JFK's assassination and the films of George Lucas into one seamless machination created by a joint Freemason/Zeta Reticulan alien organization.

INDEX

DEDICATIONS

Bill Hicks – I was once lucky enough to interview the great man. He was a keen conspiriologist. I think he would have liked this book.

Robert Vaughn – It is wonderful when a childhood hero who fought the conspiracies of THRUSH turns out to be even more heroic in real life for fighting to uncover the truth about the murder of Robert F. Kennedy..

ACKNOWLEDGEMENTS

The authors would like to offer a tip of the smoking gun to:

The Usual Suspects...............................
Surreal Girl; Cheryl Twist; Matt Adams; Annie & Luis; Steve Behan; Andrew & Suzie Collins; Storm Constantine; Tim Dedopulos; Jeff Edmundson; Stephen Grasso; Chandira Hensey the HTML Fairy; Kate Ison; J; Gareth Jones; Ian Lawton; James Muslic; Hugh & Gaetane Phillips; Staci Rolfe; Dickon Springate; Liz Swanson; Richard Ward and Sean Yorke – all of whom should know why they are on the list.

The Unusual Suspects............................
Ricky Tomlinson – a working class hero and victim of a vicious conspiracy; Ken MacLeod – Scotland's greatest novelist and someone who actually understands conspiracy theories; David Benson for general talent and his Conspiracy Cabaret; Gary Russell because he still likes conspiracy theories; Emilia Telese; Dr. Jack Sarfatti; Catherine Yronwode; Robin Ramsay; my friends at SIS; Piggy; Harry of the Yard; Inspector 'X'; Peter from the Palace; Zef Nano; Patrick Browne; Mark Pilkington; Tom Vague; Ingo Storm; Steve Rajam; the spirits of Robert Anton Wilson and PKD; Paul Weston; Nigel Beckwith; Jaye Beldo; Ben Fairhall; Greg at Occult of Personality; Dan Parker; Dr. Shaun Saunders; the other FT; Mich at the CIA and all of those grassy know-alls who helped with research on the Potere Occult who do not want to be mentioned by name.

This book was written to a soundtrack of Luke Haines, country versions of classic tracks by The Stooges and the bizarre French disco rock of Black Strobe.

PICTURE CREDITS

The publishers would like to thank the following sources for their kind permission to reproduce the pictures in this book.

Key:

T = Top, B = Bottom, L = Left, R = Right and C = Centre.

Carlton Books Ltd: 36 L, 36 R, 38 T, 41, 47, 89 L, 99, 100, 164, 165, /Stephen Behan: 148, 157, 171, /English Heritage: 105, / HOK/Don Wong: 107, /Seth Shotstak/SETI: 35.
Corbis Images: 1 BL, 55 R, 115, 119, 122 T, 145, 191, /ABC News: 139, /Alan Hindle: 181, /Bettmann: 10, 14, 17, 26, 54, 60, 94, 136 L, 143, 182, 174, /Brian A. Vikander: 103 L, /Brooks Kraft: 124, 133 L, /Christine Osborne: 38 B, /Daemmrich Bob: 125, /Darren Winter: 31, /David Turnley: 138, 189, / Dennis di Cicco: 93, /Grishkin Denis: 134, /Hulton-Deutsch Collection: 16, 49, /Jim McDonald: 150, /Joel Stettenheim: 177, /John Madere: 98, /Leif Skoogfors: 131, /Liba Taylor: 1 TR, 22, /Mark Peterson: 43, /Mitchell Gerber: 9 R, /Murdo Macleod: 159, /Patrick Robert: 1, 116, /Paul A. Souders: 89 , /Phil Schermeister: 32 , /Raab Shanna: 118, /Ralf-Finn Hestoft: 185 R, /Roger Ressmeyer: 166, /Ron Sachs/CNP: 55 L, /S.I.N.: 9 L, /Stapleton Collection: 73, /Stone Les: 21, /Sunset Boulevard: 25, /Tanguay Jockmans/Reuters: 195, /Van Parys: 122 B, /Waco Tribune Herald: 186, /Wally McNamee: 7, 110.
Getty Images: /Hulton Archive: 77, /Natasja Weitsz: 68.
Harvard-Smithsonian Center for Astrophysics: 188.
LDTV.CO.UK: 87, 87 BL.
Library of Congress: 18, 43 TL, 50, 53, 65, 82, 94, 109, 147, 152, 155 R, 155 L.
NASA: 45, 129, 130, 169, 172, 179 L, 179 R.
U.S. National Archives and Records Administration: / Ronald Reagan Library (NLRR): 120.
Naval Historical Foundation: /U.S. Naval Historical Center: 91.
PA Photos: /Khalid Tanveer/AP/PA: 71.
Photos 12.com: 167, /Bertelsmann Lexikon Verlag: 80T, / Collection Cinéma: 13 TL, 13, 34, 78, 136 R, 140, 151, 173, /Hachedé: 74, 83, /Jean Guichard: 90, /Keystone Pressedienst: 114, 133 R, /Oasis: 103 R, /Siny Most: 84, / World Religions Photo Library: 146.
Rex Features: /Dave Hartley: 58, /Paul Glover: 67, /Philippe Hays: 28, /Richard Young: 1 BR, /Scott Laperruque: 193, / Sipa Press: 141.
Topfoto.co.uk: 40, 44, 149, 168, /ImageWorks: 185 L, / Photri: 112, /PressNet: 57, 63 B, 153, /Uppa.co.uk: 63 T, 127, 161, /Charles Walker: 80.

Every effort has been made to acknowledge correctly and contact the source and/or copyright holder of each picture and Carlton Books Limited apologizes for any unintentional errors or omissions, which will be corrected in future editions of this book.